T0271125

ROUTLEDGE LIBRARY EDITIONS:
THE HISTORY OF
ECONOMIC THOUGHT

Volume 4

THE BREAKDOWN
OF CAPITALISM

THE BREAKDOWN
OF CAPITALISM

A history of the idea in
Western Marxism, 1883–1983

F. R. HANSEN

Routledge
Taylor & Francis Group

LONDON AND NEW YORK

First published in 1985 by Routledge & Kegan Paul plc

This edition first published in 2017
by Routledge
2 Park Square, Milton Park, Abingdon, Oxon OX14 4RN

and by Routledge
711 Third Avenue, New York, NY 10017

Routledge is an imprint of the Taylor & Francis Group, an informa business

British Library Cataloguing in Publication Data
A catalogue record for this book is available from the British Library

ISBN: 978-1-138-29250-5 (Set)
ISBN: 978-1-315-23288-1 (Set) (ebk)
ISBN: 978-1-138-22993-8 (Volume 4) (hbk)
ISBN: 978-1-315-38750-5 (Volume 4) (ebk)

Publisher's Note
The publisher has gone to great lengths to ensure the quality of this reprint but points out that some imperfections in the original copies may be apparent.

Disclaimer
The publisher has made every effort to trace copyright holders and would welcome correspondence from those they have been unable to trace.

The breakdown of capitalism

A history of the idea in Western Marxism, 1883–1983

F. R. Hansen

Routledge & Kegan Paul

London, Boston, Melbourne and Henley

First published in 1985
by Routledge & Kegan Paul plc

14 Leicester Square, London WC2H 7PH

9 Park Street, Boston, Mass. 02108, USA

464 St Kilda Road, Melbourne,
Victoria 3004, Australia and

Broadway House, Newtown Road,
Henley-on-Thames, Oxon RG9 1EN, England

Set in 10 on 11 point Times
by Set Fair
and printed in Great Britain
by The Thetford Press, Thetford, Norfolk

Library of Congress Cataloging in Publication Data

Hansen, F. R.,

The breakdown of capitalism.
Bibliography: p.
Includes index.
1. Capitalism. 2. Marxian economics.
3. Marx, Karl, 1818–1883. I. Title.
HB501.H346   1984   335.4'12   84–17803

British Library CIP data also available

ISBN 0–7102–0015–3

Contents

1 Breakdown theory and intellectual history:
An introduction to the relevant issues

The assertion that Marx did not propose a 'breakdown theory' is primarily attributable to the revisionist interpretation of Marx before and after the First World War. Rosa Luxemburg and Henryk Grossmann both rendered inestimable theoretical services by insisting, as against the revisionists, on breakdown theory.

Rosdolsky, *The Making of Marx's Capital*

[I]n his polemic against Bernstein, Kautsky vigorously denied that there were any traces of a breakdown theory in his earlier work. He even maintained, and there seems to be no good reason to doubt his accuracy, that the very conception of a breakdown theory as well as the term itself (Zusammenbruchs-theorie) were inventions of Bernstein.

Sweezy, *The Theory of Capitalist Development*

This study reconstructs the history of Western Marxist theories of the breakdown of capitalism. For the last hundred years, Western Marxists have devoted a significant portion of their work to speculations concerning the fate of capitalism. The history of theories of breakdown is a history of attempts to read past and present tendencies, to find the future, and to capture it in systematic speculative thought. That body of speculative thought, directed towards a specific historical event, is the object of study here.

The intellectual influence and power of theories of breakdown extend far beyond the theories themselves. The theories, their supporting concepts, their particular appropriations of Marx, and their specific perceptions of capitalist reality, have penetrated and colored a vast body of ideas related to the development of capitalism, economic crises, business cycles and class struggle.

1

Beginning with Bernstein and Kautsky, theories of breakdown have elicited a response: Lenin's works register his sharp objections to the theories as tools of revisionism. From within the Marxist camp, the theories have interpellated statements which might have otherwise been omitted and retorts which might have otherwise been silenced. In this sense, theories of breakdown have played a symbolic role in Western Marxism which has often exceeded the substantive role of the idea itself.

The history of Marxist theories of the breakdown of capitalism is marked by several curious phenomena. The theories studied here conclude that capitalism cannot survive indefinitely, and claim a common reference point for this conclusion in a specific text: Marx's *Capital*. There is, then, an 'original' text or source for theories of breakdown. But despite this common reference point, there is little agreement on the questions of when and by what process breakdown will occur. Marxist theories of breakdown encompass a large number of radically different and conflicting ideas, which continue to generate new material and show little sign of exhaustion. The existence of such a high degree of controversy, sustained over a long period of time and despite a common reference point, raises a series of questions concerning the interpretation and dissemination of ideas, the nature of influence and intentionality, and the sources of conceptual change.

A second and related series of questions arises from another curious phenomenon in the history of breakdown theories. The theories studied here were produced with some expectation of practical and predictive value. Most of the Marxist theorists trusted that their analyses and speculations would eventually correspond to some historical reality, and that the correspondence would be discernible. Most agree, however, that capitalist reality has eluded the predictive power of their theories. Judged by their own standards of verification and timeliness, theories of breakdown have been defeated at every turn. But despite the demand for discernible predictive power, and the frequent failure to meet this demand, theories of breakdown are generated and regenerated. The seeming durability and autonomy of theories of breakdown raise questions concerning the social conditions and consequences of theoretical work, and the status of critical thought in capitalist society.

This study examines the development of Western Marxist theories of the breakdown of capitalism, with their conflicting interpretations of a single text, and their invulnerability to empirical defeat, as events in the history of ideas. These events, in turn, raise questions about the reconstruction and interpretation of their history. I hope, however, that this study proves useful for purposes which go beyond intellectual history as an academic field of inquiry. Specifically, I hope that this study will allow those of us who still ponder the fate of capitalism to situate our thoughts in their historical and intellectual context, and to construct strategies with an understanding of that context. At a time when the idea of the breakdown of capitalism still finds a place in the minds of so many people, it may be worthwhile to make note of those historical moments when similar thoughts flourished, only to find their explanations incomplete, and their object unrealized.

There is a massive number of works on the development of capitalism and the future of capitalist societies. I have not attempted to provide a definitive documentation of all theories pertaining to the fate of capitalism. Rather, I have attempted to indicate the enormous range of theoretical possibilities contained in the singular idea of breakdown, and grounded in one basic text: Marx's *Capital*. In order to provide some sense of the range of possibilities, I have discussed a large number of texts. The selection of texts to be treated was a difficult and often troublesome process; several criteria for selection were used, and these are outlined below.

Specifically, this study treats the works of a number of Marxist theorists who have been influential in Western Europe and the United States, beginning with the original points of reference in Marx's works, and ending with works published in the last few years. I have selected from the vast amount of material produced by Marxist scholars only those works which make definite contributions to breakdown theory, or which play a significant role in its development. In most cases, the works under study were written by men and women like Lewis Corey and Rosa Luxemburg, for whom the breakdown of capitalism was a real and lasting concern in their intellectual lives. I have excluded writers who approached the issue from a historical or descriptive, rather than theoretical, perspective.

The attempt to limit the study to those texts produced by Western Marxist theorists proved difficult in some cases. I have included theorists like Louis Boudin and Ernst Mandel who have defined themselves as Marxists, and theorists like Jürgen Habermas and John Strachey who have not explicitly adopted the label, but have claimed Marx as a major positive influence on their theories of collapse. Also, after much deliberation, I decided to include the works of Thorstein Veblen, who rejected the Marxist label but worked in the shadow of Marx, and accepted those aspects of his thought related to crises and capitalist development.

Chapter 2 deals exclusively with the reference points for breakdown theory found in Marx's theory of capitalist development. Chapters 3, 4, and 5 treat the works of the Western European and American breakdown theorists from the time of the

3

Second International to the second Great Depression. Chapters 6 and 7 bring the study up to the present decade. Although the conclusions of the study, found in Chapter 8, indicate that there are many continuities and similarities in the works of the Western European and American theorists, I think that the small but important differences warrant the use of geographic segregation here. The comparative approach adopted by this study was inspired, in part, by my doubts about the validity of the tradition of geographic segregation in most works in intellectual history. I have maintained the tradition, but I have also attempted to indicate its deficiencies and the specific ways in which it conceals commonalities in the Western European and American experiences.

Theories of the breakdown of capitalism were initiated during the Second International. The 'breakdown controversy,' as a full-fledged theoretical debate, appeared in the early works of Bernstein and Kautsky, and set the terms for further theoretical development. Theories of breakdown soon emerged as an identifiable group of theories of the development of capitalism, characterized by certain assumptions or conclusions. First, theories of breakdown assume or conclude that, at some point, capitalism will cease to exist as a dominant mode of production. Second, the theories assume or conclude that the end of capitalism will be caused, in the final analysis, by a narrow range of contradictions internal to and inherent in the economy, without the full intervention of revolutionary forces. These two assumptions or conclusions distinguish theories of breakdown from theories of crises, theories of business cycles, and theories of social revolution.

Breakdown is commonly defined as a final and irreversible end to the capitalist order. Crises, by contrast, are usually seen as cathartic upheavals which occur in the face of defeated economic expectations and re-establish equilibrium once expectations have been adjusted. Unlike breakdown, crises are not conclusive or decisive events, but simply one of the various mechanisms of self-correction at work in the capitalist economy. Business cycles are usually defined as a series of crises and recoveries which follow a pattern produced by fluctuations in rates of investment. The low points in business cycles may be designated as crises, but do not constitute breakdown. Crises and cycles represent mutations in the economy, but not the radical change indicated by the collapse of a dominant mode of production. The concerns of this study lie with those theories that postulate breakdown as the future of the capitalist order, as the final event in capitalist history.

Theories of breakdown can also be distinguished from theories of social revolution. Theories of breakdown determine that the collapse of capitalism will be caused by forces that are largely beyond the reach of immediate human will and intervention. Theories of class struggle and revolution, by contrast, commonly determine that social upheaval will create economic or social change that might not otherwise occur. Although some theories of breakdown conclude that social revolution is a probable or necessary consequence of breakdown, they do not recognize revolution as an autonomous and sufficient causal force in the collapse of capitalism, or as a decisive element in the end of the system.

Theories of breakdown, then, are characterized by their common determination that capitalism will collapse, and that collapse will be caused by forces internal to and inherent in the mechanics of the system itself without decisive class intervention. The theories can be distinguished from other theories of capitalist development on this basis. But despite their common determination concerning the fate of capitalism, theories of breakdown offer a number of different and often conflicting interpretations and explanations of the phenomena they seek to describe. Indeed, the very factors which might act as stabilizing and unifying forces in the development of breakdown theories – their common determination of fundamental issues and their common grounding in Marx's writing – instead function as explosive points which generate controversy rather than agreement, and shatter the history of the theories into a series of seemingly discrete conceptual developments. The fragmentation of opinion, the proliferation of conflict rather than consensus in theories of breakdown, begins with the initial readings of *Capital*, and carries through later theoretical developments in Western Marxist scholarship. Initial readings of *Capital* did not produce one set of rules that governed method and content in breakdown theory and provided a solid and unchanging basis for theoretical development. Instead, breakdown theory is characterized by a set of competing interpretations, shifting between positions of dominance and subordination within individual texts, and within the Western Marxist tradition as a whole.

The sources of theoretical conflict are many. Two of the most important sources are found in a series of historical and epistemological questions generated by breakdown theories, and sustained throughout the history of their development. The most significant historical question concerns the relationship between the economic structure of capitalism and its political and ideological superstructure. The particular answers provided are crucial factors in the formulation of causal explanations in theories of breakdown. Marx argued that economic forces are primary and controlling under the conditions of liberal capitalism, but did not indicate whether this would remain the case in later stages of capitalist development. Western Marxist theorists have debated the issue of the primacy of economic forces; their theories of breakdown reflect the widespread disagreement on the specification of causal forces in capitalist society.

The determination of this substantive historical issue does not control, but certainly influences, the determination of the methodological and epistemological questions generated by theories of breakdown. The most significant epistemological question concerns the utility and validity of certain forms of data in constructing theories of breakdown. Theorists have debated the reliability of empirical data produced under the conditions of capitalist society, and have not reached any agreement on this point. Those theorists who give greater consideration to superstructural forces have challenged the relevance and reliability of data used by economic theorists. Both the historical issue of causality and the epistemological issue of the validity of certain types of empirical data are closely tied to the particular appropriation of Marx's texts that are found in the theories, and to the various perceptions of capitalist reality that mark the theories at every turn. From the determination of these two central historical and epistemological issues follows the structures of explanation, the methodological conventions, and the discursive rules that govern the development of any particular theory of breakdown.

These issues can be approached, answered and reconciled in a variety of ways; an enormous range of theoretical possibilities exists for their resolution. The ways in which Western Marxist theorists have selected and rejected possibilities within that range constitute the object of study here. Over the last century, three basic forms, three different approaches to the problem of breakdown, have emerged. These three basic forms constitute three identifiable movements within each of the texts studied here, and three identifiable traditions in the history of theories of breakdown as a whole.

The first form, which I refer to as the orthodox form or position, adopts causal explanations which assume the primacy of economic forces in shaping the fate of capitalism. The orthodox interpretation of laws of development is primarily positivistic, and more closely tied to neo-Kantianism than to Hegelian forms. In epistemological terms, the orthodox position assumes that these economic forces are subject to empirical investigation and that the relevant data is readily accessible and available. The orthodox appropriation of Marx's texts is generally selective and literal. It draws primarily from the middle-range economic theories and declarative statements found in *Capital*, and the text as a whole then stands or falls on the verifiability of certain statements contained within it. The orthodox perception of capitalist reality is that all fundamental developments can be described in economic terms and are subject to empirical documentation and middle-range analysis. The original terms for the construction of theories of breakdown were set within the context of this orthodox position.

A second form of resolving the historical and epistemological issues generated by the problem of breakdown, a second identifiable movement, also assumes the primacy of economic forces, and formulates causal statements concerning breakdown in structural terms. In this second form, however, there is some recognition of superstructural forces. I refer to this form as a neo-orthodox position. Empirical data is utilized, but with some caution, and the theories offered are generally more elaborate than those found in the orthodox theories. The neo-orthodox appropriation of Marx is selective and interpretive, and favors the middle-range economic theories and the historical analyses found in *Capital*. The neo-orthodox perception of capitalist reality is that there has been a significant change in the nature of capitalism, a change which is usually located at the turn of the century, and which necessitates a modification of the original theories and concepts found in the texts of Marx. The neo-orthodox position was initially formulated in response to the orthodox constructions of breakdown theory generated during the Second International.

The third form or position on the historical and epistemological issues related to breakdown theories, referred to in this study as the anti-orthodox position, rejects the assumption of the primacy of economic forces. Superstructural phenomena are given an equal or dominant role in causal explanations concerning the development of capitalism. Empirical data is utilized infrequently, and with extreme caution. The anti-orthodox theories of breakdown are highly speculative, abstract and rarely given concrete application. The appropriation of Marx is selective, analytical and critical, and favors the broad social theories and methodological statements found throughout Marx's works. The anti-orthodox perception of capitalist reality indicates that significant changes have occurred in the capitalist mode of production, and that these changes require a radical reconsideration of Marx's concepts and theories. Beginning with Veblen, the anti-orthodox position appears as a challenge to the orthodox and neo-orthodox theories throughout the century.

Each of these forms appears as dominant or subordinate elements in each of the texts studied here. Luxemburg's theory of breakdown, for example, is dominated by the neo-orthodox position, but occasionally admits arguments which belong to an orthodox or anti-orthodox position. The cohesion and self-referentiality of the dominant form in each text creates a resistance to interruptions from the subordinate positions; a confusion of distinct discourses occurs as conflicting positions surface and clash. The confusion is compounded when particular appropriations of Marx's thought and particular perceptions of capitalist reality are forced to co-exist. The dual commitment to an original theoretical reference point and to contemporary applicability – a commitment that informs all of the theories of breakdown studied here – creates a conflict within each of the theories, and among the theories in the Western Marxist tradition.

Mechanisms of selection, rejection, resistance and resolution come into play as each theorist approaches the range of theoretical possibilities surrounding the problem of breakdown. These mechanisms are among the central concerns of this study. The image I have attempted to reconstruct is, in part, the image of each theorist as he turns away from the temptation of possibilities which oppose his dominant position and threaten the coherency of his argument. The discursive expressions I have attempted to capture are those which reflect the ease or discomfort with which the theorists move away from the transgressive paths of conflicting viewpoints. The focus rests on those precise moments in the texts and in their history when theoretical retrieval re-establishes a dominant form, and a particular discourse on breakdown is reproduced. The seeming autonomy and the relative durability of theories of breakdown are born of those moments, and the relationship between the capitalist order and the theories of its dissolution may well be found there.

2 Points of reference in Marx's theory of capitalist development

> When capitalism's inner connections are grasped, all theoretical belief in the permanent necessity of existing conditions breaks down before their practical collapse.
>
> Marx, *Letters to Kugelman*

Over the last hundred years, Marxist theorists have turned time and time again to the text of *Capital*, in search of some theoretical understanding of the development of capitalism and its fate as an economic system. They have not found there, however, a fully unified treatise, but an enormous range of concepts, generated by Marx's theory of capitalist development, and sustained by his lifelong concern with economic and social change. This chapter surveys those sections of *Capital* which were later adopted as points of reference for theories of breakdown.

For the purposes of this study, the most important element of Marx's theory of capitalist development rests in Marx's consistent contention that capitalism is a transitory mode of production, and that its transitory character is determined by contradictions internal to and inherent in the system itself. Those sections of *Capital* adopted as reference points for breakdown theory, however, do not represent the full range of Marx's thought on the transitory nature of capitalism and the transition to socialism. Instead, theories of breakdown are based on highly selective readings of the theory of capitalist development, with some elements of the theory raised to predominant positions, and others suppressed and silenced. Marx's historical analyses of specific crises, and their intersection with particular shifts in the balance of class forces, are rarely referred to in theories of breakdown. Marx's concept of class conflict – a central concept in his characterization of capitalism as a transitory mode – largely disappears in theories of breakdown, or assumes an automatic

9

form; while the concepts of underconsumption, disproportionality, and profit rates are given determinative roles in the
promotion of the idea of mechanical collapse.

The attempt here is to describe those concepts which later
become reference points for theories of breakdown, and to
provide some sense of their larger epistemological and historical
context in *Capital*. In order to situate the points of reference
arising from Marx's theory of capitalist development, with its
central characterization of capitalism as a transitory mode, it is
necessary to turn to the site of the theory's construction. The site is
located in Marx's critique of classical political economy, where he
attempts to dissolve the assumptions that blocked the development of new economic thought, and to create a logical space for a
theory of capitalist development within the realm of economic
discourse.

Marx's critique of classical political economy: The creation of logical space

The historical and epistemological assumptions of classical political economy effectively precluded the consideration of capitalism
as a transitory mode of production. The Physiocrats, and the
classical political economists who followed them, defined and
developed many of the economic concepts that are essential to a
theory of capitalist development, including the concepts of value,
accumulation and profit; but they never contemplated the potential for an end to the system. Pre-Marxian theorists recognized the
potential for disruptive crises and for an end to accumulation
under capitalism, but did not conclude that collapse might occur.
Long before Marx developed the concept of a falling rate of profit,
the Physiocrats contemplated the possibility of a falling rate of
profit as an inherent feature of capitalist production. The
Physiocrats assumed, however, that a falling rate of profit and the
resulting decline in accumulation would produce a harmless
movement towards stationary conditions, not economic collapse.

Adam Smith studied the falling rate of profit as an effect of
interest rates and competition, but believed that its impact could
be mitigated by an expansion of trade.[1] Ricardo further developed
the concept of a falling rate of profit, but located the cause of the
fall outside the capitalist system itself, in pressures on wages and
rents resulting from population growth and scarce land resources.
Ricardo concluded that a serious fall in the rate of profit caused by
these external forces would occur only in the distant future, and
that capitalism would absorb its impact through importation.[2]
These pre-Marxian notions of economic development were contained within and limited by economic models based on the
assumption of stasis. Theories of radical economic change,

including theories of collapse, and characterizations of capitalism as a transitory mode, were largely precluded from consideration.[3] These static models of capitalism are the object of Marx's extended critique of classical political economy in his massive *Theories of Surplus Value*, written between January 1862 and July 1863. When Marx began *Theories* only the first part of *Capital* had been drafted, and Marx's intention was to integrate the historical, critical writings of *Theories* with the three theoretical parts of *Capital* itself. The eventual length of the *Theories* manuscripts, however, led Marx to the decision to produce *Theories* as a separate, final volume to *Capital*. This final volume is almost as large as the other three combined, and is the best single treatise on classical political economy available.[4] *Theories* forms what Marx calls the 'historico-critical' or 'historico-literary' part of his analysis of capitalism. It contains Marx's attempt to systematically clear the ground for a dynamic conception of capitalism through the deconstruction of static classical models.

The classical economists defined capitalism as a set of material conditions, and assumed that capitalism is an eternal and absolute mode of production, given to immediate empirical investigation. Marx's critique is based on a radical rejection of that classical definition and the assumptions it generated. Capitalism, he argues, is not a set of material conditions, but a series of social relations. As such, capitalism is not eternal and absolute, but is subject to gradual and radical change. Moreover, as a series of social relations, capitalism cannot be understood through the use of purely empirical information. Rather, Marx argues, it can only be understood through the use of abstract analyses and critical historical studies.

Marx begins *Theories* with an analysis of the Physiocrats, who thought of capital in its 'material forms of existence . . . in isolation from the social conditions in which they appear . . . and thereby made of the capitalist form of production an eternal, natural form of production.'[5] For the Physiocrats,

> [t]heir method of exposition is, of course, necessarily governed by their general view of the nature of value, which to them is not a definite social mode of existence of human activity (labor), but consists of material things – land, nature, and the various modifications of these material things.[6]

According to Marx, this conception of capitalism was continued in the works of Adam Smith, which were 'limited to fixing the abstract categories' produced by the Physiocrats.[7] Ricardo also viewed the physical, material conditions through which capitalist relations are expressed as the eternal forms of capitalism itself.[8] Under this classical conceptualization, capital was defined as a

11

'stock of commodities,' and the properties of material objects were taken as the properties of capitalism.[9] However, Marx argues that the physical, material conditions of capitalism – the use of materials, labor, and tools of their phenomenal forms – are 'common to all modes of production and do not express the specific nature of capital.'[10] Capitalism, then, as defined by the classical political economists, was mistaken for a material, atemporal, absolute form.

Marx argues that capital is the embodiment of specific, definite social relations of production, and that capitalism can only be defined as a series of social relations, not as a set of material conditions. The classical political economists, Marx determines, 'do not conceive of capital as a relation. They cannot do so without at the same time conceiving it as a historically transitory, i.e., a relative – not an absolute – form of production.'[11] Once capital is conceived as a relation, which encompasses the means of production and the labor-power that creates surplus value, 'then the historically transitory character of this relationship becomes at once evident, and the general recognition of this fact is incompatible with the continued existence of this relationship, which itself creates the means for its abolition.'[12] Marx argues that the classical political economists cannot accept any conception of capitalism that would reveal its contradictions. When confronted with such a conception, the economists revert to the representation of capital as wealth, as use-value – a material, atemporal form. The relational form, which carries with it the recognition of potential, internal, inherent limitations to the continuation of capitalism, is thereby precluded from consideration.[13]

The classical economists, Marx continues, are compelled 'to prove that capitalist production cannot lead to general crises,' and consequently, 'all its conditions and distinct forms, all its principles and specific features – in short *capitalist production* itself – are denied.'[14] In the context of this critique of the classical conception of capitalism as a static material entity, Marx once again defines capitalism as a set of historically specific and transitory conditions and relations. This definition forms the basis for a consideration of capitalism as a system subject to conflict, contradiction and termination.[15]

The epistemological consequences of this definition, however, are complex. As a series of temporal relations rather than a set of material conditions, capitalism is not subject to the empirical analysis utilized by the classical political economists; nor is it subject to their positivistic approach to economic inquiry. As Engels noted in his Preface to *Capital*, 'a theory which views modern capitalist production as a mere passing stage in the economic history of mankind, must make use of terms different from those habitual to writers who look upon that form of production as imperishable and final.'[16] In their analyses of capitalism, the classical political economists accepted as given the domain of economic 'facts' and forms presumably apparent in the material conditions of production. Marx explicitly rejects this fixation on the domain of the given. Capitalism, he determines, must be understood as a series of relations that cannot be studied through empirical means alone. The relations must be reconstructed in abstract thought. Moreover, Marx determines that the relations are not apparent, but are masked by ideological forces generated by capitalism itself.

With Adam Smith and later economists, Marx argues, 'lack of theoretical understanding needed to distinguish the different forms of economic relations remains the rule of their coarse grabbing at and interest in the empirically available material.'[17] According to Marx, the classical formulation of the laws of capitalist production is derived through a process of direct extrapolation, which presents the phenomena as the law of the phenomena, and the given 'facts' as the general laws and abstract conceptions of economic development. Ricardo is reproached 'for regarding the phenomenal form as *immediate* and *direct* proof or exposition of the general laws, and for failing to *interpret* it.'[18]

When discrepancies arise between the laws derived by the economists and further developments in the economy, the discrepancies are resolved 'by directly subordinating and immediately adopting the concrete to the abstract.'[19] In classical thought,

[c]rass empiricism turns into false metaphysics, scholasticism, which toils painfully to deduce undeniable empirical phenomena by simple formal abstraction directly from the general law, or to show by cunning argument that they are in accordance with that law.[20]

Starting from the 'facts' of capitalist production, and unable to grasp its form, which has been accepted *a priori* as self-evident, the economists 'consequently . . . examine only the magnitude' of the crucial components of capital. Their attention is thereby diverted from the relational forms which reveal the sources of contradiction.[21]

The classical political economists, Marx argues, are unaware of the ideological forces that arise from capitalism as a series of social relations, and are therefore unaware of their collusion with the system. Consequently, '[t]hey simply express in theoretical terms the notions of the practical men who are engrossed in capitalist production, dominated by it and interested in it.'[22] Marx's rejection of the empiricist notion of apparent 'facts' is part of his analysis of the mechanisms by which the economists deny the

13

possibility of a transitory capitalism – a probing of the grammatical gaps through which the economists 'cling to the concept of unity in the face of contradiction.'[23] In the works of the economists, Marx argues, a series of 'verbal fictions' function to 'transform the unity of opposites,' the transitory capitalist system, 'into the direct identity of opposites,' an eternal mode of production preserved from the anticipation of economic transition.[24]

Marx's characterization of capitalism as a transitory mode occurred in the context of the epistemological critique of classical political economy found in *Theories of Surplus Value*. Decades later, when breakdown theorists turned to *Capital* as a reference point, they extracted the characterization from its epistemological and critical underpinnings, and reverted to the classical forms. Once again, the given 'facts' of capitalist production and circulation were converted directly into general laws. As the 'facts' shifted over time, so too did readings of *Capital*, and interpretations of the general laws it provided. The definition of capital as a series of social relations was displaced by images of a mechanical economy. Marx's formulation of the tendential laws of capitalist development became fertile ground for those engaged in the construction of theories of automatic collapse.

The law of the tendency of a falling rate of profit

The characterization of capital as a series of social relations subject to conflict and contradiction is explicated in *Capital*, the site of the construction of the characterization of capitalism as a temporary mode. The construction, however, takes place at several scattered points within the text, and assumes a number of discursive forms. Generally, the dominant forms of the construction emerge through two mutually dependent but distinct discourses which recur at various points throughout *Capital*, and later provide the points of reference for theories of breakdown.

The first discourse consists of a series of general assertions concerning the contradictions of capitalism and the progressive realization of tendential laws. The second discourse consists of a more concentrated and cohesive theoretical elaboration of the law of the tendency of the rate of profit to fall, a tendential law in the development of capitalism which presumably acts like other tendencies, and serves as a link between the contradictions of capitalism and its concrete existence as a mode of production. The range of theoretical possibilities generated by these two discourses, and by their co-existence, is compounded by variations in the epistemological bases of the text.

The first discourse appears sporadically throughout *Capital*. With respect to the transitory character of capitalism, the discourse is most forcefully represented in the first volume of *Capital*, in the Preface and in Chapter XXXII, in passages which are frequently cited as reference points for theories of mechanical collapse and automatic revolution:

Intrinsically, it is not a question of the higher or lower degree of development of the social antagonisms that result from the natural laws of capitalist production. It is a question of these laws themselves, of these tendencies working with iron necessity towards inevitable results. The country that is more developed industrially only shows to the less developed, the image of its own future.[25]

The monopoly of capital becomes a fetter upon the mode of production, which has sprung up and flourished along with, and under it. Centralisation of the means of production and socialisation of labour at last reach a point where they become incompatible with their capitalist integument. Thus integument is burst asunder. The knell of capitalist private property sounds. The expropriators are expropriated.[26]

But capitalist production begets, with the inexorability of a law of Nature, its own negation. It is the negation of negation.[27]

In these passages, Marx relies on a linear causality which necessarily results in a definite, identifiable state of affairs involving the actual end of capitalism. The primary contradiction of capitalism, the contradiction between the developing forces of production and the limitations placed on this development by the relations of production, provides the setting for radical social change.

This contradiction is given another form of expression in Marx's numerous discussions of tendential laws. These discussions involve the tendency towards concentration and centralization, the tendency towards the increasing relative impoverishment of the proletariat, and the tendency towards relative overpopulation. At some points, Marx's formulations of these tendencies support the linear notion of causality found in Chapter XXXII. The laws are absolute in that their realization is necessary and inevitable; they are tendential in that they are realized progressively and with growing intensity. Epistemologically, they are grounded in a conception of economics which provides for empirical documentation of the system as a whole. These tendencies, however, are discussed in recurring passages which do not provide systematic, concentrated theoretical elaboration. The only concentrated theoretical elaboration of a tendential law occurs in Marx's discussion of the falling rate of profit.

Theoretical elaboration of the law of the falling rate of profit takes place primarily in the third volume of *Capital*, in Chapters XIV, XV and XVI, where Marx discusses 'the law itself,' the 'counteracting influences,' and the 'internal contradictions of the law.'[28] The fundamental contradiction of capitalism which forms the center of Marx's first discourse on the transitory nature of capitalism is reformulated in Volume III in the discussion of the law of the tendency of the rate of profit to fall:

> The *real barrier* to capitalist production is *capital itself*. . . . The means – unconditional development of the productive forces of society – comes continually into conflict with the limited purpose, the self-expansion of the existing capital. The capitalist mode of production is, for this reason, a historical means of developing the material forces of production and creating an appropriate world-market and is, at the same time, a continual conflict between this its historical task and its own corresponding relations of social production.[29]

This statement of the contradiction is no longer the explicit statement on the end of capitalism that is found in the discourse on contradictions exemplified in the passages quoted from Volume I. Instead, the statement from the discussion of profit rates is a statement of the 'continual conflict' between the unconditional development of productive forces and the limited purposes of expansionary capitalism. The rising social productivity of labor, as it finds expression in the higher organic composition of capital and, finally, in the falling rate of profit, is a movement which simultaneously generates barriers to capitalism and the means of their circumvention through a series of unresolved effects and counter-effects. The law of the tendency of the rate of profit to fall is thus 'an inner and necessary connection between two seeming contradictions,' a decrease in the rate accompanied by an increase in the mass of profit.[30] As such, the law loses its power as a tendency that provides a direct link between the abstract conception of contradiction and crisis and the observation of its actual occurrence in the phenomenal world.

The law of the tendency of the rate of profit to fall is one consequence of increased productivity, 'an expression peculiar to the capitalist mode of production of the progressive development of the social productivity of labor,' which is 'identical with the progressively higher organic composition of capital.'[31] Due to its importance to capitalist production, the law 'may be said to be a mystery whose solution has been the goal of all political economy since Adam Smith.'[32] Marx makes it clear that the law was not only the goal, but the great fear of the classical political economists. The 'terror' which the law inspired in them arose from its implications for the concentration of capital, and from the implication of an internal and inherent limit to capitalist production.[33] The conceptual prerequisites of its formulation, however, eluded the classical political economists. The elements of the law appear for the first time in the extended analyses of *Capital*, and include the concepts of variable capital, constant capital, and distinction between surplus value and profit, and the formula for an average rate of profit.

The law, simply stated, is straightforward. In any capitalist production process, the total capital invested is divided between constant capital (c), the value of capital consumed in the material means of production, and variable capital (v), the value of capital consumed in wage payments to productive laborers. The value of the total capital consumed in the production process is c + v = C (total capital). The organic composition of capital reflects technological advancements and is expressed in the ratio of constant to variable capital ($\frac{c}{v}$).[34] The total value emerging from the production process is expressed through the combination of constant capital, variable capital, and the surplus value (s) added to the value of the commodity through the labor process, so that c + v + s = C'.

The rate of the surplus value (s') is the ratio of surplus value to variable capital ($\frac{s}{v}$).[35] The rate of profit, or the rate of return on the total value of capital consumed in the production process, is determined by dividing the surplus value extracted during any given period, by the combined constant and variable capital consumed during that period: $\frac{s}{c+v}$ = p' (rate of profit).[36] Assuming a constant rate of surplus value, the rate of profit will decrease as the ratio of constant to variable capital increases, and will increase as the ratio decreases. In other words, with a constant rate of surplus value, a rise in the social productivity of labor is attended by a higher organic composition of capital, or by a growth of constant capital relative to variable capital, and subsequently, by a falling rate of profit.[37]

However, the same rise in productivity that increases constant capital in relation to variable capital, and results in a falling rate of profit, also produces a growing mass of profit due to expanded accumulation and production output. Moreover, expanded output also provides the conditions necessary for an increase in the population of the working class. This increase reduces the wage rate through the creation of a relative surplus population. 'Hence,' Marx concludes, 'the same laws produce for the social capital a growing absolute mass of profit, and a falling rate of profit.'[38] '[T]his not only *can* be so,' Marx argues, '[a]side from temporary fluctuations it *must* be so, on the basis of capitalist production.'[39] The law of the tendency of the rate of profit to fall is, then, a 'double-edged law' which contains its own 'internal contradictions.'

The same movement of development within capitalism produces contradictory effects, which 'mutually influence each other and are phenomena in which the same law expresses itself.'[40] The falling rate of profit is countered by developments which arise from the same increase in productivity. These include an increased mass of profits arising from accelerated accumulation; a reduction in the value of constant capital due to increased productivity; and a reduction in the cost of labor-power through a reduction in the value of its means of reproduction, and through an increased tendency towards a relative surplus population. These counteracting influences 'cross and annul the effect of the general law' of the falling rate of profit and give it 'merely the characteristic of a tendency.' The law as an 'absolute action is checked, retarded, and weakened,' by counter-effects which 'hamper, retard, and partly paralyse' the downward motion of the rate of profit.[41] 'Thus,' Marx concluded, 'the law acts only as a tendency. And it is only under certain circumstances and only after long periods that its effects become strikingly pronounced.'[42] This last statement, with all its vagueness and generality, is the most concrete anticipation of crisis that occurs in Marx's discussion of the falling rate of profit.

In *Capital*, the contradictory effects of the same basic contradiction of capitalism are resolved into a unity of opposites whose final historical destiny is never fully anticipated. Marx indicates that the tendential laws of capitalism cannot predict or be identified with a given class of events. He provides a theoretical elaboration of a tendency which seems to be posed as the movement towards a certain class of events, as the link between the contradictions of capitalism in their abstract form and the realization of those contradictions in history. But the events which would represent the end of accumulation are not specified beyond the postulation of their possibility, and the immediate qualification of that postulation through a discussion of counteracting forces. In the discussion of the falling rate of profit, the characterization of capitalism as a temporary mode of production is removed from the realm of specified events, and returned to the general conception of contradiction from which it arose.[43]

Marx maintains his rejection of empiricism, his rejection of the given and of economic 'facts' throughout his discussion of the law of the tendency of the rate of profit to fall. He finds that, '[j]ust as everything appears reversed in competition, and thus in the consciousness of the agents of competition, so also this law, this inner and necessary connection between two seeming contradictions.'[44] Moreover, Marx reminds the reader that some of the possible counteracting influences to the falling rate of profit are not discussed in *Capital* because they are not related to the 'general analysis of capital, but belong in an analysis of competition, which is not presented in this work.'[45] These qualifications and the methodological considerations they entail, however, were largely silenced in later readings of the law.

Crises and underconsumption

Beyond the characterization of capitalism as a transitory mode that appears in *Capital*, in the general statements on contradiction and the theoretical elaboration of the law of the tendency of the rate of profit to fall, there exists a continuous discussion of periodic crises as the recurrent but indecisive manifestations of the contradictions of capitalism. Marx's discussions of contradiction and the tendential law of profit are aspects of the general analysis of capitalism and, as such, are not subject to problems arising from the realization of value, or to verification through immediate empirical inquiry. The crises that punctuate the development of capitalism in its drive towards expansion, however, involve problems of circulation and realization, and draw Marx into discussions of specific historical and economic events. These events are retrieved through empirical research. At certain points, Marx provides the language through which the distinction between temporary crises and permanent breakdown would be obliterated in the hands of later theorists.

Generally, Marx presents crises as temporary suspensions in the drive towards economic expansion. As such, crises eventually redefine equilibrium and recreate the conditions for accumulation. Overproduction, the primary cause of crises, and the credit system, the basis of circulation, 'are means by which capitalist production seeks to break through its own barriers and to produce over and above its own *limits*.'[46] During crises, Marx argues, capital is devalued, prices are adjusted, the various sectors of industrial production are realigned, and the surplus working population is reapportioned.[47] Unlike the analysis of profit rates in *Capital*, the analysis of crises does not assume an absence of realization problems. Rather, crises emerge through the impact of overproduction on the circulation process, and create disruptions in the realization of surplus value and in the continued expansion of capital. Marx's initial concern with the realization of value rests only with the role of realization in the reconversion of money into capital, a prerequisite to accumulation.

Crises may arise from a general increase in the price of raw materials, from a general overproduction of capital and consumer goods, or from the disproportionate production of capital goods in

19

relation to consumer goods.[48] All result in a disruption in the flow of payments which constitute the credit system and which form the basis for a smooth continuation of accumulation. The impact of crises on the economy occurs at the point of reconversion; realization is a consideration only in the context of continued accumulation. These crises are not permanent crises, which would be synonymous with breakdown. As opposed to breakdown, Marx argues, 'the transitory over-abundance of capital, overproduction and crises are something different. Permanent crises do not exist.'[49]

Crises are realization problems which achieve significance through the reconversion process, but are rooted in the production process itself. According to Marx, their 'abstract form' is revealed through 'the examination of the general nature of capital, even without going further into the actual relations which constitute prerequisites for the real process of production.'[50] The potential for crises arises from the contradiction between the unlimited productive powers of capitalism and the limited productive purposes of capitalism, as that contradiction is reflected in the general metamorphosis of commodities and the radical separation of purchase and sale. In a crisis, the actual unity of the commodity as use-value and exchange-value, and the actual unity of purchase and sale as acts in the circulation process, forcibly assert themselves. A crisis, then, 'manifests the unity of the two phases that have become independent of each other.'[51]

But this is only the 'abstract form' of crises that exists at the level of general analysis and remains distinct from the actual or empirically accessible form that would be found in an investigation of competition, credit and the composition of existing capitalist societies. Marx argues that '[t]he factors which turn this possibility of crisis into (an actual) crisis are not contained in this [abstract] form itself; it only implies that *the framework* for a crisis exists.'[52] If empirical verification and causal explanation are desired,

> the potential crisis has to be traced – the real crisis can only be deduced from the real movement of capitalist production, competition and credit – in so far as crisis arises out of the special aspects of capital which are *peculiar* to it as capital, and are not merely comprised in its existence as commodity and money.[53]

Peculiar to capital is the role of realization in the reconversion of surplus value into capital, a special form of consumption which makes realization and consumption an integral part of the production process. Marx argues that early theories of crises, developed by Rodburtus and Sismondi, wrongly considered circulation as independent of, and a limit to, production. In an attack against the notion of crises as the result of the constant underconsumption of consumer goods, apart from the requirements of reconversion, Marx argues that:

It is sheer tautology to say that crises are caused by the scarcity of effective consumption, or of effective consumers. The capitalist system does not know any other modes of consumption other than effective ones. . . . But if one were to attempt to give this tautology the semblance of a profounder justification by saying that the working-class receives too small a portion of its own product and the evil would be remedied as soon as it receives a larger share of it and its wages increase as a consequence, one could only remark that crises are always prepared by precisely a period in which wages rise generally and the working-class actually gets a larger share of that part of the annual product which is intended for consumption.[54]

In an attack upon Ricardo's limited understanding of the nature of expanded reproduction and the relationship between production and consumption, Marx notes in *Theories of Surplus Value* that,

[i]t must never be forgotten, that in capitalist production what matters is not the immediate use-value but the exchange-value and, in particular, the expansion of surplus value. This is the driving motive of capitalist production, and it is a pretty conception that – in order to reason away the contradictions of capitalist production – abstracts from its very basis and depicts it as a production aiming at the direct satisfaction of the consumption of the producers.[55]

In this way, Marx distinguishes himself from the underconsumptionists. His conception of the rate of accumulation as the variable whose fluctuations have the decisive effect on supply and demand is at odds with the underconsumptionist position.[56]

Marx's rejection of the idea of consumer underconsumption as the central causal force in the cessation of accumulation reaffirms his commitment to the concept of production as the unity of all economic processes in their contradictory states, and as the source of contradiction and conflict in capitalism. In his attempt to illuminate the nature of crises as symptomatic events, generated by the contradictions of capitalism as a mode of production, Marx returns to general statements that reformulate the idea of contradiction. In a movement similar to that which occurs in the discussion of the falling rate of profit, Marx ends his most extended discussion of crises with a reformulation of the idea of contradiction. This reformulation provides the reference point for later attempts to link the analysis of crises as production-related phenomena with the notion of consumer underconsumption, a phenomenon of circulation and distribution alone:

> Over-production is specifically conditioned by the general law of the production of capital . . . and this is carried through continuous expansion of reproduction and accumulation, and therefore constant reconversion of revenue into capital, while on the other hand, the mass of producers remain tied to the average level of needs, and must remain tied to it according to the nature of capitalist production.[57]

The same movement continues in *Capital*:

> . . . the periods in which capitalist production exerts all its forces regularly turn out to be periods of over-production, because production potentials can never be utilised to such an extent that more value may not only be produced but realised; but the sale of commodities, the realisation of commodity-capital and thus of surplus value, is limited, not by the consumer requirements of society in general, but by the consumer requirements of a society in which the vast majority are always poor and must always remain poor.[58]

> The ultimate reason for all real crises always remains the poverty and restricted consumption of the masses as opposed to the drive of capitalist production to develop the productive forces as though only the absolute consuming power of society constituted their limit.[59]

The earlier theoretical elaboration of crises, which defined crises as disruptions in the reconversion process of accumulation, is thrown into co-existence with these general statements on contradiction, which place the question of realization through consumer consumption at the center of crisis analysis. This complex reference, and the reformulation of contradiction that accompanies it, combined with Marx's references to a tendency towards increasing relative impoverishment, were later used to convert the potential for crises into a potential for permanent crisis, or breakdown. Moreover, in other elaborations on this reference, the relationship between production, as the unity of all economic processes, and circulation, as an independent realm, became obscured. Consequently, the distinction between the realm of empirical investigation, with its focus on competition and the actual development of specific capitalist societies, and general analysis, with its focus on the economy as a theoretical construct, began to blur as theories of breakdown emerged in the twentieth century.

Breakdown and the open dialectic: The status of laws

Marx's struggle with the distinction between general analysis and empirical investigation is symptomatic of a larger struggle with the status of the laws and conditions of capitalism. His rejection of the status conferred by the classical political economists precipitated Marx's break with classical thought, and provided the basis for the characterization of capitalism as a temporary mode. This break carries broad implications for the theories of history and knowledge that inform Marx's economic thought. And yet the break is expressed through a limited group of new concepts that appear in *Capital* and do not provide an explicit statement concerning the status of the laws and conditions of capitalism. Michel Foucault offers a description of the role of these concepts in Marx's break with classical thought:

> [C]oncepts like those of surplus value or falling rate of profit, as found in Marx, may be described on the basis of the system of positivity already in operation in the works of Ricardo; but these concepts (which are new, but whose rules of formation are not) appear – in Marx himself – as belonging at the same time to a quite different discursive practice: they are formed in that discursive practice in accordance with specific laws, they occupy in it a different position, they do not figure in the same sequences: this new positivity is not a transformation of Ricardo's analyses; it is not a new political economy; it is a discourse that occurred around the derivation of certain economic concepts, but which, in turn, defines the conditions in which the discourse of economists takes place, and may therefore be valid as a theory and a critique of political economy.[60]

The derivation of the concepts of value, surplus value and profit in *Capital* marks the distance that lies between Marx and Ricardo, and the existence of a discourse that is not fully contained within the assumptions of classical political economy. The primary epistemological demand generated by the derivation of these concepts, and by Marx's rejection of Ricardo, is the demand for a new status for the laws and conditions of capitalism and a new understanding of the historical relationship between them. The framework for a new status for the laws and conditions of capitalism is provided in the critical movements of *Theories of Surplus Value* and *Capital*, but largely ignored in the Western Marxist theories of breakdown.

In *Capital*, the concepts of value, surplus value and profit describe the contradictions that characterize capitalist society. According to Marx, these contradictions are masked by the ideology of equal exchange, one form of the philosophy of identity that informs classical political economy and the status it confers on the laws of capitalism. The ideology of equal exchange and its supporting philosophical assumptions veil the creation of surplus value and the contradictions of the economic order by collapsing oppositions into false identities, or alternatively, by assuming a state of radical separation to be a natural state, properly described through immutable categories. Marx argues that in the first case, contradictions are denied, and the unity of opposites existing within an economic relation is transformed 'into the direct identity of opposites.'[61] In the second case, the separation of related categories is assumed as a given condition, and '[w]here therefore it does not in fact apply, it is presumed,' since 'separation appears as the normal relation in this society.'[62] In either case,

[t]he *determinate social character* of the means of production in capitalist production – expressing a particular *production relation* – has so grown together with, and in the mode of thought of bourgeois society is so inseparable from, the material existence of these means of production as means of production, that the same determinateness (categorical determinateness) is assumed even where the relation is in direct contradiction to it.[63]

According to Marx, then, capitalist society, the product of an economic system based on the radical separation of related economic processes, is characterized by oppositions. The existence of these oppositions is denied through a philosophy of identity that restores singularity at the level of theory through the postulation of determinate, absolute laws, and at the level of analysis through the postulation of a domain of given facts and sense-certainty. The status conferred on the laws and conditions of capitalism by the classical political economists is derived from positivistic social analysis, and the broader philosophy of identity that informs it. This same philosophy of identity, in its positivistic form, re-emerges in twentieth-century orthodox and neo-orthodox theories of breakdown.

Marx argues that the laws of capitalism postulated by the classical economists are granted an unproblematic status as absolute, atemporal, immanent movements, overtly manifested in the observable, actual facts of an accessible and given economic reality. The determinism and universality of the laws foreclose on the theoretical possibilities present in the analysis of related but different temporal phenomena, and form a premature and unselfconscious circumscription of economic categories. The philosophy of identity that informs the status of the laws postulated by the classical political economists assumes an identity between what is, what should be, and what will be. To the extent that change and contradiction appear within the philosophy of identity, they appear only as a part of larger movements towards a predetermined stasis. Foucault, following Marx, finds that '[f]or Ricardo, History fills the void produced by anthropological finitude and expressed in a perpetual scarcity, until the moment when a point of definite stabilization is attained. . . .'[64]

In classical political economy, the relationship posed between the laws and conditions of capitalism is transparent, direct, and ultimately one of full identity: the laws of economic development are assumed to correspond with apparent facts of concrete economic conditions. The substantive manifestations of the philosophy of identity in classical political economy are thus supported by a series of epistemological assumptions that deny contradiction and opposition and restore singularity at the level of method and analysis. The status of the laws of capitalism conferred by classical political economists is made possible through the assumption of an identity between appearance and reality. This assumption forecloses on the theoretical possibility of an indirect relationship between the laws of capitalist development and its concrete conditions of existence. It also displaces any consideration of the social forces within capitalism that mediate knowledge of its development; transparent forms of representation and a full complicity between subject and object are assumed to exist. On the basis of these assumptions, classical political economy posits the concept of facticity as a sufficient concept of verification, and the concept of hypothesis as a sufficient concept of theory.

Through the substantive and epistemological assumptions generated by the philosophy of identity, classical political economy moves into collusion with the capitalist economic order, and with the ideology of equal exchange that occupies its superstructural forms. Marx's break with this collusion produced the concept of surplus value as the antithesis of equal exchange, the concept of fetishism as the antithesis of transparent representation, and the concept of a transitory capitalism as the antithesis of categorical determinateness. The break can be traced to his rejection of the philosophy of identity that informed classical political economy and provided the laws it postulated with the status of an absolute knowledge of a predetermined history. This rejection was initiated by Marx's critique of the concept of value and the philosophy of identity implicit in it.

The assumption of an identity between appearance and reality allowed Ricardo to think of value as an objective reality and to postulate laws derived from the concept as absolute and immanent laws. In the first part of *Capital* Volume I, culminating with the section on commodity fetishism, Marx rejects the idea of value as an innate attribute of commodities rooted in an objective reality of needs and utility. Instead, Marx redefines value as a subjective, historically and socially determined measure, a relational term.[65] The concept of value in *Capital* refers to a social relation in the world of commodity production, and to the manner in which a temporal social order defines and redefines the relative merits of commodity-producing labor. For Marx, values are not objective realities, or transparent representations of objective realities, or imperfect representations which must draw ever closer to full correspondence with their objects. Instead, they are ideological acts which bring into play social perceptions of labor's products. The classical conception of values as objective realities denies the contradictions of capitalism, the historical specificity of labor, production, and exchange under capitalism, and the temporality of the social order.

Marx's rejection of classical political economy, demonstrated in his analysis of value and the critique of commodity fetishism, represents a rejection of the positivist form of the philosophy of identity implicit in the premises of classical thought and in its assumption of a full, direct and accessible coincidence between the laws and conditions of capitalism. During the ten years that lapsed between Marx's tenuous acceptance of the classical form of the labor theory of value in *The Poverty of Philosophy* and his refutation of any positivist conceptualization of value in *Grundrisse*, Marx sketched the plan for the critique of classical political economy that was consummated in *Capital*. He also began a self-conscious reconsideration of the most formative influence on his intellectual development by returning to the works of Hegel, which he had repudiated in the earlier writings of the *Economic and Philosophic Manuscripts of 1844* and *The German Ideology*.

Marx's recognition of the potential for a disjunction between appearance and reality, and the rejection of the philosophy of identity and of classical political economy that followed from this recognition, were largely functions of his return to Hegelian concepts. The fundamentally Hegelian concepts of alienation, inversion, opposition and dialectical ralatedness appear as the critical tools of *Capital*, turned against the positivistic formulation of the philosophy of identity found in classical political economy, and against the previously impenetrable veil of capitalist relations.

The Hegelian dialectic served Marx as a critical force which could be brought to bear against classical political economy and the philosophy of identity that informed it. But the Hegelian concepts that appear in Marx's critique appear in a vastly modified form, largely stripped of their teleological components. The presence of these components would have negated the effectiveness of Marx's use of the concepts in his attack against classical political economy and the philosophy of identity underlying classical assumptions. Hegel's dialectic, in its full unmodified form, contains elements of the same philosophy of identity that informs classical political economy. These elements mark the relationship between Hegelian idealism and positivism as the two dominant ideologies of an expanding capitalist order.

The philosophy of identity found in the works of the classical political economists is an *a priori* assumption of identity and an *a priori* denial of contradiction, upon which a linear, progressive conception of economic history can be based. The dominant, teleological conception of history found in the works of Hegel rests on a different but nonetheless equally forceful form of the philosophy of identity, with an *a priori* assumption of original identity complemented by an *a posteriori* denial of permanent and irretrievable separation and contradiction. Hegel's formulation of the philosophy of identity supports a notion of history as the dialectical process of Geist working its way towards a re-identification of opposites created during an original rupture in a generic totality. The philosophy of identity appears in the form of a closed dialectic, with a predetermined end to contradiction, opposition and difference. Like the positivist philosophy of identity that informs classical political economy, the idealist form generates a series of deterministic, atemporal, universal laws, which foreclose on the theoretical possibilities for historical development and our knowledge of it.

The philosophy of identity found in Hegel's closed dialectic of historical development is related to, and supported by, a series of epistemological assumptions which lead to conclusions similar to those found in classical political economy. In Hegel's works, the complicity of subject and object and the existence of transparent forms of representation are not assumed as already given, but are assumed as pre-existing forms which will necessarily be realized through the teleological movement of Geist in its universal quest for self-recognition. The negation of the original unity of appearance and reality will be brought to a close as Geist reaches absolute knowledge of itself. In the epistemological assumptions of the Hegelian dialectic,

> the thesis of identity was always present, a thesis in which the development of the analyses was neither corroborated nor explicated. Hegel described it with the metaphor of the circle. Such closedness, which necessarily implied that nothing remained essentially unrecognized or fortuitous outside dialectics, has been exploded, along with its constraint and unambiguity.[66]

This explosion was largely the result of Marx's rejection of the philosophy of identity in both classical and Hegelian thought, an explosion which unleashed the full range of theoretical possibilities related to the understanding of capitalist society and its future. Marx's rejection of the philosophy of identity in classical political economy was a rejection of a static and contented conception of the present and our knowledge of it. This rejection was inspired, in part, by the dynamic, dialectical analysis of relational forms offered through the use of Hegelian concepts. Marx's rejection of the philosophy of identity in Hegelian thought was a rejection of a utopian conception of the future and our knowledge of it. It was inspired, in part, by Marx's revolt against the categorical determinateness of classical political economy, by his commitment to historical analysis, and by his insistence on the ideological and representational power of the capitalist superstructure. The Hegelian anticipation of a utopian future is absent in *Capital*, as is speculation about the epistemological categories which would correspond to a society where appearance and reality coincide. The classical assumption of a static and apparent present is explicitly rejected. The critical movements of *Capital* are characterized by a simultaneous movement away from both Hegel and Ricardo, and from the philosophy of identity that marks their thought.

Marx indicates that the attempt to move beyond the reified categories of understanding that appear under capitalism, and are reflected in the this-worldliness of classical political economy and the other-worldliness of Hegelianism, cannot be achieved through ideas which rely on the philosophy of identity. Rather, the attempt must be made through the practice of science as the critique of ideology, and an understanding of the unity of opposites that play through history in an open dialectic of repetition and difference. The discourse of this open dialectic in Marx – a discourse which escapes the reified split between positivistic empirical analysis and positivistic general analysis, but avoids the absolute idealism of Hegel – appears at many points in his writings. It appears most forcefully and explicitly in the negative movements of *Capital*, in the analysis of value and the critique of commodity fetishism, and in the theory of class struggle that appears throughout Marx's works. In these movements, theoretical foreclosure and reappropriation are held at bay.

For the critique of classical discourse, Marx turned back to Hegel's dialectic of appearance and reality; but for an explicit statement on the conditions of a new discourse, he was on his own and, predictably, near silence. The creation of the discourse of the open dialectic is a consequence of critique, a consequence of the negative movements in *Capital*. However, in the context of Marx's theory of capitalist development, a demonstration of a positive construction of the open dialectic may be found in the theory of class struggle and discussion of the law of the falling rate of profit.

The theory of class struggle provides an approach to political, economic and ideological issues that is fully grounded in the specificity of a particular historical movement: the assessment of the balance of class forces within a concrete economic context. Similarly, the law of the falling rate of profit is provided with an open status and with the full range of theoretical possibilities that surround a new discourse. The discourse of the open dialectic is submerged but present in Marx's discussion of the falling rate of profit. A reading of this submerged form indicates the potential for the existence of a discursive process in Marx's theory of capitalist development which is not fully accounted for by either positivism or idealism, the epistemological counterparts of nineteenth-century libreralism and conservatism.

During the time that Marx was constructing the theory of the falling rate of profit, he was also engaged in a re-reading of Hegel's *Logic*, and wrote to Engels that 'in the *method* of treatment it was of great service' to his work on profit. With a glance back to his earlier writings, Marx continued: 'If ever a time comes again for such works, I would have great pleasure in making available to ordinary common sense in two or three printer's sheets, what is *rational* in the method Hegel discovered but at the same time mystified.'[67] The theory of profit that emerged from this period contained Hegelian overtones, with its image of a law fraught with internal contradictions arising from the singular phenomenon of increased productivity. The status of the law as an ultimate tendency is prevented from reaching teleological proportions, however, by the unresolved problem of counteracting tendencies.

The law of the tendency of the rate of profit to fall, Marx's most substantial theoretical commitment to a conceptualization of breakdown, is a law of contradictions:

> We have thus seen in a general way that the same influences which produce a tendency in the general rate of profit to fall, also call forth counter-effects, which hamper, retard, and partly paralyse this fall. The latter do not do away with the law, but impair its effect. Otherwise, it would not be the fall of the general rate of profit, but rather its relative slowness, that would be incomprehensible. Thus, the law acts only as a tendency. And it is only under certain circumstances and only after long periods that its effects become strikingly pronounced.[68]

Marx's original term in the first sentence here is not *hemmen* (hamper), a word chosen by Engels, but *aufheben*, which also appears in the next sentence: 'Sie heben das Gesetz nicht auf,' translated in the English edition as 'The latter do not do away with the law.' Literally, Marx had written that the counteracting tendencies cancel out the law, and do not cancel out the law.

29

Aufheben may mean annul, preserve, transcend, or, in its Hegelian context, a context intimately familiar to Marx, to move beyond while still retaining residues of the previous state.[69]

The submerged image of the law in this passage is not that of an ultimate tendency which will necessarily find realization after a long struggle for dominance over conflicting tendencies. Nor is it that of a logical construction defeated by the concrete existence of material obstacles or historical events. In either of these cases, the contradiction between the law and the counteracting tendencies would be resolved in the absorption of one by the other. The image that emerges is one of effect and counter-effect, engaged in a mutually dependent process of reciprocity and repetition, in an indeterminate and potentially infinite play of interactions which are similar but different. There is no final indication of full foreclosure at any point, and no final indication of impending breakdown or eventual resolution. The law of the tendency of the rate of profit to fall ends in a theoretical elaboration which entertains positivist and idealist interpretations, but contains a submerged discourse which cannot be fully accounted for by either.

In later readings of *Capital*, the discourse on contradiction was commonly appropriated in forms which assumed the progressive linearity of British classical political economy or the apocalyptic vision of Hegelian teleology. The theoretical but indeterminate discourse of the law of the falling rate of profit, which combines and supersedes the conceptual analyses of political economy and the dialectics of German idealism, fell to the same fate. The theories of breakdown generated from readings of *Capital* reverted back to the philosophy of identity Marx so desperately tried to escape. The ahistorical quality of the philosophy of identity re-emerged in theories of breakdown as the historical specificity of crises, and their role in an ongoing cyclical process was lost to a detemporalized notion of crises as permanent chronic conditions or conclusive events. The *a priori* determinism of the classical and Hegelian models reappeared in the privileged linear causality of progressively intensifying chronic crisis, or the apocalyptic teleological vision of final collapse. The discourse of the open dialectic, within which class struggle could be situated, was quickly buried beneath the resurgence of earlier forms of thought. Theories of automatic collapse simply reversed the classical conclusion of automatic continuation, silencing the concepts that provided the basis for Marx's break with positivist and idealist forms.

The orthodox and neo-orthodox theories of breakdown that were generated during the Second International and expanded throughout the new century restored the singularity of the philosophy of identity through the postulation of absolute mechanical laws and sense-certainty. The anti-orthodox theories of breakdown that soon arose to challenge the orthodox and neo-orthodox positions restored the philosophy of identity through the postulation of ontological laws and the postulation of a reversal in the roles of structure and superstructure which assumed idealist forms. In both cases, the status of the laws and conditions of capitalism was returned to the same epistemological assumptions that corresponded to the expansion of the bourgeois order and became the object of Marx's critique in *Capital*.

The epistemological and historical premises of theories of breakdown, in their return to positivist and idealist forms, required fundamental reformulations of the concepts found in *Capital*. The reference points were located through selective readings, frozen in the text, and recast to accommodate the philosophical and political requirements of the new theories. The relationships between structure and superstructure, production and circulation, and profit and exploitation, were radically reset. The laws and conditions of capitalism were no longer indirectly related through critical discourse, but fully identified or completely separated.

Breakdown theorists turned away from those concepts in *Capital* through which Marx had distanced himself from classical political economy and Hegelianism – the concepts of value, surplus value, and profit. In turning away from these concepts, the breakdown theorists also turned away from the political expression of Marx's break from the earlier forms – the analysis of exploitation, class, and class struggle. With the philosophy of identity restored through positivism and idealism, and attention diverted from concrete class relations, the last obstacles to theoretical reunification with earlier forms of thought were removed. With the concept of class struggle displaced by the concept of mechanical breakdown, the liberalism of classical political economy and the conservative fatalism of Hegelianism surfaced within the Marxist camp in the politics of breakdown theory. Historically specific analyses of historically specific crises – the objective contexts for situated class struggle – were left behind. In the process, breakdown theorists formulated and fueled a notion of 'final collapse' that set them apart from those who adopted the concept of a 'final conflict' – the guiding concept of the emerging world communist movement.

3 Breakdown theory in the Second International:
The political construction of the orthodox concept

Crises, conflicts, catastrophes of all kinds, it is this lovely
alliteration that the course of development places in prospect for
the next decade.

Kautsky, 'Krisentheorien'

If society were constituted or had developed in the manner the
socialist theory has hitherto assumed, then certainly the economic collapse would be only a question of a short span of time.

Bernstein, *Evolutionary Socialism*

The broad range of theoretical possibilities generated by Marx's
theory of breakdown overflowed the conceptual schema of *Capital*
and spilled into later manuscripts. In 1875 and 1880–81, Marx
returned to the problem of the falling rate of profit, but did not
produce significant revisions of his earlier formulations. His
intention to rewrite the 1867 draft of *Capital* Volume II was never
realized, and the promised volume on method never appeared.
When Marx died in 1883, *Capital* remained in its original state,
with the end of capitalism posed, at certain points in the text, as
the necessary result of a relatively unexplained process, and at
other points, as the necessary process of a relatively unexplained
end. Engels was left to edit and publish a manuscript which barely
managed to contain the explosive quality of the theories generated
by its unevenly mediated concepts.

When Volume III of *Capital*, with its discourse on profit rates,
finally appeared in December 1894, it collided with a constellation
of theoretical, ideological and material conditions which simultaneously exaggerated and reduced the power of its arguments at
crucial conceptual junctures. Volume III had been conceived
during the period of political retrenchment that followed the
failure of the 1848 revolutions, but was read half a century later in

the activist era of the Second International. The anarchist movement that had disturbed Marx's socialist vision in the 1860s had been displaced by the revisionist debates of the 1890s, and the long economic recession of Marx's last years in London had ended in the unprecedented economic upswing of the final decade of the nineteenth century.

Those who encountered the law of the falling rate of profit in the text of Volume III also encountered a material context of observed increases in the rate of profit, occurring in the midst of unbridled technological change, increased productivity and expanded accumulation. The economic depression that began in 1873 ended with an economic boom that seemed to demonstrate the ultimate invulnerability of capitalism. By 1895, the major industrial countries were reporting tremendous economic growth accompanied by a degree of concentration, consolidation and imperialist involvement that seemed to indicate a material shift in the very nature of capitalism itself. The relationship between the laws and conditions of capitalism set forth in *Capital* was opened to a series of elaborations that radically altered the implicit and explicit assumptions underlying Marx's formulations. Perceptions of the theoretical text clashed with perceptions of the circumstantial historical context, and the result was a sizable and significant expansion of the range of theoretical possibilities generated by Marx's theory of capitalist development, and the construction of theories of breakdown which went far beyond anything anticipated in Marx's passing references to collapse. This expansion assumed increasingly exaggerated forms as European Marxists contemplated the theory of capitalist development over the next seventy years, and pursued theories of breakdown in a multitude of forms.

Full documentation of all the theories of breakdown produced during this period would require a full-length work in itself. The purpose here is simply to provide some sense of the extremes of interpretation found in the writings of early European breakdown theorists. These extremes form the conceptual boundaries of theories of breakdown and may be used to situate the works of later European and American theorists. For the most part, later theorists were fully familiar with the development of breakdown theory at the turn of the century. Their reading of Marx was never direct, but filtered through the literature that grew out of the breakdown controversy in the Second International. This intervening body of texts, and the theoretical alternatives it suggested with respect to breakdown theory, are discussed here as part of the ongoing attempt to reconstruct the development of European and American theories of breakdown as they absorbed and resisted *Capital* itself.

Capital in the context of the first Great Depression, 1873–1895

During the last few years of Marx's life and in the decade following his death, most of the work produced by Marxist theorists was not concerned with the economic concepts of *Capital* or with the theory of capitalist development. Instead, major theoretical works focused on the interpretation and systematization of Marx's brief writings on socialism, and on the expansion of historical material-ism as a universal method of analysis. Bebel's *Women Under Socialism* appeared in 1883, Mehring's *On Historical Materialism* in 1893, Plekhanov's *The Development of the Monist Conception of History* in 1895, and Labriola's *Essays on the Materialist Conception of History* in 1896.

During the same period, Engels also devoted much of his time to promoting the concept of historical materialism and its relevance to non-economic fields of study. *Anti-Dühring* was published in 1878. Engels worked on *Dialectics of Nature* from 1873–80, and published *The Origin of the Family, Private Property, and the State* in 1884, and *Ludwig Feuerbach and the End of Classical German Philosophy* in 1886. By the time the Second International was founded in 1889, Marxism had become the dominant theory in the international workers' movement, but its key theorists remained ensconced in issues that led them far from the primary concerns of *Capital*.

Engels had been left the difficult task of editing and publishing the manuscripts for *Capital* Volumes II and III. This work occurred during the depression that had begun in 1873. The depression continued in a second full decade of decline, defying earlier cyclical patterns. Those aspects of the depression that captured Engels's attention indicated basic shifts in the capitalist order: a dramatic increase in the importance attributed to foreign markets for capital goods, a radical escalation in capital concen-tration and centralization, and a clean break, both in terms of the duration and the nature of the overproduction involved, with earlier cyclical patterns of crisis and recovery. As Engels set to work on Marx's literary estate, the consensus grew among bourgeois and Marxist economists alike that the Great Depression of the last quarter of the century was unlike any that had occurred before. Engels increasingly concurred in this judgment, and edited *Capital* accordingly.

The crisis was preceded by a period of exceptionally intense capital investment, technological development, increased pro-ductivity, and rising export demand, especially in British iron and coal.[1] Foreign trade and investments preserved profitability from the threat of overaccumulation. The initial phase of crisis that began in 1873 was associated with the collapse of foreign outlets –

bankruptcy in Spain, financial crises in Austria and South America, and defaults on payments of foreign loans. Export demand plummeted with the decline in American railroad construction and the growing ability of the American iron and steel industry to meet domestic needs. The decisive impact of the contraction in foreign trade and investment on the British economy was to stimulate a marked preoccupation with new foreign trade and investments, and the intensification of colonization in Africa, Asia, South America and the Pacific Islands. Britain was joined by France, Germany, and the United States in the rush for imperialist control over capital goods markets.

The decline of foreign trade and investments was followed by an initial rise in domestic investment, and then a dramatic decline in 1877. Prices collapsed across Europe and profit rates fell, especially in coal, iron and textiles – the industrial base of nineteenth-century expansionary capitalism. The depression was severe in Russia and Britain, but the initial crash was particularly acute in Germany. Cut-throat competition and price-cutting escalated concentration to an unprecedented degree, especially in the more flexible economies of Germany and the United States. Manufacturers' associations formed in the German iron and coal industries in the 1870s, and quickly spread to other sectors. Four hundred German cartels were in operation by 1905. In the United States, the rapid rise of trusts increased visible concentration and the capacity for a full-scale challenge to British industrial domination.

But the most striking quality of the depression, for Engels and his contemporaries, was its unprecedented duration and its break from the recognized cyclical pattern. In 1878, when the depression was still in its early stages, Engels published *Anti-Dühring*, which contained his most extensive discussion of cycles and crises. *Anti-Dühring* affirmed the model of cyclical crises set forth in *Capital*. Since the first general crisis of 1825, Engels determines, crises have recurred every ten years, and have followed a uniform pattern:

> Trade comes to a standstill, the markets are glutted, the products lie in great masses, unsalable, ready money disappears, credit vanishes, the factories are idle, the working masses go short of the means of subsistence because they have produced too much of them, bankruptcy follows upon bankruptcy, forced sale upon forced sale.[2]

Stagnation continues until the accumulated commodities have been destroyed, and then the economy revives. The pace of investment and speculation quickens until it reaches

a complete industrial, commercial, credit and speculative

steeplechase, only to land again in the end, after the most breakneck jumps – in the ditch of a crash. And so on again and again. We have now experienced it five times since 1825, and at this moment (1877) we are experiencing it for the sixth time. And the character of these crises is so clearly marked that Fourier hit them all off when he described the first as *crise pléthorique*, a crisis of superabundance.[3]

Underconsumption does not fully explain cyclical crises, Engels argues, because underconsumption is not peculiar to capitalism but exists in all societies based on exploitation. The cyclical crises of the previous fifty years cannot be linked solely to underconsumption, but must be traced to overproduction instead. Underconsumption of consumer goods is 'a necessary condition of crises, and plays a role in them which has long been recognized; but it tells us just as little why crises exist today as why they did not exist at earlier periods.'[4]

Instead, the cause of crises lies in the contradiction between social production and capitalist expropriation, and the inability of the system to control productive forces. In crises, the social character of production is revealed. The pressure to recognize the social character of production is manifested in the rise of joint-stock companies and in state take-overs of key industries like the railroads, telegraph services, and postal services. State take-overs are testimony to the necessity of the continued socialization of production, and the inability to reconcile socialization with private appropriation. Thus state take-overs are an extreme form of capitalism which occur just as capitalism is converted into its opposite.[5]

Engels does not indicate that the crash of 1873 or the ensuing depression are beyond the bounds of cyclical crisis theory. He speculates, however, that the growth preceding the crash may have pushed the contradictions of capitalism to an unprecedented point. Engels finds that 'large-scale industry has developed the contradictions lying dormant in the capitalist mode of production into such crying antagonisms that the imminent collapse of this mode of production is, so to speak, palpable. . . .'[6] In 1880, a brief period of recovery which would have invoked earlier cyclical patterns proved to be but a flashing moment. For Engels, the duration of the depression eventually called into question Marx's conceptualization of the periodicity of cyclical crises.

In 1884, a year after Marx's death, and after almost a full decade of economic decline, Engels began to speculate about a permanent crisis in the system. In his 1884 Preface to the first German edition of Marx's *Poverty of Philosophy*, Engels spoke of the 'inevitable collapse of the capitalist mode of production which is daily taking place before our eyes to an even greater degree. . . .'[7] The equalization of production and demand on the world market, previously established through periodic trade crises, seemed beyond reach. Instead, the unrelieved depression of the post-1873 period, Engels argues, may indicate the end of cyclical crises. If prosperity does not return, 'then chronic stagnation would necessarily become the normal condition of modern industry, with only insignificant fluctuations.'[8]

In his 1886 Preface to the English edition of *Capital*, Engels again speculates about the possibility of chronic depression. Engels poses the idea of a crisis removed from the cyclical framework and detemporalized, no longer a passing phase in a recurring process, but a permanent condition of capitalism:

> The decennial cycle of stagnation, prosperity, over-production and crisis, ever recurrent from 1825 to 1867, seems indeed to have run its course; but only to land us in the slough of despond of a permanent and chronic depression. The sighed-for period of prosperity will not come; as often as we seem to perceive its heralding symptoms, so often do they again vanish into air.[9]

Again in 1887–8, a partial recovery occurred, only to disappear in another new crisis in 1890. Engels was not alone in his estimation that the depression marked a unique moment in the development of capitalism. The Royal Commission on the Depression of Trade and Industry surveyed the British economy between 1870 and 1884, and concluded that 'the remarkable feature of the present situation, and that which in our opinion distinguishes it from all previous periods of depression, is the length of time during which this overproduction has continued. . . .'[10]

In Germany, where the crash had been most violent in 1873 and again in 1890, the depression inspired in the Social Democratic Party (SPD) the idea that the final moments of capitalism were at hand. In 1891, the SPD Congress adopted the *Erfurt Program*, drafted by Karl Kautsky and Eduard Bernstein and submitted to the Congress after direct approval from Engels. The *Program* included a categorical statement on the end of capitalism which neglected the tendential qualities of the laws described in *Capital*, and constructed a purely mechanistic conception of breakdown expressed in the apocalyptic imagery of collapse:

> Capitalist society has failed; its dissolution is only a question of time; irresistible economic development leads with natural necessity to the bankruptcy of the capitalist mode of production. The erection of a new form of society is no longer something merely *desirable*; it has become something *inevitable*.

The only question is: shall the system of private ownership in the means of production be allowed to pull society with itself down into the abyss; or shall society shake off that burden and then, free and strong, resume the path of progress which the evolutionary law prescribes to it?[11]

Despite the categorical statements of the *Erfurt Program*, Engels was still not prepared to endorse the idea of mechanical collapse or the concept of chronic crisis without qualification. The recovery that began in Russia in 1893 and gathered speed through the last months of Engels's work on Volume III of *Capital* provoked a new series of questions. In his long note on Marx's discussion of the business cycle in Volume III, the idea of the crisis as the end of a clear cyclical pattern in the development of capitalism re-emerges in muted form, with the cyclical character of the crisis partially restored. The periodic crises of the 1825–67 period, Engels determines, have been replaced by

a more chronic, long drawn out, alternation between a relatively short and slight business improvement and a relatively long, indecisive depression – taking place in the various industrial countries at different times. But perhaps it is only a matter of a prolongation of the duration of the cycle.[12]

On the other hand, Engels asks, 'is it possible that we are now in the preparatory stage of a new world crash of unparalleled vehemence?'[13] The 'profound changes' that occurred with the crisis induced this line of thought. These changes included the creation of the world market, the end of Britain's monopoly on industrial production, the growth of cartels and trusts, and the rise of protective tariffs and inter-imperialist rivalries. Eventually, the Great Depression led Engels to the conviction that capitalism had undergone a major change which marked the end of competition:

The daily growing speed with which production may be enlarged in all fields of large-scale industry today, is offset by the ever-greater slowness with which the market for these increased products expands. . . . The results are a general chronic over-production, depressed prices, falling and even wholly disappearing profits; in short, the old boasted freedom of competition has reached the end of its tether and must itself announce its obvious, scandalous bankruptcy.[14]

As the recovery was consolidated in Russia, Engels turned to Volume III and the theory of the falling rate of profit. The only chapter in the long-awaited text of Volume III for which there was no manuscript was Chapter IV, where Marx had intended to discuss the effect of the length of the turnover-time of constant capital on the rate of profit. In Volume II, Marx had devoted one chapter to the turnover-time of variable and constant capital considered jointly, and one chapter to the turnover-time of variable capital alone.[15] Engels decided to complete the manuscript of Volume III by writing Chapter IV himself. In the process, Engels introduced an argument that ran counter to the law of the falling rate of profit set forth in later chapters of Marx's manuscript.

In Chapter IV, Engels contends that technological advancements in production, transportation and communication increase the rate of turnover of capital investments. If the rate of turnover increases while the rate of profit remains the same, then the effective rate of profit, which determines the mass of profit available for investment and expanded accumulation, also increases. Moreover, Engels argues that increased productivity does not necessarily raise the ratio of constant to variable capital but, in many cases, lowers it. Technological improvements may involve machinery and production processes that are more simple and less costly than those replaced. The rate of profit, then, may remain the same or even increase over time. With this argument, Engels essentially introduces two counteracting tendencies to any tendency of the rate of profit to fall, and indicates that they are sufficient to maintain or increase the rate of profit during periods of increased productivity.

Engels's argument about turnover-time and its effect on the falling rate of profit, and his speculations on the end of cyclical crises, were soon seized upon by Bernstein as evidence of an admission that *Capital* no longer accurately described the development of capitalism. Although Engels never moved firmly beyond the point of speculation with respect to the end of cyclical crises, his brief inquiries into the possible significance of the depression were appropriated as a critique of Marx's theory of capitalist development. For the revisionists, these passages provided an opportunity to view the depression as a watershed period in capitalism, marking the end of unregulated production. For the orthodox defenders, Engels's speculations about chronic depression provided the reference point for a new theory of mechanical economic collapse. In both cases, the historically specific analysis of historically specific crises was left behind, and the motor role of class struggle in bringing the end of capitalism was reduced to mere rhetoric.

The revisionist assault and the postulation of breakdown theory

The Russian recovery of 1883 began with a new round of railway construction and industrial investment. Germany followed, with the electrical and chemical industries leading the revival. By 1895, recovery in Germany was in full swing. The government, still fresh with the power brought by unification, fueled the recovery through subsidies to the railroad and shipping industries. In Britain, recovery did not begin until 1896 with a boom in the domestic transport industries, consolidated by a renewal of capital export and foreign investments in Canada, India and South America.

The unprecedented recovery evident by 1895 provided bourgeois economists with an opening which had narrowed during the crisis-ridden years of the previous two decades. Reaction to the third volume of *Capital* was swift. Although Volumes I and II had been met with measured silence by bourgeois economists, a response to Volume III was provoked by the rapid growth of socialism on the continent in the last decades of the century, the consolidation of Marxism as the unrivalled theoretical foundation for the socialist movement, and the apparent vindication of capitalism provided by the recovery. The assault was launched by Eugen von Böhm-Bawerk and the marginalist theorists who had effectively expelled Marxist theory from the mainstream of economic thought in Europe.

When Böhm-Bawerk published *Karl Marx and the Close of His System* in 1896, he was already one of the most famous economists in the world, and the leading promoter of the theory of marginal utility.[16] Born in 1851 to an aristocratic family in Austria, Böhm-Bawerk served as Finance Minister in the Austrian Empire in three cabinets, and held a chair in political economy at the University of Vienna. His book was immediately influential in Europe, and was translated into Russian and English to mitigate Marx's growing influence in those countries.

Böhm-Bawerk's central criticisms of Marx focused on Marx's acceptance of what Böhm-Bawerk determined to be an empirically operational labor theory of value. Böhm-Bawerk further argued that Marx's labor theory of value was not coherent, but took diverse forms, resulting in a contradiction between the theory of value in Volume I of *Capital* and the theory of value in Volume III. Through the refutation of Marx's theory of value, and through the postulation of a 'transformation problem' in *Capital*, Böhm-Bawerk effectively undermined the calculations of profit rates found in Volume III and, consequently, the theory of the falling rate of profit.

The significance of Böhm-Bawerk's critique lies in the fact that he established an empiricist interpretation of the function of value theory, and a positivist epistemology as the appropriate framework for the evaluation of Marx's work. This interpretation, and the terms of debate set by its acceptance, went unchallenged for a full decade. In the intervening years, with the authority of Böhm-Bawerk cited in support and the recovery of 1895 as the key issue, debates within the Second International promoted the empirical testing of *Capital* within the Marxist camp. Marx's theory of capitalist development, and the epistemological considerations it entailed, were soon displaced by concepts that were tied to *Capital* by thin and twisted threads. In the process, the idea of breakdown was transformed from a fleeting image into a full-blown theory that influenced Western Marxist thought throughout the twentieth century.

Engels's death in 1895 cleared the path for this radical reformulation of Marx's concepts. Within a decade, an orthodox version of breakdown theory was firmly established as a distinctive element in Marxist debates. The establishment of this theory required the displacement of the dialectic by models which more clearly resembled those of classical political economy. Hegel was replaced by Kant and Darwin; revolutionary class struggle by reformism or fatalism. By the end of the Second International, Marxist thought, as it appeared in the works of the revisionists and in the works of the orthodox defenders, bore little resemblance to the theory of capitalist development in Marx. At the center of this dramatic theoretical shift, breakdown theory first appeared as a coherent and lasting concept in Western Marxism. Beginning with the Second International, the theory functioned as the fulcrum for the broader theoretical shift which shaped the development of Marxism in the West. This broader shift, and the central role of breakdown theory in its development, is nowhere more evident than in Eduard Bernstein's *Presuppositions of Social Democracy* and the debates it inspired.

Soon after Böhm-Bawerk's critique appeared, Bernstein published a series of articles in *Die Neue Zeit*, the official organ of the German SPD. The articles ran from 1896 until 1898, punctuated by heated rebuttals from Kautsky, Cunow and Luxemburg, who defended Marx against Bernstein's attack. Bernstein's articles were expanded and published in book form in 1899 as *Presuppositions of Socialism and the Tasks of Social Democracy*, the first extended refutation of Marx's theory of capitalist development.[17] In this work, Bernstein constructs a theory of breakdown, attributes the theory to Marx, and then refutes the theory as an empirically unverified notion of capitalist development.

Bernstein locates the origins of breakdown theory in *The Communist Manifesto*, and rejects the political conclusions that Marx provides. Bernstein claims that the 'presuppositions of socialism' provided in the *Manifesto* are based on the idea that a catastrophic economic collapse will usher in socialism. The 'tasks of social democracy' are to re-evaluate the presuppositions in the light of empirical evidence and to construct the proper political strategies dictated by the results. The *Manifesto* was correct in its general description of the 'social evolution' of capitalism, but mistaken in its claim that the end of capitalism was imminent:

> I set myself against the notion that we have to expect shortly a collapse of the bourgeois economy, and that social democracy should be induced by the prospect of such an imminent, great social catastrophe to adapt its tactics to that assumption. That I maintain most emphatically. The adherents of this theory of a catastrophe, base it especially on the conclusions of the *Communist Manifesto*. This is a mistake in every respect.[18]

Bernstein asserts that Engels had admitted this mistake in his Preface to *Class Struggles in France*. According to Bernstein, the error was not a simple miscalculation, but an indication of a fundamental flaw in Marx's thought. The concept of breakdown was part of Marx's fatalistic Hegelianism, and the result of the 'excessive abstraction' and 'theoretical phraseology' that marked the 'conflict between scientificity and tendency' in *Capital*.[19] The theory had been disproven by the continued development of capitalism: collapse had not occurred in timely fashion. 'If the universal crisis is the inherent law of capitalist production,' Bernstein writes, 'it must prove its reality now or in the near future.' Without empirical demonstration, the theory is more 'abstract speculation.'[20]

Moreover, Bernstein claims that the material conditions of capitalism in the late nineteenth century preclude the continued applicability of Marx's theory of capitalist development. In the context of the growth of cartels and credit, of a fully developed world market, and of new democratic institutions, which Bernstein describes in a summary presentation of empirical data, any form of breakdown theory is erroneous. Instead, he argues, the tendency of capitalism is towards a decrease in conflicts and crises, and the gradual elimination of contradiction.

Bernstein systematically recounts Marx's discussion of centralization, periodic crises, underconsumption, the law of the tendency of the rate of profit to fall, and disproportionality, and refutes their conclusions with a series of statistical sketches concerning the empirical conditions of capitalism in late nineteenth-century England and Europe. In his 'purification' of the 'principles' of Marxism, Bernstein counters the concept of the falling rate of profit with a discussion of the equalization of the distribution of wealth through shareholding and real wage increases. Periodic crises resulting from overproduction and underconsumption occur with less frequency and severity, Bernstein claims, due to the decreased turnover-time of capital, the flexibility provided by a sophisticated system of credit, and the development of foreign trade.[21]

There is then, according to Bernstein, no reason 'to expect shortly a collapse of the bourgeois economy,' despite the predictions of Marx, his orthodox followers, and the Socialist Congress.[22] The 'catastrophic theory of evolution' set forth by those who dwell on the rhetoric of *The Communist Manifesto* and the economic calculations of *Capital* have been disproven, Bernstein argues, by the actual development of capitalism since *Capital* was drafted. Capitalism will end, he concludes, not through economic breakdown, but through a gradual process of democratization in all economic and political institutions.[23]

With breakdown theory, one of the 'presuppositions of socialism,' discredited by empirical evidence, political tactics based on the expectation of imminent collapse must be rejected:

> The point at issue is between the theory of a social cataclysm and the question whether with the given social development in Germany and the present advanced state of its working classes in the towns and the country, a sudden catastrophe would be in the interest of the social democracy. I have denied it and deny it again, because in my judgment a greater security for lasting success lies in a steady advance than in the possibilities offered by a catastrophic crash.[24]

> But it is evident that if social evolution takes a much greater period of time than was assumed, it must also take upon itself *forms* and lead to forms that were not foreseen and could not have been foreseen.[25]

Rarely has the nexus between breakdown theory and a political program been so clearly stated. The new 'forms' enumerated are components of social democracy, already established as a substantial part of the program of the SPD, and limited only by their incompatibility with the Marxist theory that still wielded a strong influence within the party. The political content of the debate over breakdown theory within the Second International was clear from the outset: the expansion of social democratic practice required a break from the intellectual demands of Marx's theory of capitalist development.

The break required a rejection of the conceptual and epistemological underpinnings of the theory. Bernstein again led the way. Through his postulation of a breakdown theory in Marx and his subsequent critique of the theory, Bernstein reset the epistemological boundaries for debate. By sweeping aside all of the considerations generated by Marx's critique of classical political economy, and pursuing a purely empirical evaluation of the tendential laws of capitalism, Bernstein pushed Marxist debate into the positivist arena. The tendencies towards concentration, centralization, a falling rate of profit, and increasing relative impoverishment are all systematically reformulated in absolute terms and then summarily dismissed through the selective application of empirical data.[26] The labor theory of value, and the theory of surplus value, are rejected as no more relevant or valid than other theories of value, such as Böhm-Bawerk's theory of marginal utility. All can be tested through empirical verification.[27] The labor theory of value, Bernstein finds, 'refuses services over and above a certain point, and therefore it has become disastrous to nearly every disciple of Marx.' The theory can be empirically disproved by the existence of 'the "aristocracy of labour" just in those trades with a very high rate of surplus value. . . .'[28]

The rejection of Marx's theory of capitalist development and the political conclusions that arise from that theory also required a rejection of historical materialism. In a movement that parallels his treatment of the theory of capitalist development, Bernstein reduces historical materialism to a set of untenable postulates to facilitate his wholesale rejection of the method. According to Bernstein, historical materialism is based on the 'necessary movements of matter' which are viewed 'from beginning to end as a mechanical process, each individual process being the necessary result of preceding mechanical facts.'[29] This doctrine led Marx 'to all kinds of false conclusions,' including the theory of automatic, mechanical economic breakdown.[30]

The economic determinism entailed in historical materialism is no longer appropriate in a society where 'the interdependency of cause and effect between technical, economic evolution, and the evolution of other social tendencies is becoming always more indirect. . . .'[31] With the dialectical model for social change replaced by the evolutionary model, and epistemological considerations displaced by crude empirical verification, the Hegelian content of Marx's thought is quickly dissolved. Instead, Kant provides all of the epistemological guidance that is necessary, and 'ethical imperatives' replace objective social forces as the basis for social change.

With the dialectic removed, class struggle was easily converted into the prescription for parliamentary socialism. Bernstein's contention that crises are improbable allows him to minimize the potential for social revolution. In his empirical refutation of the theory of growing relative impoverishment, Bernstein redefines class as a common standard of living rather than a relation to the means of production. With this new definition, Bernstein finds that the proletariat is decreasing in size and strength, while the middle classes are increasing. Political reform and gradualism are the obvious responses to the new constellation of class forces. Marx and Engels, Bernstein writes, 'left to their successors the duty of bringing unity again into their theory and of co-ordinating theory and practice.'[32] In the context of Bernstein's Germany, 'co-ordinating theory and practice' meant reformulating Marx's revolutionary thought to coincide with the growing strength of reformist politics.

When *Presuppositions* was published, Bernstein was firmly established as a central figure in the SPD, co-author of the *Erfurt Program*, and executor of Engels's literary estate. Those who might have provided more than formal opposition – Kautsky, Liebknecht, Bebel – were all moving to the right. Kautsky was editor of *Die Neue Zeit* when Bernstein's articles were published and made no attempt to block them, although he would later silence Luxemburg's submissions on the mass strike.

Presuppositions generated three days of debate at the Hanover Congress of the SPD in 1899. Its findings were rejected in a resolution passed by delegates. The revisionist position was rejected a second time at the Lübeck Congress in 1901, but motions to expel the revisionists were defeated, and Bernstein received the full support of the SPD in his successful bid for the Reichstag. Bernstein's base within the SPD was composed of those who wanted to form new alliances with other political parties, and the moderate wing of the trade unions.[33]

With his position in the SPD fundamentally unchallenged, and the SPD clearly posed as the dominant force in the international socialist movement, Bernstein's formulations gained wide influence in Marxist circles throughout the West. Despite the denunciations from leaders within the SPD, the theoretical and political victory ultimately belonged to Bernstein. From his position of exile in England, he had launched a controversy that preoccupied the Second International, fed the brewing split within the SPD, and introduced a theory of breakdown in terms which pushed Marxist debates far from Marx's theory of capitalist development and the critique of political economy. The theoretical development of the concepts found in *Capital*, and the political development of the conclusions generated by Marx's analysis of capitalism, were temporarily suspended, and permanently skewed.

The orthodox response

Heinrich Cunow fired a response to Bernstein in *Die Neue Zeit*, which made no attempt to refute Bernstein's reading of Marx or his construction of breakdown theory.[34] Cunow simply refuted Bernstein's arguments with his own notion of shrinking markets as the cause of collapse. Cunow also defended the prospects of imminent revolution induced by increasing impoverishment, posed in relative terms, although Bernstein had already rejected any relative formulation of the theory.[35] The official SPD response was left to Karl Kautsky, widely recognized as the chief theoretician of the party during his long tenure as editor of *Die Neue Zeit*.

In 1887 Kautsky had published *The Economic Doctrines of Karl Marx*, which was translated into several languages and quickly became the official SPD commentary on Marx.[36] *Economic Doctrines* endorsed a linear model of crises occurring with increasing intensity and severity until the 'final crisis' of capitalism arrived and the system was overthrown. The path to socialism was paved by the progressive concentration of capital and socialization of labor until the irresistible moment of revolution occurred. In *Economic Doctrines*, the tendential laws described by Marx appear in absolute form, as mechanical, deterministic linear movements, progressively realized and empirically verifiable. The peculiar brand of 'historical materialism' that Bernstein erroneously claimed to find in Marx was more likely taken from Kautsky.

In 1899, when the recovery in Europe was fully consolidated, Kautsky was called upon to issue the orthodox response to revisionist interpretations of Marx and to Bernstein's postulation and refutation of breakdown theory. By this time, he had modified his position on the end of capitalism. In response to Bernstein's empirical attack against the theory of breakdown, Kautsky argued that 'a distinct collapse theory was never established by Marx and Engels.'[37] Bernstein attributed to Marx an idea that was 'ridiculous.'[38] Kautsky went on to argue that there was no theory of breakdown in the *Erfurt Program*, a claim that undermined his defense of Marx.[39]

A few years later, Kautsky developed the notion of 'chronic depression,' which served as a surrogate for the concept of breakdown, but was more concrete and predictive. The notion of chronic depression was introduced in an article for *Die Neue Zeit* in 1902. Here Kautsky argues that 'in general, crises are becoming ever more severe and extensive in scope,' and that,

[a]ccording to our theory this development is a necessity, and it is proved by this alone that the capitalist method of production has limits beyond which it cannot go. There must come a time, and it may be very soon, when it will be impossible for the world market even temporarily to expand more rapidly than society's productive forces, a time when overproduction is chronic for *all* industrial nations. . . . The continued existence of capitalist production remains possible, of course, even in such a state of

chronic depression, but it becomes completely intolerable for the masses of the population; the latter are forced to seek a way out of the general misery, and they can find it only in socialism.[40]

Periodic crises that fall into a cyclical pattern, Kautsky argues, are caused by the ebb and flow of outlets as new markets are discovered and then exhausted. Centralization will not alleviate crises, as Bernstein argued, but will intensify the problem as cartels reduce domestic demand and increase dependency on foreign outlets. Capitalism is threatened by a chronic shortage of markets produced by its own internal contradictions. These contradictions, Kautsky argues, cannot be contained by expansion, planning, or the credit system, as the revisionists claim, but will increasingly disrupt the economy until revolution becomes the inevitable response to impoverishment and unemployment. 'Crises, conflicts, catastrophes of all kinds, it is this lovely alliteration that the course of development places in prospect for the next decades.'[41]

Kautsky endorsed the crude form of the notion of economic primacy that had become associated with Marx through superficial readings of *Capital* and through interpretations of Engels's later works. Although Kautsky eventually developed a theory of imperialism that linked economic problems to political policies, he never fully considered the potential for interaction between the economic structure and the political and ideological superstructure that Marx had discussed at so many points in his writings. Kautsky framed breakdown theory as a purely economic and empirical problem. The predictive power he assigned to it is evident in his conclusions concerning the immediate fate of capitalism.

Kautsky adopts a mechanistic conception of the economy as an autonomous and isolated force in history and bases his notion of breakdown on this conception. Throughout his discussions of capitalism, Kautsky draws from the general analyses of *Capital*. He then supplements these analyses with large quantities of empirical data intended to meet the arguments of the revisionists and to establish a direct correlation between the laws and material conditions of capitalism. In this way, Kautsky reinforces the revisionist tendency to view the conditions of capitalism and economics in general as a series of 'facts', readily apparent and available for immediate utilization. And in this sense, Kautsky and the revisionists he sought to discredit fall into the same epistemological and conceptual patterns of thought that had characterized classical political economy, and become the object of Marx's critique in *Theories of Surplus Value*. Although both Kautsky and Bernstein claimed allegiance to Marx's ideas, and grounded their work in *Capital* itself, both ultimately came to depend on a conception of the economic order and on a form of analysis that Marx refuted throughout his works.

As capitalism continued to expand without significant difficulties, Kautsky repudiated his theory of chronic depression, and concluded that there was no longer support for the expectation that crises would render the continuation of capitalist production impossible and its replacement by socialism unavoidable. Eventually, Kautsky perceived a permanent end to the crisis-ridden era of 1873–95, and rejected breakdown theory completely:

> Indeed, we expected much more from the crisis at that time [1885]. . . . Not only the revival of the socialist movement in Britain, but the breakdown of capitalism throughout the world. This hope proved illusory. Capitalism survived the crisis, despite its considerable extension in space and time and its inordinate intensity. A new phase of capitalist prosperity ensued. But what emerged was an entirely altered capitalism. The older form of capitalism had been eclipsed.[42]

The positivist epistemology that informed Kautsky's thought and the breakdown controversy as a whole throughout the Second International represented a return to the assumptions and methods of classical political economy. The terms of the debate were largely set by theorists who were unable or unwilling to continue the critique of the philosophy of identity or the theory of capitalist development initiated by Marx. For all their seeming disagreement about the ultimate fate of capitalism, the revisionists and the orthodox Marxists of the Second International adopted a common epistemology and common political concerns. Both found in breakdown theory a convenient construct for the pursuit of their theoretical and practical goals.

Both rejected the Hegelian aspects of Marx's thought that had served as a tool in his critique of Ricardo. Both turned back to Kant and to the neo-positivist epistemologies of the day for support in their displacement of the dialectic and the epistemological and political considerations it entailed. Both produced static or linear models of capitalism, rejected cyclical patterns, and detemporalized crises. Several lasting consequences resulted. The debates of the Second International firmly established the concept of mechanical breakdown and claimed a reference point for the concept in Marx. The rejection of Hegel, the installation of a positivist epistemology, and the adoption of a gradualist political program were necessary prerequisites for the construction of the concept and, in turn, were furthered by its promotion.

The breakdown controversy also established the perception of the Great Depression of the last quarter of the nineteenth century and the recovery of 1895 as constituting a watershed in the development of capitalism, from which a 'new capitalism' emerged. Engels's hypotheses were transformed into statements of fact. For the revisionists, the 'new capitalism' was subject to regulation and control, and crises were reduced or obliterated. For the orthodox Marxists, the 'new capitalism' was marked by permanent, detemporalized crisis. The perception of a 'new capitalism,' which emerged in full form in Bernstein's refutation of breakdown theory and Kautsky's theory of chronic depression, exercised enormous influence over the development of Marxist theory for the next thirty years, until the second Great Depression muted the memory of the first. The perception provided the material justification for radical reformulations of Marx's theory of capitalist development and his theory of the relationship between structure and superstructure – reformulations that went far beyond anything Engels imagined in his speculative asides on joint-stock companies.

These reformulations, combined with the displacement of the dialectic, were part of a larger political movement away from the concepts of class and class struggle and towards reformism and fatalism as the emerging political alternatives to revolutionary struggle. According to Bernstein, in the absence of crises, economic exploitation and inequality will be overcome through the steady expansion of political democracy, not through class struggle. For Kautsky, the conditions of permanent crisis inevitably push the working class to revolt: political organization and the development of a revolutionary movement are of less force than the weight of the crisis itself. In the breakdown controversy of the Second International, reformism and fatalism were secured as alternatives to class struggle within the Western Marxist camp. Breakdown theory provided a vehicle for maintaining certain aspects of Marx's thought and a justification for abandoning his political conclusions – a way of contemplating the end of the system without engaging the class struggle. Much of the attention of the next generation of Marxist theorists was focused on reversing the process that had led to this political retreat.

4 Neo-orthodoxy and the general analysis of a politicized economy

Capitalism only became imperialism at a definite and very high stage in its development, when certain of its fundamental attributes began to be transformed into their opposites.

Lenin, *Imperialism*

Imperialism is simultaneously a historical method of prolonging the existence of capitalism and the most certain means of putting an end to its existence in the shortest possible time.

Luxemburg, *Accumulation of Capital*

In the first decade of the twentieth century, the Second International began to crumble. Simultaneously, the downside of the business cycle reappeared with the slump of 1905. In comparison to the long and deep depressions of the last quarter of the nineteenth century, the brief and shallow recession of 1905 did not present a challenge to the static economic models that emerged in the debates of the Second International. Bernstein and Kautsky continued to draw on empirical data largely limited to Britain and Germany; their parochial political interests restricted their theoretical pursuits.

The first theoretical attempt to rethink *Capital* on an international scale after the first Great Depression came from Rudolf Hilferding in his *Finance Capital*, published in 1910. As an SPD organizer, Hilferding worked closely with Bauer, Kautsky and Bebel, but rejected their theoretical views. Hilferding moved the debates of the Second International beyond the boundaries set by Bernstein and Kautsky in their war of statistics, and beyond their positivist interpretation of the concept of 'laws.' Hilferding's first attack against positivist interpretations of *Capital* was directed at Böhm-Bawerk and the marginalist theorists.

Hilferding's *Böhm-Bawerk's Criticism of Marx*, a highly lucid and closely argued work on the labor theory of value, was originally published in 1904 as part of *Marx Studien*.[1] Hilferding's central claim is that the concerns of Marx and those of the marginalists, including Böhm-Bawerk, share no common ground from which comparisons might be drawn. According to Hilferding, Marx defined economics as part of a social structure and attempted to determine its laws of development. Böhm-Bawerk, however, used the individual as the base unit of economics and was more concerned with problems like price determination than with general forms of analysis. Hilferding criticizes the marginalists for their ahistorical view of capitalism, for their neglect of the 'social determinateness' of the relations of production, and for their empiricist definition of economics, which leads them to misinterpret Marx's labor theory of value.

The object of Marx's studies, and of political economy, Hilferding argues, is not the determination of price, but 'the social aspect of the commodity, of the good, in so far as it is a symbol of social interconnection.'[2] In Hilferding's writings, political economy as a specific social science is partially retrieved from the purely economic and empirical considerations that mark the works of the revisionists, the marginalists and the orthodox Marxists who followed Kautsky's lead.

Finance capital: Reinstating the dialectic

Hilferding's critique of Böhm-Bawerk was followed by the publication of *Finance Capital* in 1910.[3] *Finance Capital* was the most important work in Marxist economic theory to appear during the immediate pre-war period, and gained wide attention in Europe. Unlike Kautsky, who had attempted to apply the economic concepts of *Capital* to specific geographic regions, Hilferding worked on an international scale, and attempted to adjust the conclusions of *Capital* to what was perceived to be a new capitalism, characterized by the emergence of banker control, increased monopolization and growing state regulation of the economy.

Finance capitalism is defined as a specific phase of capitalist development, which Hilferding believed was anticipated by Marx, but which requires a modification of the general laws of capitalist development outlined in *Capital*. Finance capitalism is characterized by three tendencies: the increasing control of banks over industry through their financing of capital investments, the increasing centralization and concentration of capital, and the increasing centralization of finance. As the rising organic composition of capital lengthens the turnover-time of capital and decreases the ability of capitalists to respond to short-term

51

changes, capital becomes increasingly dependent on credit. Banks, in turn, protect their interests by encouraging the formation of cartels and trusts. In addition, the growing size of industrial enterprises and their investments requires larger and more centralized banks to provide adequate credit, thereby increasing the tendency towards the concentration and centralization of finance.

These changes require a dramatic increase in the power of the state and the level of state intervention in the economy. The elimination of internal competition leads to the demand for tariff protections against external competition to protect monopoly pricing. The state must have sufficient political and military power to secure suitable treaties and protect monopoly interests abroad. Moreover, the state must be prepared to 'transform the whole world into a sphere of investment for its own finance capital,' and to 'pursue an expansionist policy and the annexation of new colonies.'[4] The principal cause behind imperialism, Hilferding argued against Luxemburg, is higher profits, not a shortage of profits. Just as Hilferding's analysis of the economy is infused with the political understanding of the state, his theory of imperialism, which had previously been construed as a political phenomenon, analyzed imperialism as the economic policy of finance capitalism, a response to the needs of a changing capitalist economic order.[5]

Hilferding refuted Bernstein's claim that the organization and regulation of capitalism through cartels and trusts would put an end to the business cycle. Crises, Hilferding argues, arise from disproportionalities in investments between the two departments of production, not from overproduction. Cartels cannot prevent crises or reduce their effects, but can mitigate the effects by transferring them to unorganized industries. Marx had argued that financial crises arise from and intersect with industrial crises, but Hilferding determines that financial crises are improbable under finance capitalism. Nonetheless, industrial crises will continue. The idea that cartels will end crises 'ignores completely the inherent nature of crises.'[6]

The real threat to the continued existence of capitalism does not arise from cyclical crises but from proletariat revolution. Finance capitalism 'knows well that competition is becoming increasingly a political power struggle.'[7] Ideologically, finance capitalism is justified through 'an extraordinary perversion of the national idea,' and through racial ideologies which support the requirement for imperial expansion.[8] The proletariat must oppose imperialist policy, 'for only then will the proletariat become the beneficiary of the collapse to which it must lead, a collapse which will be political and social, not economic. . . .'[9] But class antagonisms unavoidably increase as centralization grows.

As an ever smaller number of capitalists face an ever growing number of the economically dependent, class relations become more explicit. Eventually, antagonisms build to the point of revolution. The proletariat takes control over the state and therefore, over the economy.[10] Capitalism will end when '[i]n the violent clash of these hostile interests the dictatorship of the magnates of capital will finally be transformed into the dictatorship of the proletariat.'[11] With this argument, Hilferding restored the dialectic between the conditions of capitalism and the historical agency of the proletariat that had been lost in the revisionism and fatalism of the Second International. Simultaneously, he marginalized the concept of mechanical collapse that had been set in play by Bernstein.

The concept of finance capitalism as a new economic order, and the level of inquiry required by its international application, continued to push Hilferding away from the purely empirical forms of analysis that he had already denounced in his earlier works, and towards a general analysis of the development of capitalism. This theoretical movement redefined the relationship between the laws and conditions of capitalism and became the dominant approach of Marxist theorists during the World War I era.

Morever, Hilferding's particular characterization of capitalism infused his economic analyses with political considerations. In his works, economic and political theory are merged in a way which far exceeds Bernstein's discussion of democratic institutions as a factor in economic change or Kautsky's discussions of imperialism as an economic force. Breakdown theory, or its rejection, was no longer a purely economic and empirical problem. Hilferding's refusal to treat it as such in *Finance Capital* arose from his perception of a changing capitalist reality, and foreshadowed the direction that Marxist theory was soon to take in the writings of Lenin and Luxemburg.

Hilferding's characterizations of a new capitalist reality, and the approach that accompanied this new characterization, were accepted by Lenin and Luxemburg, and the generation of Marxist theorists who contemplated breakdown theory during the period between the first revolutionary waves in Russia and the collapse of the proletariat movement in Germany two decades later. Like Hilferding, Lenin and Luxemburg sought a correspondence between the laws of capitalism and its material development, but resisted the crude empirical correlations utilized by Bernstein and Kautsky.

As the level of state intervention in the economy became more and more apparent with the spread of imperialism and the approach of World War I, Lenin and Luxemburg increasingly infused their economic analyses with political considerations forced by their perception of a new relationship between the economic structure and the political superstructure of capitalism. But they went far beyond Hilferding in their attempts to find solutions to the seeming impenetrability of finance capitalism. These attempts led them to a reconsideration of the role of class struggle in the development of capitalism, and to a re-evaluation of the nature of ideology in the context of a new capitalist order. By the end of their generation, the assumption of the primacy of economic forces still dominated Marxist thought and breakdown theory, but in a far different form than the mechanistic assumptions that had been the accepted common ground of revisionists and orthodox Marxists during the era of the Second International.

Lenin's earliest and most systematic writings on breakdown arose in response to the extreme form of underconsumptionist theory advanced by the Narodniki, who had considerable influence in socialist circles in the 1890s. In his 1899 *The Development of Capitalism in Russia*, the first extended application of *Capital* to a specific historical problem, Lenin argues against the Narodniki contention that capitalism could not expand in Russia without access to foreign markets.[12] However, Lenin simultaneously rejects Tugan-Baranowsky's claim that unlimited capitalist expansion is possible in a closed but proportionate economy. In an essay written in 1908, after the prosperity of the recovery had been broken by the new slump in the United States and Europe, Lenin refuted the revisionist position on crises and breakdown:

> The position of revisionism was even worse as regards the theory of crises and the theory of collapse. Only for a very short time could people, and then only the most short-sighted, think of refashioning the foundations of Marx's theory under the influence of a few years of industrial boom and prosperity. Realities soon made it clear to the revisionists that crises were not a thing of the past: prosperity was followed by a crisis. The forms, the sequence, the picture of particular crises changed, but crises remained an inevitable component of the capitalist system.[13]

But Lenin also rejects the purely mechanistic notion of collapse that he had originally encountered and disputed in his debates with the Narodniki and in the controversies of the Second International. The growth of cartels will not put an end to crises or cause mechanical economic collapse, he determines, but will accentuate class divisions and provide the context for political action:

> While uniting production, the cartels and trusts at the same

time, and in a way that was obvious to all, aggravated the anarchy of production, the insecurity of existence of the proletariat and the oppression of capital, thereby intensifying class antagonism to an unprecedented degree. That capitalism is heading for a breakdown – in the sense both of individual political and economic crises and of the complete collapse of the entire capitalist system – has been made particularly clear, and on a particularly large scale, precisely by the new giant trusts.[14]

Realization problems cannot be ignored, Lenin argues, but consumption is not a controlling factor in crises. Imperialism will delay the downward movement of accumulation, but will not provide a full resolution to the contradiction between unlimited production and the process of reconversion. In his attempt to reinstate the dialectic of objective economic developments and proletarian revolt, Lenin avoided resolutions directed towards the overtly economic aspects of the contradictions of capitalism and turned instead to political considerations. These considerations redefined the grounds of the controversy and, eventually, returned to challenge the assumption of economic primacy that had always provided its foundation.

In *Imperialism: The Highest Stage of Capitalism* (1916), Lenin readily agrees with Hilferding's characterization of capitalist reality, and finds that 'the beginning of the twentieth century marks the turning point from the old capitalism to the new, from the domination of capital in general to the domination of finance capital.'[15] According to Lenin, the 'new capitalism' is characterized by the monopolization of capital, the subsequent socialization of production, and the emergence of imperialist policies as an integral part of the economic order.[16] Lenin argues that the 'new capitalism' is a modification of competitive capitalism intended to compensate for its contradictory and destructive elements. But it is not, he contends, immune to crises and breakdown. Rather, Lenin describes the 'new capitalism' as:

a shell which is no longer suitable for its contents, a shell which must inevitably begin to decay if its destruction be delayed by artificial means; a shell which may continue in a state of decay for a fairly long period, but which will inevitably be removed.[17]

But despite this pronouncement, the end of capitalism in *Imperialism* appears only through this formulation, as a phenomenon that is unavoidable but virtually unimaginable apart from Lenin's anticipation of social revolution.

The primary purpose of imperialism and the first demand of finance capitalism, Lenin claims, is the export of capital. Capital investments abroad can be set in motion by sub-standard wage payments to produce high profits, otherwise unattainable due to the congestion of capital and the falling rate of profit in developed capitalist economies. Part of the profits obtained abroad, he argues, are used to maintain economic prosperity and to buttress wage rates at home, minimizing the discontent among important sectors of the working class and reducing the class tensions that threaten the capitalist order. Through this argument, the theory of imperialism is linked to Lenin's theory of the vanguard party as the causal force in revolution at a time when capitalism strengthens its grip on the masses, and gradualist elements pervade the ranks of the proletariat.

The theory of the vanguard party contains Lenin's most explicit statement on the interaction between structure and superstructure at the deepest levels of capitalism's economic development. The 'new capitalism,' he argues, is directly linked to problems of consciousness and ideology, and subject to understanding only through the critique of capitalism generated by professional revolutionaries who are distanced from its direct influence on those involved in the production process. Through the efforts of the vanguard party, the proletariat can be organized and directed towards the realization of its true class interests. In his discussion of the need for a vanguard party in *What Is To Be Done?* Lenin concludes:

> we shall never be able to develop the political consciousness of the workers by confining ourselves to the economic struggle, for the limits of this task are too narrow. . . . The workers can acquire class political consciousness only from without, that is, outside the economic struggle, outside the sphere of relations between workers and employers.[18]

According to Lenin, the contradictions of finance capitalism, supported by the political institutions of imperialism and government intervention, require and generate a political response, not an economic resolution. And the political response, Lenin indicates, comes only through the mechanisms of critique, and an understanding of the particular forms of reification that arise with the emergence of a new relationship between the economic structure and the political and ideological superstructure.

As a new economic order, finance capitalism demanded a series of theoretical elaborations and an understanding of the relationship between the laws and conditions of capitalism that would go beyond the crude empiricism and positivism of the orthodox works. A few years before Lenin wrote *Imperialism*, he studied Hegel, and renounced positivist epistemologies in *Materialism and Empirio-Criticism*, published in 1908. Lenin recognized the significance of the revisionists' turn to neo-Kantian epistem-

56

ologies, and their rejection of the dialectic. But Lenin's influence in the West was circumscribed by political schisms in Europe and the United States after the Russian Revolution, and later, by the waves of anti-Sovietism that swept through Western Marxism. Lenin's critique of positivism, his analysis of capitalism, and his restoration of the dialectic were overshadowed by his writings on the state and political organization. Luxemburg was adopted as the authority on accumulation and crisis, and it was her conception of capitalist development, rather than Hilferding's or Lenin's, that captured Western Marxism.

Permanent crisis and class consciousness

The most powerful response to Bernstein came from Rosa Luxemburg, one of the founding members of the Polish Socialist Party, and the Social Democratic Party of Poland and Lithuania. Luxemburg moved to Berlin and became active in the German SPD in 1898, just as the controversy generated by Bernstein reached its peak. From the floor of the Hanover Congress, Luxemburg denounced Bernstein, and argued that 'the concept of breakdown, of a social catastrophe' is the crucial factor in separating reformism from revolutionary Marxism.[19] Luxemburg's formal response was published in an article in the *Leipziger Volkszeitung* in September of 1898. Bernstein replied with criticisms of Luxemburg's 'false dialectics' in *Presuppositions*.[20] Luxemburg wrote a second article refuting *Presuppositions* in 1899; both articles were published as *Reform or Revolution* in 1900.

Unlike Kautsky and Cunow, Luxemburg recognized the breadth and depth of Bernstein's rejection of Marx. Kautsky and Cunow remained tied to the terms of debate dictated by Bernstein and, with him, formulated their concepts of breakdown within a positivist, classical framework. Luxemburg, however, immediately recognized the resurrection of static classical models and bourgeois epistemology in Bernstein's work, and removed herself from the boundaries of debate that had circumscribed the controversy. Bernstein's 'vulgar bourgeois economics,' Luxemburg argues, produced 'a theory of standing still in the socialist movement, built, with the aid of vulgar economy, on a theory of capitalist standstill.'[21]

Moreover, Luxemburg reinstates the distinction between cyclical crises and conclusive breakdown – a distinction eroded by Engels, Bernstein and Kautsky. The theory of collapse, 'the cornerstone of scientific socialism,' consists of a fundamental idea, which may take 'exterior forms.'[22] The fundamental idea 'consists of the affirmation that capitalism, as a result of its own inner contradictions, moves toward a point when it will simply become impossible.'[23] The 'exterior forms,' which include the particular form that collapse may assume and cyclical crises, must be carefully distinguished from fundamental, inevitable breakdown in the accumulation process.

Refuting Bernstein's interpretation of the 1895 recovery, Luxemburg determines that 'the people who abandoned Marx's theory of crisis only because no crisis occurred within a certain space of time merely confused the essence of the theory with one of its secondary exterior aspects – the ten-year cycle.'[24] The elongation of the cycle, noted by Engels and interpreted as a sign of a new non-cyclical capitalism, is not, according to Luxemburg, of consequence, since the schedule of crises, and the decennial pattern that characterized mid-nineteenth century capitalism, 'was a purely exterior fact, a matter of chance.'[25]

Later, in *The Accumulation of Capital* (1913), Luxemburg notes that a similar form of confusion takes place among classical political economists. Whereas Bernstein confuses the absence of cyclical crises with the absence of conditions for general collapse, other economists mistake the fundamental and decisive contradictions of accumulation for inconclusive cyclical crises: 'As soon as economic theory gets an inkling of the problem of reproduction. . . . it reveals a persistent tendency suddenly to transform the problem of reproduction into the problem of crises, thus barring its own way to the solution of the question.'[26]

Luxemburg argues against Bernstein's claim that the expansion of the credit system and the growth of cartels and trusts will attenuate the problems of reproduction and the anarchy of capitalist production. Instead, 'they appear to be an instrument of greater anarchy' and 'accelerate the coming of a great decline of capitalism.'[27] Bernstein's rejection of breakdown theory undermines the scientific basis of socialism. Socialist theory, Luxemburg finds, holds that 'the point of departure for a transformation to socialism would be a general and catastrophic crisis.'[28]

The ideas recorded in *Reform or Revolution* were expanded in the 1909–10 debates between Luxemburg and Kautsky, where the political alternatives for socialist activities were outlined, and the political elements of breakdown theory under the conditions of the 'new capitalism' were finally made explicit. Theoretical support for Luxemburg's theory of breakdown was provided in *The Accumulation of Capital*, a book that placed theories of imperialism at the center of the development of neo-orthodox breakdown theory.

In *Accumulation*, the role of critique – so central to Marx's work but lost in the positivist debates of the Second International – is reinstated. Luxemburg formulates a critique of classical political economy, of Marx's schemes of reproduction, and of Tugan-Baranowsky's elaboration of Marx's schemes. Accumulation, Luxemburg argues, 'is more than an internal relationship between the branches of capitalist economy; it is primarily a relationship between capital and a non-capitalist environment. . . .'[29] From this criticism, Luxemburg formulates the concept of crisis and breakdown employed in *Accumulation*.

Although Luxemburg is commonly considered an underconsumptionist, she does not argue that the final contradictions of capitalism rest on an insufficient demand for consumption goods. Instead, she finds an inherent, chronic insufficiency of demand and markets in all branches of production. Luxemburg determines that the collapse of capitalism is a logical consequence of the process of accumulation at a time when there is a serious shortage of markets. She rejects Marx's law of the falling rate of profit, arguing that the tendency is automatically neutralized by counteracting forces, and may even be reversed if real wage rates are constant.

The main contention of Luxemburg's book is that accumulation can continue only so long as non-capitalist markets are available to absorb economic surplus and insure the expansion necessary for continued accumulation. *Accumulation* is a sharp critique of the colonialist and imperialist policies that arose from the continuous need for new markets, as outlying home markets and older foreign markets were converted into capitalist economies. In *Accumulation*, Luxemburg concludes that the expanded reproduction schemes of *Capital* Volume II do not accurately account for capitalist development because they do not take realization problems into consideration. Realization problems, she contends, are crucial in the context of a closed capitalist society fraught with increasingly limited market outlets.

Luxemburg argues that capitalism must turn to non-capitalist societies in order to realize the surplus value necessary to continue accumulation. Capitalism, she claims, has survived into the twentieth century only by virtue of colonialism and imperialism. Once all non-capitalist societies are converted to capitalism through imperialism, the collapse of capitalism becomes a logical necessity. 'For capital,' Luxemburg writes, 'the standstill of accumulation means that the development of productive forces is arrested, and the collapse of capitalism follows inevitably, as an objective historical necessity.'[30]

But Luxemburg argues that proletariat revolt, which reflects the decay of the capitalist system, may bring about collapse before the society reaches 'this natural economic impasse.'[31] The financial and military investments required by imperialism combine with domestic stagnation until 'after a certain stage the conditions for the accumulation of capital both at home and abroad turn into their very opposites – they become conditions for the decline of capitalism.'[32]

According to Luxemburg, the collapse of capitalism would not be followed by an automatic transition to socialism, but could result in barbarism if the proletariat failed to intervene in an appropriate manner. However, the exact nature of proletariat intervention, Luxemburg argues, must not be crystallized prior to collapse; predetermined forms of intervention increase the risk of duplicating capitalist forms of domination and reification. Like Lenin's theory of the vanguard party, Luxemburg's political theory arose from her understanding of the interaction between structure and superstructure. Her argument for the necessity of spontaneity reflects her recognition of the relationship between capitalism and consciousness, and precludes any consideration of the economy or its corresponding ideology as autonomous forces. In her analyses of the actual process of breakdown, Luxemburg infuses economic theory with the political considerations of imperialism. In her analyses of collapse and the probable nature of its aftermath, Luxemburg infuses economic theory with the considerations of ideological residues and the limits of consciousness.

Luxemburg's method in *Accumulation* follows the form of general analysis found in *Capital*. The bulk of her study is a critique of earlier theories of accumulation, beginning with the classical political economists, and including Marx and the revisionists. Luxemburg's theoretical work takes place within this context of critique, and appears sporadically throughout the text. Where the critique ends, Luxemburg does not move into a predominantly theoretical discussion, but intersperses generalizations and theoretical elaborations with a series of historical accounts of imperialism and colonialism. Theoretical and reflexive statements concerning the relationship between these elaborations and their objects emerge and then disappear again into a narrative history of the British economy.

Despite her consistent rejection of the crude positivism of Bernstein, Luxemburg never locates an epistemology that would serve to support her theoretical claims, or to describe the nature of the relationship between the laws of capitalism and its material conditions. However, Luxemburg's theory of breakdown, with its mechanistic formulation of collapse, its full-fledged analysis of imperialism, its focus on realization problems and its references to spontaneous forms of revolt, ultimately wielded greater influence in the development of Western Marxist theories of breakdown than Hilferding's and Lenin's more theoretically complex and more politically demanding analyses of capitalist development.

The dissemination of her theory of breakdown in the West was accelerated by Georg Lukács's promotion of the idea.

Lukács's purpose in *History and Class Consciousness*, written in 1922, was to restore Marx and reinstate Hegel and the dialectic after the revisionist onslaught.[33] More so than Lenin or Luxemburg, Lukács recognized the political consequences of Bernstein's rejection of the Hegelian dialectic, the turn to positivism, the central role of crisis theory in this epistemological shift, and the nexus between revisionism and classical political economy. Following Marx's *Theories of Surplus Value*, Lukács notes that Ricardo's methods and concepts precluded the idea of inevitable crises in capitalism. Bernstein's revisionism is a 'theoretical relapse into the methodology of vulgar economics,' but with an important political difference. The denial of crises and contradiction becomes a self-conscious political act in Bernstein's hands:

> What was good faith in Ricardo became a consciously misleading apologia of bourgeois society in the writings of the vulgar economists. The vulgar Marxists arrived at the same results by seeking either the thorough-going elimination of dialectics from proletarian science, or at best its 'critical' refinement.[34]

Bernstein's self-serving empiricism allows him to 'stand "firmly on the facts" so as to be able to ignore the general trends' toward contradiction and decline in the system.[35] The rejection of the dialectic is a necessary prerequisite for Bernstein's 'theory of "evolution" without revolution,' the first political requirement of opportunistic social democracy. The revisionist installation of immutable evolutionary laws, Lukács argues, promotes a return to Kantian ethical imperatives as the only basis for socialism.[36] Lenin's *The State and Revolution* and Luxemburg's *The Accumulation of Capital* reversed this trend by reinstating the objective conditions for crises and revolution, and the 'literary-historical' methodology of *Capital* – a methodology that recognizes the dialectic and the central role of epistemology in reaching proper political conclusions.[37]

Although Lukács claims to follow Luxemburg's theory of breakdown, in *History and Class Consciousness*, his interpretation of Luxemburg mutes the more deterministic and mechanical aspects of her theory, and emphasizes the role of proletariat revolution to the point that a significantly different theory appears. For Lukács, as for Luxemburg, recurring crises are not a cyclical process apart from the 'permanent crisis' of capitalism – the objective limits to accumulation – but are simply acute moments in an ongoing movement towards decline.[38] The 'permanent crisis' does not become fully realized in the actual cessation of accumulation – a situation which Lukács finds 'empirically still remote' – but is revealed by forced changes in capitalism itself: the intensification of colonization, the struggle for markets and materials, inter-imperialist rivalries and wars. But for Lukács the development is non-linear: 'For dialectical trends do not constitute an infinite progression that gradually nears its goal in a series of quantitative stages. They are rather expressed in terms of an unbroken qualitative revolution in the structure of society. . . .'[39] These changes, however, 'simply hasten the course of events that destroy it.'[40] The 'course of events' is the deepening crisis in accumulation and the rise of proletarian class consciousness driven by crisis. The expansionary capitalism of the nineteenth century made it possible to mask the contradictions of the system. The reality of world economic crisis – a unified and coherent phenomenon – was concealed by the appearance of disparate events in different branches of industry and different countries, occurring at different times. With the end of expansion and the beginning of general decline, marked by the rise of imperialism, the underlying unity of apparently diverse aspects of crisis becomes comprehensible to the bourgeoisie and proletariat alike. The bourgeoisie respond with the acceptance of regulation and economic planning as necessary to preserve the system. This acceptance, however, creates an ideological crisis, 'an unfailing sign of decay,' as liberal free-market values and the pre-eminence of the bourgeoisie are shown to be bankrupt.[41]

For the proletariat, acute crisis means that revolution 'has now become objectively possible.'[42] Class consciousness takes an authentic visible form only when 'an acute crisis in the economy drives it to action.' Otherwise, class consciousness 'remains theoretical and latent, corresponding to the latent and permanent crisis of capitalism. . . .'[43] As long as class consciousness is lacking, 'the crisis remains permanent, it goes back to its starting point, repeats the cycle' until, through long suffering, the proletariat is forced to act.[44]

For Lukács, then, the end of capitalism comes only with proletariat revolution, and revolution comes only with the class consciousness fermented by inevitable economic crises. The central role of class consciousness moves Lukács into the detailed discussion of reification and ideology that comprises most of the book, and becomes the central point for Lukács's influence on later generations of Marxists in the West. The attack on revisionism – Lukács's inspiration and purpose in *History and Class Consciousness* – and the central role of economic crisis, were quickly swept aside in the attempt to install Lukács as the 'origin' of Western Marxism, with its growing concern for consciousness, ideology, methodology, and philosophy, and the displacement of the study of the economy and analyses of the objective conditions of capitalism. Despite his neo-orthodox position on the end of capitalism, Lukács's works provided the foundations for the emerging anti-orthodox theories of collapse that dominated Western breakdown theories in the next generation.

The emergence of anti-orthodox forms in Europe

Within a year of Luxemburg's death in 1919, the social, institutional and theoretical conditions that had supported the attempt to combine theories of mechanical breakdown with theories of class conflict came to an end. The German revolution, the last hope of Lenin and Luxemburg for the imminent end of capitalism in Europe, was defeated by 1920. In Hungary, Romanian troops toppled the Commune and installed a counter-revolutionary government. The Austrian socialists broke their reformist coalition with the bourgeois regime, but capitalism was already restored, and no longer susceptible to destabilization. In Italy, the workers' revolt in Turin fell to the joint efforts of the factory owners and the Liberal government. What had appeared to be a massive proletariat move towards power in Europe collapsed into a series of brief and unsuccessful incidents, long before the Russian Revolution was safely secured and able to influence revolutionary efforts in other countries. The Third International, established in Moscow in 1919, did not clear its own organizational grounds until the Second Congress of July 1920, after the revolutionary wave had already passed through Europe. Capitalism, and the bourgeois governments which were so closely entangled in its fate, had survived the war and the revolutions that followed in its wake.

The Soviet Union itself was devastated by the war and by civil war, cut off from Europe by the imperialist blockade, and untouched by the aid that restored the economies of the continent. When Lenin's role as an effective leader ended in 1923, the realities of October 1917, and the impact of the theoretical contributions associated with that time, were gone. Western Marxism, isolated from intellectual life in the Soviet Union, developed without knowledge of the long debates about crisis theory and the development of capitalism that preoccupied Soviet scholars.[45]

But the isolation was not complete. When the Marx-Engels Institute in Moscow began the compilation of the first volume of the *Collected Works*, it worked in conjunction with the Institute of Social Research, founded in Frankfurt in the year of Lenin's death to promote Marxist scholarship. Under the direction of Carl Grünberg, a member of the Austro-Marxist school and a historian originally based at the University of Vienna, the Frankfurt

Institute accommodated communists and social democrats, and published a journal entitled *History of Socialism and the Workers' Movement*. The first volume of the *Marx-Engels Gesamtausgabe* (MEGA) was published in Frankfurt in 1927 under the joint auspices of the Institute and its Moscow counterpart. Despite the proliferation of material and political conditions that ran counter to a neo-orthodox perspective, Grünberg maintained a neo-orthodox position on the central issues of Marxism, and hoped that the Institute would become the mainstay of Marxist scholarship in a hostile Europe.

While Grünberg was still in Vienna, before assuming his position at the Institute, he met Henryk Grossmann, who was studying economics under Böhm-Bawerk. In 1925, Grünberg offered Grossmann a position at the Institute. Grossmann's lectures there between 1926 and 1929 were published in 1929, the year of the stock-market crisis, as *The Law of Accumulation and Collapse in the Capitalist System*, the first volume of the Institute's *Schriften*.[46] Grossmann claimed a strict orthodox adherence to Marx's economic theories, and adopted Marx's method of moving from abstract conceptualizations to concrete explanations. In *The Law of Accumulation*, the most detailed and elaborate study of breakdown since Luxemburg's *Accumulation* and the most significant product of Marxist scholarship during the inter-war years, Grossmann returned to the notion of the falling rate of profit, long neglected or rejected by Marxist theorists.

Grossmann claims that capitalism contains a material set of contradictions that necessarily result in breakdown and are located in the realm of production, apart from problems of realization. These contradictions, Grossmann argues, are not manifested in underconsumption or disproportionality, but in the tendency of the rate of profit to fall that arises from the absolute and unavoidable overaccumulation of capital. In the face of the suppression of proletarian revolution in Europe and the political isolation of the Soviet Union, breakdown theory was once again returned to the realm of economic determination and mechanical collapse.

Drawing from the third volume of *Capital* and from Otto Bauer's mathematical models, Grossmann plots the rise of the organic composition of capital and the corresponding fall in the rate of profit for a period of thirty-five years. He concludes that the profit rate cannot maintain a satisfactory level of accumulation past the second decade of development in the hypothetical scheme. Although Grossmann gives careful consideration to the offsetting force of a growing mass of profits, he remains convinced that the new markets provided by imperialist policies would not suffice to raise the mass to a point where overaccumulation would be mitigated. According to Grossmann, the counteracting tendencies outlined by Marx could delay the collapse of capitalism, and the presence of intense class struggle could speed its arrival, but the system itself contains an absolute economic limit that could not be avoided indefinitely or met long before its time.

Grossmann was never explicit about the exact relationship between this three decade scheme and the material conditions of capitalist development in the twentieth century. But he was careful to note that different levels of abstraction account for the relevance and power of certain predictive factors in economic analysis, and was adamant about the distinction between materialism and empiricism. The quietistic implications of his emphasis on objective conditions and his steadfast denial of the relevance of realization problems drew sharp criticism from theorists like Fritz Sternberg, who more closely followed the neo-orthodox positions of Lenin and Luxemburg. Moreover, his insistence on the primacy of economic forces was quickly rejected by the Institute's inner circle, a group of younger scholars who had already expressed disapproval of the neo-orthodox positions of Grünberg, Neumann and Wittfogel, all older Institute members.

The Institute's most direct response to Grossmann was issued by Friedrich Pollock in the second volume of the Institute's *Schriften*, *Experiments in Economic Planning in the Soviet Union 1917–1927* (1929) – a book which, it should be noted, served as the object of Paul Baran's apprenticeship at the Institute. Here Pollock argues that the growing use of government controls can contain the economic contradictions of capitalism for an indefinite period, and that the trend is towards a proliferation and stabilization of state capitalism, not towards the collapse of capitalist economies. Pollock emphasizes the role of technological advancements and increased defense spending in absorbing surplus and raising profit levels.[47]

Although he depends heavily on economic analysis, Pollock stresses the politicization of the economic realm in a way that implicitly challenges the notion of economic primacy. Members of the Institute's inner circle supported Pollock against Grossmann, and the Institute ceased to publish Grossmann's work after 1934. In 1937, Grossmann emigrated to the United States to join his colleagues in New York, but his relationship to the members of the Institute became increasingly fragile. Grossmann maintained his association with the Institute until 1940, but during his fourteen years as a member he had never functioned as a significant force in its intellectual development.[48]

Pollock's emphasis on the politicization of the economy, and the Institute's general support for his position, did not constitute a simple extension of the shift in breakdown theory that began with studies of state intervention and imperialism by Hilferding, Lenin and Luxemburg. The politicization of breakdown theory in the work of these earlier writers retained the essential elements of the concept of economic primacy. The realm of the economic was infused with political considerations, and breakdown theory was necessarily modified by this infusion, but it remained a fundamentally economic problem. At no point did Hilferding, Lenin or Luxemburg suggest that the relationship between the economic structure and the political superstructure had been radically altered with the emergence of a 'new capitalism.' Their recognition of state intervention, and their concern with ideology, led them to an understanding of the interactions between structure and superstructure that had escaped the revisionists and the orthodox Marxists of the Second International.

But this understanding did not bear significant consequences for their commitment to the concept of the primacy of economic forces and the method of general analysis that Hilferding, Lenin and Luxemburg adopted from *Capital*. In reaction to Bernstein and Kautsky, and their empiricist testing of the works of Marx, Hilferding, Lenin and Luxemburg pushed general analysis to its final form. Luxemburg, whose influence ultimately prevailed, remained caught in the positivistic schism between empirical and general analysis that obscured the discourse of the open dialectic in Marx's thought. Her understanding of the interaction between structure and superstructure faltered on an unresolved epistemological problem that left the laws and conditions of capitalism unmediated, and the range of theoretical possibilities enlarged but even less clearly defined.

However, Pollock, and to an even greater degree, other members of the Institute such as Marcuse and Adorno, used the politicization argument, which stressed the interplay between structure and superstructure in the context of economic determinacy, as the primacy justification for a much more dramatic shift towards superstructural analysis. Their analysis placed a new emphasis on the superstructural aspects of capitalism as the key to its functional reality and its continued survival and expansion in the twentieth century. With this shift, superstructural phenomena were seen as the locus of capitalist development and as the proper point of inquiry for breakdown theory.

The concept of breakdown, where it survived at all in this new theoretical context, survived in an anti-orthodox form, radically different from the earlier neo-orthodox theories, with the economic origins of the concept buried far beneath new political and ideological definitions. The economic conception of the 'internal contradictions of capitalism,' so central to the development of the theory of capitalist development, was eventually displaced. And the economic analysis of the survival mechanisms of capitalism under bourgeois state control, so important to the theorists of the revolutionary period, was radically reformulated. The considerations that preoccupied the new generation of European Marxist theorists strayed far from an immediate reading of *Capital,* and even farther from any anticipation of the imminent collapse of capitalism or the imminent rise of proletariat revolution. Theoretical developments in the United States did little to stay the trend.

5 Breakdown theory and the American Marxists:
The theoretical spectrum of the early years

> The crisis and breakdown were foreseen by Karl Marx. His foresight was dismissed as the mere wish-fulfilment of his revolutionary purposes. Now it has been verified by life itself.
>
> Corey, *The Crisis of the Middle Class*

> Whatever approves itself to us on any grounds at the outset, presently comes to appeal to us as a gratifying thing in itself; it comes to rest in our habits of thought as substantially right.
>
> Veblen, *Theory of the Leisure Class*

> The things themselves, which only the limited brains of men and animals believe fixed and stationary, have no real existence at all. They are the flashing and sparks of drawn swords, the glow of victory in the conflict of opposing qualities.
>
> Nietzsche, *Philosophy in the Age of the Greeks*

The American theorists who contemplated the end of capitalism during the first few decades of the twentieth century were confronted by an expanding body of European interpretations and by heightened perceptions of a changing capitalist reality. The revisionist debates and the orthodox defense in Europe, the continued monopolization of capital and the rise of imperialism, all combined to form an explosive context for the American theorists as they viewed the text of *Capital*. The three theorists studied in this chapter – Thorstein Veblen, Louis Boudin and Lewis Corey – represent three very different attempts to measure Marx's thought against the theoretical demands of a seemingly new social order.

Although these three theorists responded to a common set of concerns and conditions, their perspectives and positions differed considerably. Veblen, a philosopher by training, pursued his studies of capitalism from a position that more closely resembled the academic setting of the Frankfurt scholars than the revolutionary world of the neo-orthodox theorists. Although Veblen was never fully integrated into the American university system, he remained even more distanced from the political organizations and movements of his time. Boudin, by contrast, was a practicing attorney throughout the period when his theoretical efforts were consolidated, and assumed a leadship role in the American Socialist Party. He was immersed in the practical affairs of everyday life and in the radical politics of the early socialist drive.

Corey, however, did not share Veblen's ties to the academic world or Boudin's entanglements in the complexities of the bourgeois legal system, but was a professional revolutionary. With little or no connection to the larger society until relatively late in his life, Corey lived out a practical commitment that eventually evaded his theoretical understanding. Despite these differences of training and purpose, however, these three theorists were linked by their common interest in the fate of capitalism, their common perception of a changing social order, and their common use of Marx as a reference point in their attempts to comprehend economic developments.

The works of these three theorists appeared at a time when Marx's influence was first felt with full force in the United States. Their writings should be placed in that context. It was also a time, however, when perceptions of a changing capitalist reality were first articulated, and the revisionist controversy set the terms of the debate. Marx's thought was simultaneously appropriated and subjected to modification. No full assimilation of the original texts occurred with the assumption of their complete and immediate applicability; initial readings were already marked by a revisionist eye. Like the European theorists of the same era, the American theorists were writing at a point when the disjuncture of Marx's texts and the context of capitalist development seemed to be well established for a significant group of writers with a particular political agenda.

There is no linear movement in the development of American Marxist theory during this early period, nothing that might resemble what has been construed as a progression from orthodoxy to anti-orthodoxy in the European experience.[1] Instead, there is a much more complex diffusion of concepts of breakdown, one that does not easily fit traditional models of conceptual change. Anti-orthodox concepts appeared at an early point in the intellectual history of American Marxism, but remained subordinate to the uneasy but entrenched orthodox and neo-orthodox positions.

Boudin, who openly struggled to reconstruct an orthodox theory in the face of the revisionist challenge, inadvertently moved into a confused amalgamation of the discourses of *Capital*, forcing together empirical and general modes of analysis, and silencing the undeterministic and anti-positivist theoretical position of Marx's work on profit rates. Veblen, who placed himself outside the Marxist camp and made a deliberate effort to rewrite Marx in conjunction with a perceived change in the economic order, produced texts that anticipated the anti-orthodox position of the Frankfurt theorists. His work was never fully assimilated by the neo-orthodox theorists despite his duplication of many of Marx's basic concepts. Corey, whose claims of allegiance to Marx were unequivocal, eventually fell into an apocalyptic determinism that resonates most clearly with the general statements on contradiction in *Capital*, and yet relies on the elaborate analysis of profit rates found in Volume III for theoretical support.

The result of the works of these three American writers is an expansion of the range of theoretical possibilities generated by the concept of breakdown. This expansion duplicates the European experience at certain points and defies it at others, simultaneously affirming and defeating European perceptions of historical change and the theoretical adjustments that followed. In the works of the early American Marxist theorists, the history of the theories of breakdown is played out in a series of duplications and exaggerations, magnifications and retractions, repetitions and differences. The original texts of Marx are shattered and scattered in a discourse that strains to capture change itself.

Resistance to revisionism

Although Victor Berger and the Wisconsin Socialists adopted Bernstein's interpretations of the first Great Depression and recovery and openly accepted the revisionist label, most leaders in the American Socialist Party at the turn of the century believed that socialism in the United States and Europe was imminent. With the rise of trusts and the rapid increase in the size of the industrial proletariat, many American Marxist theorists thought that capitalism in the United States was already deep in decline, and might soon move into the final stages of collapse.[2] When the revisionist assault spread from Europe to the United States, Louis Boudin, the chief theoretician for the American Socialist Party, quickly issued a response.

Boudin was born in Russia but emigrated to the United States at an early age. He was one of the founders of the radical faction of the Socialist Party, and a key contributor to *New Review* and *The Class Struggle*.[3] Boudin's *The Theoretical System of Karl Marx, In the Light of Recent Criticism* was published in 1907 in response to the revisionist debates of the Second International.[4] The book originally appeared in 1905–6 as a series of articles in the *International Socialist Review*, a periodical that served the Marxists and syndicalists of the Socialist Party in the United States. *Theoretical System* was translated into German and Russian soon after it appeared in book form. With *Theoretical System*, Boudin's position as the chief theoretician for the Socialist Party was solidified, and he became an internationally known Marxist writer. Luxemburg cites Boudin's 'brilliant review' of Tugan-Baranowsky.[5] Lenin was familiar with Boudin's work, and included *Theoretical System* in his 1914 bibliography of Marxism.

One of the most striking features of *Theoretical System* is its detailed dialogue with the European and Russian Marxist theorists of the revisionist era. Boudin was fluent in German and Russian, and had access to the foreign-language press and to the German editions of Marx's writings. He was familiar with the works of the classical political economists, with Marx's early works and all three volumes of *Capital*, and with the voluminous reports emerging from the revisionist controversy. Boudin was in full command of the works of Böhm-Bawerk, Bernstein, Kautsky, and Tugan-Baranowsky. Few other American Marxists have written from such a complete knowledge of their European counterparts.

Boudin's explicit purpose in *Theoretical System* is to re-establish an orthodox reading of *Capital* in the face of the revisionist onslaught. *Theoretical System* is marked by a polemical and defensive style. Throughout, Boudin relies on a reading of Marx that demands complete consistency and coherence from *Capital*. Conceptual variations and divergent styles within the original text are flattened in the commentary as Boudin increasingly sacrifices the logic of his own position for a forced clarity in his reading of Marx. The highest level of confusion and fragmentation in Boudin's work occurs in those portions of the text that attempt to circumscribe and limit the range of theoretical possibilities arising from Marx's theory of capitalist development.

Boudin begins *Theoretical System* with a long and detailed defense of the labor theory of value against the charges leveled by the marginalists. He then moves into a discussion of surplus value and Marx's chapters on profit, where Marxist theory scores its 'greatest triumph.'[6] Boudin approaches the law of the tendency of the rate of profit to fall as the pivotal point in Marx's understanding of the contradictions of capitalism. At this point in *Theoretical System*, Boudin's reading of Marx begins to falter. In his discussion of the falling rate of profit, Boudin loses sight of the complexity of *Capital*, and forces an argument that is not sustained by Marx's writings in Volume III.

In an attempt to answer the revisionists, Boudin determines that

71

he will present the law of the falling rate of profit in the context of 'the actual facts of capitalist production' rather than discuss the 'tendency in its purity.'[7] Although Marx holds the rate of surplus value constant throughout his formulation of the tendency towards a falling rate of profit, the 'actual facts' of capitalism lead Boudin to associate a fall in the rate of profit with a rise in the rate of surplus value, and to adopt these two movements as the manifestations of the 'cross-tendencies' at work in profit rates. This is a fundamental misreading of Marx's theory, and one that appears all the more striking due to Boudin's claim that his work 'is merely intended to present the Marxian theory as *stated* by Marx.'[8]

With a rise in the rate of surplus value rather than a rise in the mass of profit posed as the counter-tendency to the falling rate of profit, Boudin denies the effect of the counter-tendency and discounts its ability to slow the falling rate of profit. Although Boudin acknowledges the increase in the mass of profits as a movement which accompanies a decrease in the rate, he does not acknowledge this increase as the effective counter-tendency that Marx posed as an off-setting force in the law. This failure to acknowledge the central counter-tendency leads Boudin to re-formulate the law of the tendency of the rate of profit to fall as an absolute and inevitable law, rather than the tendential movement that Marx described with great qualification in Volume III of *Capital*. In *Theoretical System*, Marx's only full theoretical elaboration of the contradictions of capitalism is given a deterministic and mechanistic voice, and linked to the general statements on contradiction. Subsequently, the open dialectic of effect and counter-effect is irrevocably lost in Boudin's interpretation of profit rates.

With the law of the falling rate of profit firmly established as an absolute movement towards the collapse of capitalism, Boudin does not pursue the significance of this movement or present the predictions that logically follow from his position. Instead, he abruptly shifts into a detailed and faithful discussion of average rates of profit in an attempt to refute the revisionist argument that posed a contradiction between the concepts of value utilized in *Capital*. When the discussion of the fate of capitalism re-emerges in the next chapter, the law of the falling rate of profit is mentioned only in the context of the higher organic composition of capital and its role in the creation of a reserve army of workers.[9] Without a glance back to Volume III and the discourse surrounding the discussion of profits, Boudin turns to the popular passages of Volume I, where the general statements on contradiction are combined with the statements on a proletariat revolution. At this point, Boudin's discussion of the contradictions of capitalism becomes largely rhetorical, and his conception of breakdown becomes an unwitting confusion of what he describes as 'economic' and 'moral' categories, a merging of distinct and, according to Boudin, incompatible discourses. The theoretical power of *Capital* Volume III, with its postulation of tendencies and counter-tendencies, is suddenly and completely replaced by the predictive position of Marx's general statements on contradiction.

What follows is a confused argument that predicts the absolute and automatic breakdown of the capitalist system. Boudin argues that collapse is already under way, but will eventually take one of three forms. First, he argues that a purely mechanical collapse will occur as the inevitable consequence of the irremediable development of contradictions stemming from centralization and concentration, and properly understood as an entirely economic problem. Then, Boudin goes on to argue that these contradictions produce 'sociological' conditions such as increased unemployment and exploitation which will force a 'moral' imperative to revolt among members of the working class. Finally, he argues that a fatal underconsumption crisis will occur before the full development of economic contradictions brings about mechanical breakdown. With this assortment of causes for the inevitable breakdown of capitalism enumerated, Boudin then fills the rest of *Theoretical System* with arguments that qualify and ultimately retract his claims.

Working from *Capital* Volume I, Boudin contends that a mode of production can continue only as long as it 'does not hinder the unfolding and full exploitation of the productive forces of society.'[10] According to Boudin, the concentration and centralization of capital, which occur as an unavoidable result of the process of capital accumulation, constitute a set of fetters on the mode of production and provide the necessary and sufficient cause for the collapse of the capitalist system. 'If this process should be permitted freely to work out its tendencies' towards accumulation, concentration, and centralization, Boudin argues, the concentration of wealth would become so great that the economic system could not continue to function.[11] The 'purely economico-mechanical existence' of capitalism 'is put in jeopardy by the laws of its own development.'[12]

But this development, which leads to mechanical collapse, Boudin claims, may be 'arrested' by the 'sociological results' to which the processes of concentration and centralization 'must inevitably lead.'[13] The 'sociological expression' of the 'mechanical law of accumulation' is the 'capitalistic law of relative overpopulation,' which leads to the creation of a reserve army of workers and increased exploitation of the proletariat.[14] These 'sociological conditions' generate dissatisfaction with the capitalist system in large sectors of the population. The revolutionary response to oppressive conditions is a 'moral' response, which arises from the very nature of man. Boudin assumes that man may be 'depended upon to make a moral issue of, and lead a crusade against, anything that will stand in the way of his economic progress.'[15]

This ontological assumption allows Boudin to adopt the general statements on contradiction from Volume I of *Capital* without specifying the historical conditions for proletariat revolution. The 'purely economico-mechanical' causes of breakdown can then be combined with causes arising from the 'moral nature' of the proletariat as an active and decisive historical agent. The famous passage from *Capital* Volume I, Boudin argues, does not describe two separate movements in the breakdown of capitalism, but 'one process' containing both the 'economic conditions and the psychological effects which these conditions produce upon the working-man,' effects which guarantee that revolution will occur.[16] Boudin concludes with an ambiguous statement that mixes the 'econ-omico-mechanical' causes of breakdown with the equally deterministic 'sociological' or 'moral' causes of breakdown in a way which undermines any further distinction between the two:

> While the facts themselves which will lead to the displacement of the capitalist system must be strictly economic in their nature, that is to say the capitalist mode of production and distribution must become a fetter upon production before it can be overthrown, the actual power which will overthrow it, or at least the form which this will assume in the consciousness of the men who will do this work, may be of a moral or ethical character.[17]

However, Boudin then claims that the full development of the contradictions of capitalism and the actual occurrence of social revolution may be precluded by breakdown arising from yet another source. He argues that consumer goods underconsumption crises will increase in severity as exploitation intensifies. Surplus consumer goods 'will clog the wheels of production and bring the whole economic machinery of society to a stop.'[18] Underconsumption cannot be counteracted, Boudin continues, by the absorption of workers into means-of-production industries or by an increase in capitalist class consumption, as the revisionists had claimed. However, Boudin later states that underconsumption crises are not the cause of breakdown but only symptoms of the decaying capitalist order.[19] The question of the causal force of underconsumption crises is never resolved in the text as Boudin wavers between a sharp distinction between crises and breakdown and none at all.

Boudin insists throughout *Theoretical System* that the break-down of capitalism is inevitable and imminent. Although he perceives several changes in capitalism, he consistently refutes the revisionist position that these changes counteract the contra-dictions of capitalism and necessitate a reformulation of Marx's theory. Imperialism, an extension of capitalist policy, can prolong the decline of the economy but cannot cancel the effects of underconsumption since foreign markets soon begin to produce the consumer goods they once absorbed.[20] Waste, the 'safety-valve of capitalism,' absorbs surplus and may delay collapse, but cannot diminish the long-run effects of accumulation. Boudin concludes that 'it is on waste that the capitalist system now depends for the continuance of its existence.'[21]

Even if it could be demonstrated that the economic conditions for collapse have been mitigated, Boudin continues, the 'Marxian philosophy does not require the arrival at an economic impossi-bility,' but only a state of fettered production, before proletariat revolution becomes the inevitable impetus to collapse.[22] Capital-ism in its fettered state is a system which 'has become *historically impossible*, even though mechanically it may still be possible.'[23] The 'economic' and 'moral' causes of breakdown that Boudin merges in his earlier discussion are once again separated. Caught within the terms of the revisionist debate, Boudin incorporates the moral imperatives introduced by Bernstein and the economic imperatives defended by Kautsky, but understandably, is unable to accommodate both within a coherent logical argument.

Boudin was never seriously tempted to rethink his commitment to the concept of economic primacy. A decade after *Theoretical System* appeared, Boudin once again turned to the problem of breakdown in his *Socialism and War*, published in 1916.[24] Although Boudin discusses imperialism in a way that clearly indicates the need for a reconsideration of the theory of structural and superstructural formations, he retains his original theory of capitalist development. Boudin argues that the involvement of the state in economic affairs is a 'physical necessity,' endorsed through the creation of an ethical imperative. Imperialism, he argues, is possible only by virtue of the existence of ideological forces that convert foreign involvements into issues of 'individual morality.'

Boudin's ontological argument about the inevitability of revol-ution as a moral response to oppression is part of Boudin's attempt to undermine revisionist claims concerning a change in the objective conditions of capitalism. If the idea of mechanical collapse no longer gained wide acceptance, the inevitability of an ontological law could provide irrefutable proof of the imminent end of the system. Unwittingly, Boudin adopted Bernstein's idea of socialism as a moral rather than economic necessity, and further eroded the analysis of class as an integral part of the analysis of objective conditions.

When the radical wing of the American Socialist Party broke to form the Communist Party in 1919, Boudin did not follow. After the crash of 1929 and the second Great Depression failed to bring down capitalism or to elicit the 'moral response' that Boudin thought inevitable, he left the socialist movement entirely. The best theoretical mind of the Socialist Party had been squandered on the revisionist debates, and ultimately, became a captive of the same political assumptions that left Western Marxism in ruins on the Continent.

Anti-orthodox beginnings

Veblen's writings on capitalism, published during the same period as Boudin's works, were part of his attempt to redefine the discipline of economics. Veblen discounts the marginalist school as theoretically misguided and criticizes classical political economy for its narrow approach to economic problems. Classical political economy, Veblen argues, cannot develop a concept of 'evolutionary economics' because it lacks an understanding of anthropology. 'Evolution' for Veblen, however, did not carry the same connotations of gradual self-propelled social reform that the term carried for Bernstein, or the meaning of deterministic laws progressively realized that Kautsky adopted.

Veblen recognized in clear and explicit terms that Darwinism had displaced Marx's theory of history in the hands of the revisionists and orthodox Marxists, and took a critical position against this reformulation.[25] Veblen's commitment to an 'evolutionary' and anthropological formulation of economic problems eventually provides his work with a model that closely resembles Marx's structure/superstructure scheme. Evolutionary economics, Veblen writes, 'must be the theory of a process of cultural growth as determined by the economic interest, a theory of a cumulative sequence of economic institutions stated in terms of the process itself.'[26]

Veblen, however, was not committed to the concept of economic primacy, and indicates that the relationship between structure and superstructure is one of interaction and mutual determination. Economic life, he says,

> affects the cultural structure at all points, so that all institutions may be said to be in some measure economic institutions. This is necessarily the case, since the base of action – the point of departure – at any step in the process is the entire organic

complex of habits of thought that have been shaped by the past process.[27]

Veblen's willingness to rethink the relationship between structure and superstructure led him to reformulate Marx's theory of capitalist development in anti-orthodox terms.

Veblen's theory of the breakdown of capitalism appears in *The Theory of Business Enterprise*, written in 1904, long after he had completed his study of Marx.[28] In this work, Veblen distinguishes between crises, which occur as part of the business cycle, and depressions, which do not necessarily follow a cyclical pattern. Both are linked to profit rates. According to Veblen, crises are 'periods of price disturbance' inherent in capitalist economies. But no 'tenable theory' of these crises has been produced because 'it has been customary to approach the problem from the side of the industrial phenomena involved – the mechanical facts of production and consumption; rather than from the side of business enterprise – the phenomena of prices, earnings, and capitalization.'[29]

Veblen contends that crises are preceded by periods of prosperity, marked by rising prices and high profit rates, and caused by progressive demand and decreases or relatively slow increases in the cost of production. Investments made during periods of prosperity are financed on the prospect of increased profit rates. Veblen argues that '[i]n the ordinary course, however, the necessary expenses of production presently overtake or nearly overtake the prospective selling price of the output.'[30] Profit rates then begin to fall.

At this point in the economic cycle 'the enhanced capitalization based on enhanced putative earnings proves greater than the earnings realized,' and a drastic readjustment of values follows.[31] A crisis, then, represents the discrepancy between the value of projected and effective capital as shown through profit rates.[32] The onset of a crisis is marked by a falling rate of profit, followed by 'liquidation, cancelment of credits, high discount rates, falling prices, and "forced sales", and shrinkage of values,' and a subsequent decrease in existing capital and capital investments.[33] The concentration of capital is increased as the result of defaulted loans and reduced credit.[34]

Veblen claims that prior to the 1880s, crises normally were followed by a renewal of prosperity, stimulated by increased demand in one sector of the economy. But Veblen, like Engels, argues that capitalism underwent a fundamental transformation in the last quarter of the nineteenth century, and that the business cycle no longer followed a stable pattern of inflation, crisis, and recovery. Instead, the post-1880 period of capitalist development

77

is marked by a tendency towards what Veblen calls 'chronic depression,' or the consistent divergence of capitalization and profit rates. After 1880,

> the advancing efficiency and articulation of the processes of the machine industry reached such a pitch that the cost of production of productive goods has since then persistently outstripped such readjustment of capitalization as has from time to time been made. The persistent decline of profits, due to this relative overproduction of industrial apparatus, has not permitted a consistent speculative expansion, of the kind which abounds in the earlier half of the nineteenth century, to get under way.[35]

The increasing efficiency of the production process, represented by the increase of constant capital over variable capital, results in a chronic depression which is 'normal to business under the fully developed régime of the machine industry.'[36] Chronic depression displaces cyclical crises; economic development is detemporalized.

Veblen argues that the only remedy to chronic depression is to restore the rate of profit to a level above the rate of interest through direct control over output and price levels. This control can be exerted through the formation of trusts, or 'thoroughgoing coalition in those lines of business in which coalition is practicable.'[37] Veblen does not indicate that chronic depression will end in the economic breakdown of capitalism, but simply implies that a state of repetition has been reached in capitalist development. Since coalition is possible in the 'greater part of those lines of industry which are dominated by the machine process, it seems reasonable to expect that the remedy should be efficacious.'[38]

According to Veblen, then, the breakdown of capitalism will not be caused by a mechanical failure in the economic sphere. Instead, capitalism is ultimately threatened by a structural contradiction that manifests itself in superstructural forms. The consequences of the transformation of capitalism that occurred in the last quarter of the nineteenth century, Veblen argues, go far beyond the onset of chronic depression in the economic realm. The transformation also effected a fundamental change in the political realm and altered the relationship between structural and superstructural forces. Consequently, a new conception of economic breakdown is required. In an attempt to respond to this requirement, Veblen recounts the development of the political order during the pre-capitalist and liberal capitalist eras.

In pre-capitalist societies, Veblen claims, the state was 'an organization for the control of affairs in the interest of princely or dynastic ends,' preoccupied with 'dynastic prestige and security,' and legitimized by direct appeals to political lineage and loyalty.[39]

In these societies, the economic order was subsumed under and supported by the political hierarchy and its traditional forms of legitimation. Since the advent of liberal capitalism, however, constitutional governments have replaced dynastic governments and 'business ends have taken the lead of dynastic ends in statecraft.'[40] Constitutional government and liberal capitalism developed simultaneously, and both sought legitimation in the concept of natural rights and the ideology of equal exchange that grew out of the natural rights concepts. Their legitimation was buttressed by 'institutional survivals' from the pre-capitalist era in the form of the ideologies of patriotism and private property. But, Veblen continues, liberal capitalism rests on the machine process as the primary force of production, a process that facilitates certain 'habits of mind,' and these 'habits' are ultimately incompatible with the legitimating ideologies of the economic system.

According to Veblen, the machine process that serves as the basis of industry and engages large sectors of the population inculcates a belief in 'impersonal cause and effect' and technical forms of rationality. The mental 'discipline' and 'habits of mind' associated with the machine process are further manifested in the growth of science, which is 'single-minded in its pursuit of impersonal relations of causal sequence in the phenomena with which it is occupied,' and fully contained within 'lines marked out by technological thinking.'[41] This technical rationality, induced by contact with modern industrial science and technology, is fundamentally at odds with the legitimating ideologies of the economic order: the sovereignty of private property under natural rights, liberal values and the laws of civil society. Bourgeois governments, and the capitalist economies that support them, are thus threatened by a contradiction within their own borders.

This contradiction, arising from the machine process itself, is manifested in the socialist movement, which Veblen describes as 'an animus of dissent from received traditions.'[42] The discipline of machine technology 'is peculiarly designed to inculcate such iconoclastic habits of thought as come to a head in the socialistic bias.'[43] The socialist challenge to capitalism represents a growing disloyalty to the natural rights philosophy and other antiquated institutions, and a 'demand [for] organization on industrial as contrasted with business lines.'[44] Veblen claims that the socialist movement, originally seduced by the natural rights philosophy, moved into a fully scientific position by the end of the nineteenth century. Within the socialist movement, Veblen argues, '[t]he claim to the full product of labor . . . has gradually fallen into abeyance,' and has been replaced by a commitment to complete worker control over the industrial system and the government it supports.[45]

According to Veblen, the machine process is both the foundation of industry and a force that cuts away the institutional basis of the very system that industry is intended to serve. A further complication arises with the transformation of capitalism into a system hounded by chronic depression. A system that must fight for markets and armaments expenditures develops warlike tendencies which have an enormous impact on bourgeois governments. Persistent preparation for and engagement in warfare generates militaristic ideological forces which, with their emphasis on authority and subordination, counteract the growth of technical rationality.

The ideological forces associated with warfare, however, do not constitute a return to the natural rights system of legitimation but a reversion to the dynastic forms that preceded the liberal capitalist constitutional state. Veblen claims that the future may lie in 'dynastic politics and armament again played to a finish in popular squalor, aristocratic virtues, and universal bankruptcy. . . .' This reversion would not be truly 'reactionary' but would contain and carry with it an inescapable measure of the technical rationality inherent in the experience of the machine process. In this sense, it would be 'less closely bound by authentic conventions,' and would constitute a historical movement of repetition and difference rather than a new order.[46]

According to Veblen, then, capitalism generates and is subsequently threatned by two competing ideological or 'cultural' tendencies, both of which stand in direct opposition to the continuation of the economic system under its present forms of legitimation. Veblen determines that 'modern technology has, in a manner, cut away the ground out of which it first grew and from which it gathered force to reshape the course of history.'[47] Veblen ends *The Theory of Business Enterprise* with a statement that anticipates, in a cautious way, the collapse of the capitalist system:

> It seems possible to say this much, that the full dominion of business enterprise is necessarily a transitory dominion. It stands to lose in the end whether the one or the other of the two divergent cultural tendencies wins, because it is incompatible with the ascendancy of either.[48]

This statement contains the crux of Veblen's concept of breakdown and represents the full meaning of his well-known prophecy that the future lies in socialism or barbarism – a prophecy that originated in Engels. When the conceptual context of this prophecy is understood, the resonance between the works of Veblen and Marx becomes unmistakably apparent, and the extent to which Veblen's explicit interpretation of Marx conceals this underlying resonance becomes clear.

Veblen's concept of chronic depression as the result of an inherent tendency towards a rising organic composition of capital and a subsequent decrease in profit rates duplicates Marx's concept of the tendency of a falling rate of profit. Both theorists claim that the decline in profit rates is an inherent part of capitalist economies – the economic consequence of technological advancement. Both argue that the decline in profit rates can be counteracted through an increase in market size and control achieved through monopolization and imperialism. Both indicate that the process of effect and counter-effect in profit rates need not result in a decisive economic disequilibrium. The points of similarity between the two arguments extend to detail.

But despite these similarities and duplications, Veblen explicitly rejects Marx's concept of a falling rate of profit, claiming that Marx shared with Tugan-Baranowsky the classical fallacy of viewing capitalism as the 'mechanical facts of production and consumption' rather than the 'phenomena of price, earnings, and capitalization.' Veblen, then, accuses Marx of the same empiricist failing that Marx had laid at the door of classical political economy when he denounced Smith and Ricardo for mistaking the material facts of capital for its laws.[49] In Veblen's reading of Marx, the discourse of the open dialectic is lost in the shift from empirical to general analysis that marks many parts of *Capital*. Veblen locates a positivistic voice in *Capital* Volume I, and then carries it over into his reading of Volume III, where it is used to obliterate Marx's concept of the falling rate of profit.

As Paul Sweezy notes, Veblen's writings on Marx are based on 'a knowledge of the literature of Marxism which is so far ahead of that of anything of his contemporaries in the US that there is simply no ground for comparison.'[50] In his most extended critique of Marx, Veblen argues that Marx's system of thought 'differs characteristically from all systems of theory that had preceded it, both in its premises and in its aims.'[51] According to Veblen, however, Marx remains the captive of materialistic Hegelianism, combined with a natural rights philosophy and British utilitarianism. Marx adopts a dialectical vision of history from Hegel and a modified version of the labor theory of value from the classical political economists. The modification, Veblen argues, occurs in Marx's rejection of Ricardo's reliance on the repugnancy of labor as a measure of its value, which had prevented Ricardo from recognizing and calculating surplus value. Veblen concludes that Marx's labor theory of value is 'self-evident' and not subject to the marginalist critique waged by Böhm-Bawerk.[52] The theory of surplus value allows Marx to pursue the problem of accumulation and to rightfully reject the underconsumptionist theory of crises and breakdown.[53]

Veblen finds that Marx's theory of capitalist development and the transitory character of capitalism rests on his notion of inevitable increases in unemployment due to technological advancement, and the inevitable response of the proletariat to unemployment and low wages.[54] His reading of Marx's theory of development relies entirely on Volume I, where Marx links social revolution to the economic contradictions of capitalism. Veblen explicitly turns away from the second and third volumes of *Capital*, simply stating that '[t]hey add nothing essential, although many of the details of the processes concerned in the working out of the capitalist scheme are treated with greater fullness, and the analysis is carried out with great consistency and with admirable results.'[55] Marx's concept of the falling rate of profit, and the open dialectic of the discourse on the falling rate of profit, never surface in Veblen's discussion.

The theory of development that Veblen takes from *Capital* Volume I, is then dismissed as inaccurate, along with its 'Hegelian philosophical postulates.' Veblen concludes that Marx's theory suffers from a 'romantic' vision of final resolution through class conflict.[56] In his most concentrated and conclusive consideration of Marx, Veblen privileges the Hegelian content of Marx's general statements on contradiction and silences the discourse on profits in Volume III. Veblen was not unfamiliar with Volume III, however, and had written a 'Note' for the *Journal of Political Economy* when the volume appeared in 1894. The article does not discuss Marx's concept of a falling rate of profit, but simply attempts to defend Marx's theory of surplus value against those critics who had refuted it through empirical research on profit rates. Veblen correctly argues that the rate of surplus value cannot be identified with the rate of profit, but does not move past this important but limited discussion of Volume III. What might have been a crucial point of theoretical recognition is lost to a technical corrective.[57]

Veblen places his own analysis of capitalist development, with its emphasis on superstructural rather than structural primacy, beyond the theoretical reach of *Capital*. In the process, Veblen obscures the meaning of Marx's texts, and the nature of his own intellectual context. The unfailing and highly systematic misreading of Marx that occurs in his works belies the tension that exists between his thought and Marx's theories.

Veblen's primary concern throughout his studies of capitalism revolves around the processes of abstraction through which economic symbols are reified and distorted. His analysis of animism, central to so much of his work, closely parallels Marx's analysis of commodity fetishism. Both analyses provide a basis for a critique of ideology that is grounded in an understanding of the particular processes of signification arising from the economic realm. Similarly, Veblen's critique of classical political economy closely follows the critique formulated in Marx's *Theories of Surplus Value*. Both Veblen and Marx reject the process of abstraction involved in the construction of economic ideal types, and both reject the naturalistic and animistic metaphors employed in classical explanations of economic development. Moreover, both Veblen and Marx attempt to insure their escape from classical categories through the use of structural, rather than linear or teleological, concepts of causality, and through the use of a parodic prose style.

As has been noted, however, Veblen's interpretation of Marx emphasizes the Hegelian content of *Capital* and leads Veblen to distinguish between his own 'institutional' perspective and Marx's 'romantic' views. Veblen situates his break from Marx in his discovery of these Hegelian residues, the 'metaphysical' shadows cast across *Capital*. The Hegelian content he discovers and exaggerates in Marx, however, reappears in his own works, at exactly those points where his thought diverges most sharply from that of Marx. In his theory of the instinct of workmanship, Veblen introduces into his work an anthropological component of precisely the type that Marx expelled from his own when he formalized his break from Hegel in *Capital*.

Veblen's concept of an instinct of workmanship functions as the site where the objective and normative aspects of his social theory explicitly overlap. The point of overlap is established through the postulation of an anthropological *a priori* which falls into a Hegelian framework. This framework was rejected by Marx in his later works and normatively displaced by the concept of surplus value in *Capital*. Veblen attempts to disassociate his own theory of capitalist development from Marx through a misdirected critique of Hegelianism. In the process, he falls into an appropriation of Hegelian forms. Consequently, his critique of Marx effaces itself, his theory suffers, and the intellectual history of theories of breakdown is once again obscured by a series of unrealized intentions and contextual evasions.

Neo-orthodoxy and the second Great Depression, 1929–1939

The cyclical crises and preparations for war that provided the context for Veblen's works were replaced by unprecedented prosperity and civilian-sector growth in the United States economy throughout the 1922–9 period. The successful suppression of the proletarian revolutions in Europe at the beginning of the decade was followed by rapid increases in industrial production, productivity, and the level of trade across the Continent. Once again, theories of breakdown seemed misplaced.

But reconstruction had not fully resolved the economic instability created by World War I. War debts and reparations caused disequilibrium in international payments, and protectionism accelerated trade imbalances. New technologies and new lands brought under production during the war induced relative world overproduction in agriculture and depressed farm prices. When the second Great Depression occurred, the United States economy fell first, followed by France and England and, to an even greater degree, Germany.

The stock-market crash in October of 1929, and the unchecked downward trend that continued until 1933, offered a new opportunity for the revitalization of breakdown theories. In the four years between 1929 and 1933, United States industrial production contracted by one-half and wholesale prices fell by one-third. Investment plummeted, the value of trade products collapsed, and bankruptcies rose to record rates. Conservative estimates placed unemployment at 14,000,000 by March of 1933.

The Depression inspired a flood of writings on crises and collapse. The most influential Marxist analysis of the crash to appear in the United States was a book called *The Decline of American Capitalism*. Louis Fraina wrote *Decline* in 1934 under the name of Lewis Corey, an alias assumed by Fraina when he formalized his break with the Communist Party. In the first decades of the century, Corey had worked closely with Boudin on the *New Review*, and was an editor for a series of American Socialist Party publications, including *The Internationalist*, *Class Struggle*, *Revolutionary Age* and *The Communist*. He also directed the American Bolshevik Bureau of Information, founded in 1918, and edited Lenin's and Trotsky's *Proletariat Revolution in Russia*.

Decline quickly won the praise of the Communist Party and gained acceptance in popular circles, and Corey was asked to rejoin the CPUSA. Instead, he aligned himself with the expelled Lovestoneites, and gradually moved towards democratic socialism.[58] Throughout this period, Corey maintained his claim to orthodox Marxism. *Decline* was the most complete study in the new genre of crisis studies in the United States after the crash of 1929, and the most influential Marxist analysis of the Depression.

Decline is a massive history of American capitalism since the Civil War, with emphasis placed on the prosperity of the 1920s and the ensuing depression. Corey relies heavily on detailed statistical reports concerning the development of corporate holdings. Unlike Boudin, Corey does not enter into a dialogue with the European theorists of the time. Beyond the constant theoretical references to Marx and infrequent references to Lenin, Corey's writings are most clearly situated in a distinctly American context of economic and political commentary. His antagonists are not the European revisionists but the American apologists.

Writers like Luxemburg and Grossmann, who might have been cited as sources for Corey's positions, are passed over in favor of American writers like Fredrick Jackson Turner, Charles Beard, Walter Lippman and Brooks Adams. Corey's purpose is not to extend the theoretical discussion of the fate of capitalism, but to study the development of the depression of the 1930s and, in doing so, to provide support for Marx's analysis of capitalism. Corey writes:

> Precisely because it is the most highly developed, American industry offers the fullest confirmation of the analysis Karl Marx made of the laws of capitalist production. It is one of the tasks of this book, using the American statistical material, the most abundant in the world, to make a quantitative, as well as a qualitative, demonstration of the Marxist conception of the fundamental aspects of capitalism. . . .[59]

Marx is present throughout the text. Corey does not rely on the entire corpus of Marx's writings, however, but draws almost exclusively from *Capital* Volume III, and from those passages from Volumes I and II that relate to Marx's theory of crises. The tone of *Decline* is not the apocalyptic note that reaches its full force in Corey's later *Crisis of the Middle Class*, but a reasoned and undeterministic discussion of profits taken from *Capital* Volume III. Corey begins by distinguishing the cyclical crises of a growing capitalist order from the permanent stagnation that he claims characterizes the post-1929 period. He concludes, however, by reinstituting the cyclical pattern in a passage that resembles the indeterminate theory of Volume III:

> The decline and decay of capitalism do not exclude a revival of prosperity. For the cyclical movement goes on and contradictions are still 'solved' by the alternation of prosperity and depression. But on a lower level: prosperity is more incomplete than formerly, accompanied by limitation of production and disemployment, developing swiftly toward a new crisis, while depression is more prolonged and grinding.[60]

This passage does not anticipate final and complete breakdown, or restoration of a strong capitalist economy. Instead, Corey argues that the 'tendency is toward a condition of chronic depression, interrupted by fitful revivals of prosperity,' in a cyclical pattern which is 'an aspect of decline and not of growth.'[61]

This conclusion is reached after a long discussion of the transition from the industrial capitalism of the nineteenth century to the state capitalism of the twentieth. The transition is marked by a shift from cyclical growth to the cyclical decline that Corey describes as the fate of state capitalism. The state capitalism of the depression era is characterized by the 'exhaustion of capitalism as a progressive economic force,' and the inability of the system to reverse a downward trend toward permanent stagnation. The depression serves as Corey's evidence that the 'decline of capitalism' has begun. Decline is not synonymous with breakdown, but constitutes a necessary preliminary to the collapse of the system as a whole.

> Decline is not collapse. The decline of capitalism does not mean that the economic order is unable to function, but that it must function on a lower level. It does not mean an inability to restore production and prosperity, but an inability to restore them on any considerable scale. While the decline may be interrupted, the downward movement will persist.[62]

Decline is characterized by international disturbances, instability, permanent unemployment, and the social ills which, in *The Crisis of the Middle Class*, threaten to bring down the system.

According to Corey, decline is inherent and inevitable due to the nature of accumulation and the inability to expand accumulation over time. It is 'determined by the high development of the productive forces and the relative exhaustion of the long-time factors of expansion.' Decline is the dominant force in the 'perpetual struggle between the forces of expansion and decline' which marks the capitalist system and arises from three contradictions within capitalism itself.[63] The first two contradictions are the fundamental causes of the cyclical crises that occur in the industrial phase of capitalist development; the third is responsible for the permanent decline that characterizes state capitalism. The first contradiction is manifested in the overproduction of means-of-production goods, arising from the profit motive and the tendency towards excessive accumulation of capital, which limits outlets for profitable investments and creates profit realization problems. The second contradiction is manifested in the overproduction of consumer goods, arising from the tendency to develop the forces of production beyond the potential for consumption, and resulting in a standard underconsumption crisis in the realization of profits. This contradiction, Corey notes, is the most common cause of periodic crises during the industrial phase.

The third contradiction of capitalism is the cause of non-cyclical decline and the state intervention in the economy that decline inspires. This contradiction is manifested in a falling rate of profit that cannot be overcome through continued expansion of markets. The problems of overproduction and underconsumption that arise during the industrial phase of capitalism can be counteracted through increased consumption stimulated by the expansion of markets, so that the crises are relative, temporary, and cyclical in occurrence. However, with the exhaustion of markets, 'the limits to the development of capitalist production and prosperity become absolute.'[64] State intervention, monopolization and imperialism are all responses to this exhaustion of markets and the ensuing fall in profits. But these forces, Corey indicates, cannot postpone the movement towards permanent and unrelieved stagnation for an indefinite period of time. Corey concludes that '[w]here industrial capitalism was identified with economic progress and upswing, monopoly capitalism is identified with retrogression and decline.'[65]

In order for the capitalist system to survive, Corey argues, 'capitalist production *must* yield profits and these profits *must* be converted into capital by means of increasing output and absorption of capital goods.'[66] As the possibilities for expansion are exhausted, as domestic and foreign markets are saturated, the compensatory force that fights the tendency towards falling rates of profits is lost. Corey adopts the formulation of this contradiction found in *Capital* Volume III, as the basis for his theory of decline and breakdown, and the theoretical grounding for *Decline*.

According to Corey, the tendency for the organic composition of capital to increase is the 'basic objective factor in the contradictions of accumulation,' which leads to falling rates of profit that are not always offset by a sufficiently significant rise in the mass.[67] Like Grossmann, who was writing in Germany during the same years that Corey produced *Decline*, Corey finds that the falling rate of profit is the central tendency in the contradictions of capitalism that threatens the continuation of the system. Corey determines that 'capitalist production is an unceasing struggle against the tendency.'[68] The falling rate of profit, however, is not absolute and may be checked, primarily through increases in mass stimulated by increased consumption.

The exhaustion of expansion that occurs under monopoly capitalism may indicate an inability to counteract the tendency; Corey links the persistent problem of underconsumption with the disruption of counteraction. For Corey, the falling rate of profit is tied to underconsumption through the decrease in employment that follows increases in the organic composition of capital. The falling rate of profit, then, which Marx had pursued in the realm of production alone and did not formulate in cyclical terms, is linked to consumption and combined with the theory of cyclical crises in Corey's *Decline*. Despite his constant references to *Capital* Volume III, and his claims to orthodoxy, Corey essentially rewrites profit theory to enlarge its theoretical scope.[69]

In 1935, one year after the appearance of *Decline*, Corey published *The Crisis of the Middle Class*, a book which forms a logical if somewhat extreme extension of Corey's earlier arguments. *Decline* is cited throughout *Crisis* and provides the primary reference for the work. Other references, including those made to Marx, are largely rhetorical. *Crisis* does not draw from the statistical material included in *Decline*; nor does it attempt to provide a detailed empirical analysis of events. Instead, in *Crisis* Corey shifts into a self-referential and speculative general analysis of the ideological and political effects of state capitalism. With this new self-referentiality and this new focus on the superstructural manifestations of a declining economy, Corey moves to the brink of an apocalyptic vision based on an anti-orthodox interpretation of crisis and breakdown.

The world, Corey claims in *Crisis*, is in 'critical condition,' threatened by 'the death of civilization itself.'[70] This state of affairs, he argues, is the superstructural result of the economic decline and decay outlined in his earlier writings. In *Crisis*, Corey reiterates the idea that decline has become a permanent part of capitalism. The state capitalism of the twentieth century is marked by

> an *absolute limitation of capitalist production and accumulation in terms of increasing profits and their conversion into capital.* Capitalism is strangled by its objective economic limits and must decline and decay. It is the crisis and breakdown of the system.[71]

The economic transition from growth under nineteenth-century industrial capitalism to decline under twentieth-century state capitalism, presented in Corey's *Decline*, is reformulated as a series of political, social and ideological transformations in *Crisis*. Corey locates the point of transformation in the progressive era, when continued monopolization and consolidation resulted in a decrease in the number of middle-class property owners and an increase in the number of middle-class salaried employees. According to Corey, the presence of this 'new middle class' of employees produces a 'split personality' within the middle class as a whole and induces a 'crisis of the middle class.' The petty bourgeois property owners are left to maintain the liberal values of economic individualism that characterized the nineteenth century. These values conflict with those of the new middle class of salaried employees, who identify with corporate management and represent 'the *dominant system of economic collectivism*,' the monopolies of state capitalism.[72] The 'new' middle class, which increasingly displaces the old middle class of the industrial phase, operates under a set of values that displace nineteenth-century commitments to liberty, democracy, and equality of opportunity. The new values, Corey writes, consist of:

the identification of democracy and middle class interests with the acceptance of 'regulated' monopoly, a state capitalism dependent on bureaucracy and caste, and an aggressive nationalism and imperialism. Petty-bourgeois democracy was reacting against itself.[73]

According to Corey, then, state capitalism is characterized by superstructural forms that destroy the liberal values of the industrial phase and revert back to the pre-capitalist values of status, hierarchy, and militarism. This ideological transformation is represented by the rise of fascism in Europe and in the United States. 'Fascism,' Corey argues, is the 'last desperate resort of capitalism to maintain its rule,' and 'openly seeks inspiration in the medieval ideals out of the destruction of which modern civilization arose.'[74] The reversion back to feudal values constitutes a 'new barbarism,' a superstructural response to a declining economy which threatens to destroy the civilized world. Fascism may prevent a socialist revolution from overthrowing the capitalist system, Corey argues, but it cannot save the system from continued decline and 'eventual collapse, for no national economy can indefinitely exist on such a program.'[75]

Crisis, however, provides no explanation of the imperative behind Corey's argument for continued economic decline. The astute and insightful analysis of the ideological transformation that accompanies the transition from nineteenth-century industrial capitalism to twentieth-century state capitalism is marred by a theoretical silence on the issue of causality. In *Crisis*, Corey's superstructural analyses are replete with assumptions concerning causal forces in history. At those points in the text where theoretical explanations would be appropriate, Corey substitutes simplistic statements on the dialectical 'laws' of social development as the basis for his belief in the breakdown of the new barbarism:

The decline of capitalism, in its historical aspects, is the negative expression of the law of social progress: no society based upon class rule and exploitation is eternal. One social order succeeds another in the upward and onward march of humanity.[76]

In *Crisis*, the confusion that plagued the economic analysis of breakdown in *Decline* is displaced by silencing the theoretical effort and replacing it with a series of assumptions about the progressive course of history. Moreover, the determinism that fills the theoretical gap is fed by a stylistic shift. The reasoned prose of *Decline* is replaced by a highly metaphorical and graphic depiction of the 'new barbarism' which will 'consume our blood and bones.'[77] If civilization is to survive, Corey writes in one of his dramatic passages, 'the forces of life must rally against an approaching death,' in the face of an economic order that is capable of creating only 'reaction and death.'[78]

In *Crisis*, Corey's theory of breakdown shifts from the orthodox position of economic primacy to the anti-orthodox position of superstructural primacy. His description of the twentieth-century reversion back to feudal values resonates with Veblen's analysis of the rise of militarism. Corey anticipates the anti-orthodox position when he writes that, 'the state is constantly called upon to perform economic functions, to make good the shortcomings of corporate enterprise. It was the state which, in 1933, saved the American economic structure from complete breakdown.'[79] However, Corey does not fully recognize the implications of this shift in his analysis of capitalism, or attempt to reconcile the superstructural focus of *Crisis* with the structural focus of *Decline*. He does not turn back to Marx for guidance or to Veblen for support. The self-referentiality and general level of analysis in *Crisis* limit Corey's theoretical reach.

Corey was familiar with Veblen's writings and viewed them favorably. When Corey reviewed a collection of Veblen's essays for the *Marxist Quarterly* in 1937, he referred to Veblen as 'incomparably the greatest American thinker in the social sciences.'[80] Corey notes Veblen's 'prophecy that the system of business enterprise, or capitalism, must inevitably decay,' and finds that Veblen offers 'the beginnings of a practical revolutionary approach to the problem of social reconstruction.'[81] For these reasons, Veblen, 'more than any other American thinker offers material and ideas of the utmost significance to Marxism.'[82]

Corey discusses Veblen's relationship to Marx and rightly concludes that Veblen's critique of Marx arises from Veblen's narrow conception of science, his more thoroughgoing determinism, and his commitment to a concept of human nature. But, Corey argues, Veblen's work compensates for a lack of understanding of superstructural forces among Marxists, and offers a necessary corrective to Marx's work on the cultural impact of technology. Corey concludes that '[t]he value of Veblen's analysis is not destroyed by the fact that he is unaware of the pressure capitalist production exerts, through the fetishism of commodities, on the re-creation of irrationalism.'[83] With this crucial combination of Marx and Veblen completed, Corey walks away from any application of the insight contained in this corrective to Veblen's theory of the instinct of workmanship, and its bearing on Veblen's theory of breakdown.

Veblen's writings draw Corey out of the logical space of neo-orthodox speculation and into a more complex and suggestive line of interpretation. This line of interpretation draws from Marx's concept of commodity fetishism and Veblen's concept of reciprocal social action, concepts which challenge positivist epistemologies and linear, progressive conceptions of history. The confrontation of neo-orthodox and anti-orthodox writings, where it occurs at all, results in a significant if not entirely self-conscious theoretical reconsideration of the neo-orthodox position. Corey's reconsideration, however, never reached the proportions that would have been necessary to fill the theoretical gaps in his thought.

Despite his appreciation of Veblen's emphasis on superstructural forces, and despite his recognition of the potential effects of state intervention in the economy, Corey never moves into a fully anti-orthodox position based on a reversal of structural and superstructural relations. Throughout *Decline*, Corey assumes that structural forces are primary in the development and maintenance of capitalism. In *Crisis*, he turns to a superstructural definition of breakdown but is unable to provide theoretical support for his claims. Corey does not seem to recognize the enormous implications of the shift from a structural to a superstructural focus between *Decline* and *Crisis*. Moreover, *Crisis* is far too weak to sustain the theoretical weight of the new position. What might have been a fruitful and creative reconsideration of Veblen's anti-orthodoxy and the meaning of 'state capitalism' is lost in the blood imagery of the apocalyptic vision of *Crisis*.

Corey's theory of breakdown is best compared to Grossmann's, with their common return to the law of the falling rate of profit. But Corey's commitment to the concept of economic primacy seems to be the result of a theoretical default rather than the self-conscious determination that Grossmann displays in his pursuit of what he considered to be the orthodoxy of the economic approach. Corey caught sight of the anti-orthodox position and turned away from it, not so much from a desire to maintain his neo-orthodox position, but in a long flash of confusion stimulated by his obsession with impending collapse.

The transition from structural analysis in *Decline* to superstructural analysis in *Crisis* was in some part linked to the growing significance Corey placed on the rise of fascism. When *Crisis* was written, Corey was confronted by a system that had staggered through the financial crisis of 1933 and survived the highest levels of production capacity destruction in history. The threat of mechanical economic collapse was displaced by the threat of full state control and fascism. Corey's faith in the potential for proletarian revolution was diminished a decade earlier during his break with the Communist Party, and further diminished as he turned his attention to ideology and the spread of fascism. In the process, Corey's concept of breakdown was transformed from the neo-orthodoxy of *Decline* to the tendencies towards anti-ortho-doxy exhibited in *Crisis*, in a movement that resembled the shift in the works of the Frankfurt scholars as they too faced a fascist Europe.

6 The anti-orthodox response to crash and recovery: Superstructural models of collapse

> Liberation from capitalism is liberation from the rule of the economy. When the autonomy of the economy is ended, 'political economy' as an independent science also disappears.
>
> Lukács, *History and Class Consciousness*

> Are we always within the capitalist mode of production? Are we within a later mode? Are we within a mode of production at all, and have we even been in one?
>
> Baudrillard, *The Mirror of Production*

In 1930, soon after Pollock's work was published, Horkheimer replaced Grünberg as the director of the Frankfurt Institute, now well established as the center of serious social inquiry in Europe. Horkheimer was a philosopher by training, and a rigorous critic of the German Social Democratic Party and the German Communist Party. His efforts as the new director were supported by Herbert Marcuse and Theodor Adorno, central members of the Institute who shared Horkheimer's political and theoretical views. The development of Marxist theory in the West over the next forty years was largely the work of intellectuals who, like the central members of the Institute, had little in common with orthodox Marxists or the neo-orthodox theorists who had constructed the dominant forms of breakdown theory in the period before 1930.

The failure of the proletarian revolution in Germany and the rise of fascism in Europe were formative political experiences for the theorists associated with the Frankfurt Institute in Germany and the academies in France. Unlike the generation of Lenin and Luxemburg, which had been marked by internationalism and activism, the anti-orthodox Marxists of Frankfurt and Paris were characterized by parochialism and intellectual isolation, and by their uneasy, sporadic and indirect contact with worker organizations. With what may well have been a glance back to the theoretical failures forced by proximity to particularistic political activity, Horkheimer once wrote, '[o]n the identity of theory and practice, is not to be forgotten their difference.'[1]

The anti-orthodox theorists were trained as philosophers, with their immediate attention turned away from economics and politics, and towards a discourse on method and aesthetics. Their interest in non-Marxist ideas was intense rather than superficial, and their relationship to Marx was critical rather than committed. Their Marxism was spoken in a code that served the dual purpose of eluding political censorship and avoiding the positivistic terminology of the orthodox and neo-orthodox schools. Their analyses of capitalism appeared in works which were both betrayals and affirmations of Marx's most fundamental ideas. In the writings of the anti-orthodox theorists, the concepts of *Capital* were mediated by a series of perceptions and new theoretical elaborations that pressed Marx's thought to its most extreme, but nonetheless logical, conclusions. As Adorno said, their work did not represent 'the replacement of one theory by another, but the immanent drawing out of certain of the fundamentals of the materialist dialectic.'[2]

The result of their work was a fundamental shift in the nature of Marxist theory and, consequently, in the formulation of concepts of breakdown, after 1930. This theoretical shift was characterized by a pessimism about the possibility of an end to capitalism, and a certain apprehension about what might follow if it should collapse. In the age of the complete consolidation of capitalism, the rise of fascism, and the profound isolation of Western Marxists from the communist parties of Europe and the Soviet Union, economic breakdown seemed unlikely, and revolution seemed impossible. Within this context of new and less favorable conditions, Marx's thought was recast to accommodate a world that now seemed to exist in an inverted state. Theories of breakdown emerged in a superstructural form, and contained visions of the future that were less concrete, but much more awesome, than the visions found in earlier forms.

Anti-orthodoxy and the rejection of economic primacy: Critical theory

In 1941, Pollock published an essay on state capitalism which assumed a more thoroughgoing anti-orthodox position than his earlier writings. Pollock describes state capitalism as the emerging dominant mode of production. Before World War I, Pollock finds private capitalism, guided by the market mechanism, was still functional. But monopolization and the dislocation of the world market, combined with the market's failure to regulate the increasingly destructive business cycle, weakened private capitalism after the war.[3] Europe now faces 'transitional processes transforming private capitalism into state capitalism.'[4] In the United States economy, marked by high unemployment and a disfunctional market system, '[a]nalogous developments may reach a point where no measures short of a reorganization of the economic system can prevent the complete disintegration of the social structure.'[5]

State capitalism, long visible in Europe and America, emerged in full form in Nazi Germany. Under state capitalism, production facilities are privately owned but production and distribution are controlled by the state. The state is an instrument of a ruling class composed of management, the state bureaucracy and the military and party bureaucracies. Planning takes place on a national scale, with individual profit interests subordinated to the general interests of the group. Production is rationalized, prices are administered, and the business cycle is brought to an end through government control over the economy.[6]

With state capitalism, Pollock argues, economic primacy no longer exists:

> The replacement of the economic means by political means as the last guarantee for the reproduction of economic life, changes the character of the whole historic period. It signifies the transition from a predominantly economic to an essentially political era.[7]

The economic phenomena which produced crises under private capitalism become 'mere problems of administration.'[8] Economic theories of breakdown are misplaced under state capitalism; Pollock is 'unable to discover any inherent economic forces, "economic laws" of the old or new type, which could prevent the functioning of state capitalism.'[9] State capitalism, however, cannot survive in a peacetime economy; war or war preparations are necessary to avoid unemployment and overproduction without raising the standard of living to levels which breed the potential for politicization and revolution. The threat of collapse, however, arises from the political and military sphere, not from the economy.[10] With Pollock and the concept of state capitalism, the relationship between structure and superstructure in crises and collapse was reversed; economic primacy was transformed into political primacy.

Apart from Pollock's studies of state capitalism and technology, the concerns of the anti-orthodox Marxists in the post-war years rested primarily with the study of consciousness, ideology and the linguistic forces that coincided with the advance of world capitalism and the seeming suspension of overt class conflict in the West. Drawing from non-Marxist sources, and from the resurgence of Hegelian thought stimulated by the appearance of Lukács's *History and Class Consciousness*, and Marx's *Paris Manuscripts* (published for the first time in 1932), the Institute members began a series of studies of ideology and aesthetics in advanced capitalist society, and a long commentary on Marx and methodology. These projects were marked by a new emphasis on the capitalist superstructure as the force that holds the power to threaten or reinforce the economic order through ideological and linguistic control. Theories of the breakdown of capitalism competed with theories of the perpetuation of capitalism, and with a series of surrogate concepts designed to explain the absence of crises rather than their presence.[11]

According to the Institute studies, the false consciousness that blinds the working class to its own interests is not only an expression of capitalist society in an advanced and decayed state of development, but also an expression of that society's successful attempt to reorganize itself in a way that mitigates and forestalls its self-destructive capacities. Throughout the works of the Institute members, the general statements on contradiction found in *Capital* are largely displaced by a notion of history based on repetition and difference. The intellectual movement entailed resembles the open dialectic found in Marx's discussion of profit rates, but far exceeds its pessimism and minimizes its implications for the possibility of genuine change and disruption.

These studies are reinforced by a second-order discourse on Marx that is critical, anti-positivist, anti-productivist and abstract. This discourse is directed towards an attempt to revitalize the long-neglected part of Marx's thought that is conductive to an explanation of the ideological consolidation of the bourgeois order. The most complete and fruitful critique and extension of Marx's thought to arise from the Institute appears in the works of Jürgen Habermas, one of the Institute's post-immigration members, and one of the most influential Marxist theorists in West Germany today. With Habermas, the origins, meanings and consequences of anti-orthodox interpretations of breakdown theory are most clearly revealed.[12]

Habermas was a student in Frankfurt in the 1950s, after the Institute returned to Germany from its exile in America. He taught at the Institute from 1964 to 1970, and continued to identify with the critical theory school associated with the Institute despite his move to the Max Planck Institute in 1970, where he served as director. Habermas continues the critique of Marx that had been initiated by Horkheimer and Adorno in their contention that Marx relied on assumptions involving the ontological centrality of labor and a positivistic understanding of the social sciences. But Habermas remains in fundamental agreement with Marx's critique of classical political economy and with his assessment of the origins and conditions of the capitalist mode of production. Habermas returns to these points in Marx's thought for the foundations for his theory of capitalist development.

Marx was correct, Habermas contends, in his analysis of the relationship between the economic structure and the political superstructure under liberal capitalism, and in his analysis of the ideology of equal exchange as the mechanism that conceals the actual source of domination. Habermas also agrees with Marx's claim that the primary characteristic of liberal capitalism is its ability to legitimize domination through the market, rather than through the traditional institutional forums that provided justification for political domination and economic stratification in precapitalist societies. With the advent of capitalism, Habermas argues, the property order changed from a political relation to a production relation, with the economic sphere legitimized by its own system of exchange. Under liberal capitalism, he claims, 'the institutional framework of society is only mediately political and immediately economic (the bourgeois constitutional state as "superstructure").'[13]

But Habermas shares with the great majority of Western Marxist scholars the perception of a changed capitalist order, and locates the origins of that change at the turn of the century, as did Bernstein, Lenin and Horkheimer before him. Like the earlier anti-orthodox theorists, Habermas determines that the change was sufficiently dramatic to require a radical reformulation of Marx's thought, one that would redefine the relationship between structure and superstructure. Habermas specifies two major 'tendencies' that mark the 'advanced' capitalism that has come to dominate the world economy since *Capital* was written. With the neo-orthodox theorists, Habermas identifies a tendency towards an increase in the degree of state intervention in the economy, successfully introduced to reduce economic instability. With the earlier anti-orthodox Marxists, he identifies a second tendency towards an increase in the role of the sciences in the forces of production. As Habermas interprets it, the first tendency indicates that Marx's analysis of the relationship between the economic structure and the political superstructure is no longer accurate. The second tendency indicates that Marx's labor theory of value is no longer applicable, and that his concept of ideology is no longer sufficient to describe conditions under advanced capitalism. The open dialectic of *Capital* is reproduced in an exaggerated form in Habermas's thought, and ultimately turned back against itself as Marx gradually disappears from the frame of reference.

Habermas rejects the neo-orthodox analysis of a politicized economy found in Lenin's *Imperialism* and in Luxemburg's *The Accumulation of Capital*. The economy, Habermas argues, has not been 'politicized,' but 'repoliticized,' to a degree that makes its role in the social order comparable to the economies of the pre-capitalist world, and undermines any comparison with the nineteenth century. The relationship between structure and superstructure under advanced capitalism more closely resembles the relationship as it appeared under feudalism than under liberal capitalism. Habermas asserts that 'if society no longer "autonomously" perpetuates itself through self-regulation as a sphere preceding and lying at the basis of the state . . . then society and the state are no longer in the relationship that Marxian theory had defined as base and superstructure.'[14] Any theory that assumes the primacy of economics is 'inapplicable when the "base" has to be comprehended as in itself a function of governmental activity and political conflicts.'[15]

This perception of a reversal in the relationship between structure and superstructure bears far-reaching consequences for breakdown theory in Habermas's works. State intervention in the economy began, he determines, 'as a defense mechanism against dysfunctional tendencies, which threaten the system, that capitalism generates when left to itself.'[16] These dysfunctional tendencies stem from recurring crises and from the collapse of the ideology of equal exchange. In order to maintain an economic system based on the private ownership and utilization of capital, the economy, which had functioned as an autonomous force in nineteenth-century capitalism, was repoliticized, and the need for direct political legitimation reappeared.

With the relationship between the economy and the political system now reversed, the political system is directed toward the negative purpose of minimizing the occurrence and impact of economic dysfunctions, and 'government activity is restricted to administratively soluble technical problems,' rather than the realization of societal goals.[17] The consequence of this restriction, Habermas finds, is the 'abolition of politics through administration,' the depoliticization of the masses, and the transformation of science and technology into the basis of a new ideological order.[18] Crises still arise in the economic realm, but the real threat to the perpetuation of capitalism arises in the political sphere, and involves the potential for a breakdown in the ability to legitimize the governments invested with the responsibility of buttressing a flawed social order. According to Habermas, crises and breakdown in the economic realm are displaced by disruptions in the political realm.

Because the 'dysfunctional side-effects of the economic process could less and less be segmented from one another and neutralized in relation to the state,' there developed '*a general responsibility of the state for deficiencies* and a presumption of its competence to eliminate them.'[19] Habermas argues that crises in the political realm 'can be averted only if the state can credibly present itself as a social welfare state which intercepts the dysfunctional side-effects of the economic process and renders them harmless for the individual. . . .'[20] Economic contradictions and crises, and the class conflict associated with them, are increasingly displaced by crises in the political realm. This occurs when state administration necessarily fails to fulfill the expectations and demands of competing groups, and the ideological forms fail to regenerate motivation:

> Today the state has to fulfill functions that can be neither explained with reference to prerequisites of the continued existence of the mode of production, nor derived from the immanent movement of capital. This movement is no longer realized through a market mechanism that can be compre-hended in the theory of value, but is a result of the still effective economic driving forces and a political countercontrol in which a *displacement of the relations of production* finds expression.[21]

Under advanced capitalism, Habermas continues, the problem of economic breakdown is administratively processed, but not administratively controlled in a way that insures the long-term perpetuation of the system. Perpetuation is guaranteed only so long as the substitutive relation between economic surplus, political efficacy, and social motivation is maintained.[22]

If the legitimacy of the system is to continue unchallenged, Habermas argues, the dysfunctions arising from interruptions in accumulation and a pattern of unequal distribution must be corrected through governmental policies that insure growth, meet minimal collective needs and provide an acceptable standard of living. If these corrections are not possible, a crisis will occur and must be defused or concealed. When a crisis generated in the economic realm cannot be forestalled, the state 'no longer allows the crisis to come to light in an *immediately* economic form,' but shifts it into the cultural and social realms.[23] Economic crises that cannot be controlled are 'shifted towards sectors and zones marginal to the system,' so that 'other conflicts are brought into play to replace the central one.'[24] Given this state of affairs,

> [t]he real, indeed, the only, question is whether economic problems will become of such a magnitude that this model thriving on 'small crises' will be unable to function any longer and, consequently, precipitate a crisis of classic dimensions. It

remains to be seen how this is all going to end. But, on the other hand, in view of the strong probabilities of a fatal outcome, I do not think we could lightheartedly wish or hope for a 'great crisis.'[25]

The second tendency of advanced capitalism, the tendency towards the increased role of science in the forces of production, is related to the first tendency in that it contributes to this process of displacement and concealment. According to Habermas, the displacement of economic conflict by political conflict, and the subsequent 'abolition of politics through administration,' induced by the level of technological achievement in the mode of production, shifts the basis of ideology to technology and science. Technology and science then 'take on the function of legitimating political power.'[26] Habermas claims that the ideology of equal exchange collapsed with the end of liberal capitalism. The need for state intervention includes a need to 'secure the private form of capital utilization and bind the masses' loyalty to this form' through the ideological installation of science and technology as the new determinants of social advancement. Marx's labor theory of value, he argues, is inapplicable in a society where technical innovation shifts the focus away from labor and towards capital investments. Moreover, Habermas finds that Marx's concept of ideology is inappropriate in a society where science, as the critique of ideology, becomes the basis for a new ideological system which posits instrumental action as the total realm of human interaction, and technical rationality as the total realm of human rationality.

Habermas concludes that 'the laws of the economic system are no longer identical to those analyzed by Marx.'[27] The economic system of advanced capitalism is a system

about which we still have not developed adequate analyses. It is a very complex system which brings about the interaction between economy, politics, and culture. We might say that we would need a functional equivalent of Marx's theory. But we do not have it. As for the internal mechanisms of the economic system pure and simple, one can say that today they are relatively transparent and that there is not further need for a critique of ideology.[28]

The 'functional equivalent' that Habermas initiates in his account of capitalist development provides a forum for the use of empirical data, but remains thoroughly anti-positivist. The methodological and epistemological positions assumed by Habermas's critical theory preclude the possibility of linking his work to the revisionist, orthodox, or neo-orthodox schools, all of which worked within the confines of the positivistic split between empirical and general analysis. Moreover, Habermas's reversal of the structure/superstructure relationship removes him from any association with the neo-orthodox theorists who recognized the 'new capitalism' but not its full implications for Marxist thought and breakdown theory. Habermas's writings can only be situated within the discourse of the open dialectic found in the negative movements of *Capital*, in the discussion of profit rates, and in the anti-orthodox movement that first recognized that submerged voice in the works of Marx.

The substance of Habermas's analysis, and the determination with which he distances his analysis from that of Marx, combine to create a critical point of juncture between the works of Veblen and Habermas. Like Veblen, Habermas roots his reformulation of the relationship between structure and superstructure in the late nineteenth-century movement towards mechanization and concentration. Veblen's description of a return to 'dynastic' government resonates with Habermas's depiction of 'repoliticization,' a movement towards direct political legitimation, fueled by militaristic ideologies and subsequently dominated by technical rationality in depoliticized administrative sectors.

The emphasis on superstructure in the works of Veblen and Habermas leads both theorists to extensive considerations of ideological and communicative forms. Habermas's studies of distorted communication are well known, as are Veblen's writings on symbolic systems.[29] In both cases, Veblen and Habermas once again disassociate their work from its Marxist origins. Epistemologically, Veblen distances himself from Marx by exaggerating the Hegelian content of *Capital*. Similarly, Habermas's early critique of Marx rests on a reading of Marx's concept of labor that emphasizes its Hegelian origins; the later critique privileges the positivist tendencies of Marx's economic analyses. But like Veblen, the Hegelian element that Habermas exaggerates in Marx's thought reappears in his own. In his work on communicative competence, Habermas pushes dangerously close to a Hegelian notion of an ideal speech situation, in which full recovery from distorted communication is assumed to be possible. Here, Habermas moves much closer to Hegel than Marx ever ventured.

In Habermas's works, however, the open dialectic is given an exaggerated form that eventually undermines the attempt to provide a 'functional equivalent' to Marx's theory of capitalist development. In his flight from positivism, Habermas overstates the positivist content of *Capital*, and too readily rejects portions of the text that serve as a corrective against idealist interpretations of social phenomena. Consequently, Habermas's attempt to reformulate breakdown theory in superstructural terms is infused with concerns that threaten to destroy the specificity of the theory and its critical relationship to the capitalist order.

With breakdown redefined as the collapse of all forms of intellectual life, Habermas retreats into a political passivism that defeats the critical intent of his work, and reproduces a form of absolute idealism that he explicitly rejects at other points in his writings. The discourse of the open dialectic quickly becomes a discourse without an object and without an objective. In many ways, Habermas's simultaneous rejection of the positivist and idealist content of *Capital*, which exists for him in an exaggerated form, creates in his thought a series of gaps that cannot be filled.

Anti-orthodoxy and the rejection of historical specificity: French structuralism

Habermas's theory of breakdown represents the culmination of a fundamental shift in Marxist thought in twentieth-century West Germany. This shift occurred simultaneously in the academies of France, but with different consequences for the development of breakdown theory. Henri Lefebvre, the most important theoretician to work within the ranks of the French Communist Party of the 1930s, translated Marx's *1844 Manuscripts* as soon as they were released from Moscow, and immediately wrote *Dialectical Materialism*, the first full-length study to appear under their influence. Shortly afterwards, Alexandre Kojève's lectures on Hegel began to attract the generation of French intellectuals who became the forefront of anti-orthodox Marxism in France: Jean-Paul Sartre, Maurice Merleau-Ponty, and Simone de Beauvoir. Among these, Sartre achieved the most influential position, and his existentialist Marxism dominated French socialist thought for the next decade. Discussions of the economic concepts of *Capital*, or of the political problems outlined in Lenin's *Imperialism*, were lost in a flood of works on aesthetics and methodology.

The existentialist and humanist Marxism that evolved from the works of Sartre eventually collided with the structuralist perspective emerging from works in literary criticism and anthropology. A debate between humanist Marxists, best represented by Lucien Sève, and structuralist Marxists, best represented by Maurice Godelier, developed around the issue of the compatibility of two competing methodologies.[30] The humanist emphasis on history and the role of historical agents, and the structuralist emphasis on synchronic forms and economic primacy, found their fullest expression in interpretations of Marx's theory of the transition of modes of production. The concern with methodology, the original point of the debate and the central focus of French Marxist thought up to this point, once again merged with substantive issues related to the problems of economic transformations, crises, and breakdown. The merging of these interpretive, methodological and substantive issues is nowhere more complete than in the works of Louis Althusser, the most formidable Marxist theorist of post-war France.

Throughout his works, Althusser's central concern has been with the concept of ideology and its relationship to an economy which is determinative 'in the last instance.' Although Althusser has distanced himself from other structuralist Marxists, he nonetheless joins forces with figures like Godelier in his insistence on the validity of the concepts of economic primacy and structural determinacy. The concept of breakdown that emerges from his works and the works of his collaborators is the most rigorous, and yet the most elusive, to appear in the post-war period.[31]

Althusser's analysis of capitalism and his conception of econ-omic primacy rest on his idea of a structure in dominance, or the idea of an economic structure as a set of contradictions that determines the force with which other aspects of the social order control social development. Because of its position as a structure that determines the dominant forces in social development at any point in time, the economy is, according to Althusser, determinat-ive in the last instance. Superstructural forces are not epiphenom-ena of the economy, but in unity with it, and may be of superior immediate force even though that force is itself both a product and a condition of the economy.[32] Although Althusser does not directly address the problem of economic collapse, Étienne Balibar, in a lengthy essay published with Althusser's *Reading Capital*, attempts to extend Althusser's concepts of economic primacy and structural determinacy to the problem of breakdown.

Focusing on Volume III of *Capital*, Balibar treats the falling rate of profit as the necessary process of an unexplained end, as an effect of the economic structure rather than an empirically and progressively realized law of development resulting in a certain defined event. Rejecting those aspects of the law of the falling rate of profit that appear to be 'empiricist and mechanistic in character,' Balibar claims that the law of the falling rate of profit does not indicate the breakdown of capitalism but a potentially endless repetition of crises and recoveries.[33] 'Thus,' Balibar writes, 'the only intrinsic result of the contradiction, which is completely immanent to the economic structure, does not tend towards the supersession of the contradiction, but to the perpetu-ation of its conditions.'[34] The law of falling rate of profit is the theoretical elaboration of the cycle of capitalist development, not of its impending collapse. The tendencies of capitalism that express its contradictions as a mode of production never reach a climactic point or limit.

The potential for collapse, Balibar contends, does not arise from the falling rate of profit, but from the coincidence of this condition with class conflict so that the repetition of economic crises 'can be the occasion for a – revolutionary – transformation of the structure of production. . . .'[35] In this way, Balibar combines the discourse of the open dialectic from the discussion of profit rates in Volume III of *Capital* – with its notion of repetition and the potential perpetuation of contradiction – with the idea of proletarian revolution found in the general statements on contradiction in Volume I. But Balibar's contention that the falling rate of profit creates a cyclical pattern of economic development is theoretically unsupported. Moreover, Balibar's conceptualization of crises as an 'occasion' for revolutionary activity remains undeveloped: there is no attempt to specify the conditions for revolution.

Althusser does not take up the issue of breakdown or proletarian revolution, but submerges both in his discussion of the state and ideology in advanced capitalist society. His critique of capitalism and the ideological systems that support its perpetuation is initially derived from Marx's concepts of fetishism and false consciousness.[36] Like Lukács and Korsch, Althusser reacts against the idea of ideology as an illusion, an idea that was widespread during the era of the Second International. In an attempt to return to Marx's concept of ideology as a necessary illusion, Althusser emphasizes the objective role of ideology in social formations.

In doing so, Althusser moves away from the historical analyses of fetishism and ideology found in *Capital*, and turns to the concept of ideology as a necessary illusion in all societies, apart from the specific contradictions of capitalism, and the economic grounding of Marx's analyses. In *Capital*, the ideological superstructure is related to a variable economic structure. In the works of Althusser, ideology is a consequence of an invariant social structure – the universal need for social cohesion. Unlike Lenin and Luxemburg, whose interest in ideology remained tied to their analyses of the survival of capitalism and the role of the working class, Althusser's interest in ideology lies in general theories of consciousness formation. The relationship between the theory of capitalist development and the study of ideologies, a relationship implicitly affirmed in Marx's discussions of critique and fetishism, becomes obscure in Althusser's writings.

With the works of Habermas and Althusser, the leading Western Marxist theorists of the post-war era, the concept of breakdown is re-established, but in a form radically different from that which appeared in the writings of Bernstein and Kautsky, or in the works of Lenin and Luxemburg. To the extent that the orthodox and neo-orthodox theorists recognized the interaction between structure and superstructure, their recognition was motivated by their attempts to introduce the motor role of class struggle into a theory of breakdown which seemed to have lost its validity under the conditions of monopoly capitalism and imperialism. Lenin turned to the problem of consciousness in search of a theoretical guide to the development of a class struggle that would compensate for capitalism's new invulnerability to problems of realization and accumulation. With Habermas and Althusser, however, the roles of structure and superstructure are not defined by perceptions of economic problems or by political requirements, but by a much more abstract model of the ways in which causal forces shift and merge over time.

Although the conclusions drawn by Habermas and Althusser conflict at crucial points, their mutual and central concern with ideology, and their particular interpretation of Marx's discussions of fetishism and false consciousness, follow similar lines of development. Marx's specific and historically legitimate concern with consciousness and communication as parts of the capitalist labor process is transformed by Habermas and Althusser into a concept of consciousness and communication as rationalizations of the capitalist labor process increasingly external to the process itself.

Similarly, Marx's critique of a discourse devoted to the maintenance of the economic order is converted into the critique of a discourse devoted to the maintenance of superstructural forms which now assume primary responsibility for the perpetuation of an economic order no longer able to insure its existence through force of economic equilibrium. Both Habermas and Althusser explore the discourse of the open dialectic in a way that leads them to an appreciation of Marx and an understanding of his works unknown to the theorists of the pre-war period. But this understanding also leads them in directions that ultimately diverge from Marx's consistent concern with the history and development of capitalism as a specific and temporal mode of production.

The logical extreme of the modification of breakdown theory that began with the fundamental shift in Marxist thought in the 1930s and reached its penultimate form in the works of Habermas and Althusser, is found in the writings of Jean Baudrillard. A French leftist who broke from the domination of the Althusserian school, Baudrillard produced the ultimate semiological reformulation of breakdown theory in *The Mirror of Production*, first published in 1973. Here Baudrillard sets forth the most explicit and total rejection of Marxist concepts of economic primacy yet to appear in the intellectual history of breakdown theory. His work represents the most radical attempt to argue that the rule of the economy has ended, and political economy with it.

Crises, Baudrillard argues, are no longer an economic problem, but a linguistic one. Capitalism is threatened with imminent collapse, but through semiological rather than economic forces. Baudrillard concludes that Marx, and the entire system of thought generated by his writings, must be cast out of the minds of those who wish to understand capitalism today. In *The Mirror of Production*, Marx's thought is not subjected to modification or mediation, but to dismissal, and breakdown theory appears in full apocalyptic form as a purely semiological affair in a capitalist society that bears little or no resemblance to the world of Marx or Lenin.

The anti-productivist critique of Marx that preoccupied the members of the Frankfurt School, and the epistemological critique of Marx that preoccupied Althusser, reappear in Baudrillard as central points in his rejection of Marx's analysis of capitalism. According to Baudrillard, Marx never escaped from the conceptual boundaries of classical political economy and, consequently, did not succeed in his attempt to provide the logical space necessary for an understanding of the contradictory existence of capitalism and the nature of its inevitable collapse. Baudrillard argues that Marx accepted the classical assumptions of the ontological centrality of labor, the linearity of historical development, and the representational nature of language, in a way that forced the concept of economic primacy beyond its historically accurate and relevant context. As a result, Baudrillard claims, Marx's system of thought functions in collusion with capitalist society rather than as a critique of it, and fails to comprehend the dynamics of a system torn apart by its own semiological contradictions.

The concept of economic primacy, which is central to both capitalist and Marxist ideologies, Baudrillard contends, is nothing more than 'the theorization of the rupture with symbolic exchange,' the reflection of a social order that is 'structurally incapable of liberating human potentials except as *productive* forces.'[37] Theorists who support the concept of economic primacy, from Marx to Althusser, are '"objectively" idealist and reactionary.'[38] Baudrillard argues that with the transition from competitive capitalism to monopoly capitalism, a transition that began in Marx's own era, there was also a radical change in the function of the linguistic sign.

The 'classical era' of representational signification was lost to a new era where the signifier no longer referred back to any subjective or objective reality but to its own logic.[39] This transition, Baudrillard claims, constitutes a basic transformation in the nature of capitalist society, and the end of the primacy of economic forces. Through this perception of a shift in the nature of capitalism, Baudrillard posits a form of breakdown theory that claims an anti-Marxist status, and calls for an end to the use of *Capital* as the fundamental text, the intellectual origin, of the analysis of the contradictions of capitalism and its ultimate fate as a social system.

The 'epicenter of the contemporary system,' Baudrillard argues, 'is no longer the process of material production.'[40] The primary contradiction of capitalism is not economic, he claims, but symbolic, and derives from the non-reciprocity of social relations within the capitalist order. 'The symbolic social relation,' according to Baudrillard, 'is the uninterrupted cycle of giving and receiving, which, in primitive exchange, includes the consumption of the "surplus" and deliberate anti-production whenever accumulation . . . risks breaking the reciprocity and begins to generate power.'[41] Disequilibrium of power in the political realm, overtly manifested in the symbolic power of certain social groups, threatens to collapse the system, and to destroy its basic premises and institutions. Baudrillard concludes that, '[j]ust as in 1929, when the system almost died from an inability to circulate production, so today it is perishing from an inability to circulate the spoken word.'[42] When attempts to increase participation in the political and symbolic processes fail, Baudrillard argues, capitalism will fall. The vanguard of the struggle that will hasten the collapse of capitalism consists of those who have remained outside its distorted symbolic code: women, students and blacks.

With Baudrillard, the intellectual history of Western Marxist theories of breakdown appears to reach a disjuncture in an otherwise consistent allegiance to the range of theoretical possibilities generated by *Capital*. Baudrillard's escape from Marx, however, is not as complete as his claims indicate. The discourse of the open dialectic in *Capital* contains, exceeds and ultimately defeats the central points of Baudrillard's critique of Marx. Baudrillard's rejection of Marx, and his perception of the uniqueness of his own analyses, are based on a selective reading of Marx's works that silences one part of the range of theoretical possibilities and exaggerates another.

Baudrillard's work, then, does not constitute a rupture in the intellectual history of breakdown theory, but the last and most transparent point in a long series of attempts to reconcile Marx's theory of capitalist development with perceptions of a changing capitalist order. None of the attempts fully account for or contain the full range of theoretical possibilities generated by the original texts. Instead, each duplicates or exaggerates one or several of the discourses that arise from the concepts of *Capital* itself. But the range of theoretical possibilities generated by Marx's theory of capitalist development is expanded with each exaggeration, in a way that offers an ever-increasing array of alternatives to the concepts presented in the original texts. The conceptual boundaries of *Capital* are not situated by the works of the European theorists, but exploded into a confusing and conflicting series of perspectives on the nature of capitalism, its laws and conditions of development, and its ultimate fate as a mode of production.

Neo-orthodox continuations: The submerged tradition

After 1930, neo-orthodox concepts of breakdown did not disappear but were subordinate, in both quantitative and qualitative terms, to the anti-orthodox interpretations that dominated theoretical work in Europe. In England and on the Continent, Marxists continued to rewrite the history of capitalism in a way that revealed an allegiance to the assumption of linear causality found in the works of Kautsky and Luxemburg. These neo-orthodox Marxists drew from the concepts of underconsumption, disproportionality and profit that had generated confusion and conflict in the debates of the Second International. Preoccupied by the same general form of analysis that had served other theorists, and committed to a positivist epistemology that had become a dominant tradition in philosophy and the social sciences, the neo-orthodox school of Marxist theory survived the anti-orthodox onslaught in a decidedly weakened but nonetheless influential state.

In England, Marxist scholars like John Strachey believed that their neo-orthodox theories of breakdown had been verified by the depression of the 1930s. They remained impervious to anti-orthodox arguments. Strachey responded to the 1929 crash with a book entitled *The Coming Struggle for Power*, published in 1933. In this work, Strachey draws heavily from Lenin in his depiction of a 'new capitalism' characterized by the growth of monopolies and nationalism, and marked by economic instability and cultural decay. In this 'imperialist phase' of capitalist development, Strachey argues, the only future for capitalism 'will consist in the working out of the last possibilities of imperialism.'[43] For Strachey, the end of capitalism is clearly in sight:

> When capitalism has taken on its last and most monstrous form, when commercial competition has evolved into inter-imperial war, at this very moment the conflict between the two classes in society, the workers and the capitalists, is reaching its final stage.[44]

Moreover, Strachey viewed the fascist movement in Europe as the capitalists' 'last attempt to resist workers and external aggressors.'[45] The general statements on contradiction from

Capital resound in this passage, and throughout Strachey's early works. Once again in the history of Marxist thought, the mechanical, economic collapse of capitalism, acting as an automatic stimulus to a conclusive but unsituated class revolt, appeared as the inevitable future.

By 1935, Strachey had completed a lengthy manuscript on breakdown theory to support his earlier conclusions concerning the collapse of capitalism. With his expectation of imminent revolution still unfulfilled, Strachey now turned to a theory of breakdown that circumvented the issue of class struggle and relied on economic forces alone. In *The Nature of Capitalist Crisis*, Strachey combined the notion of a falling rate of profit with underconsumption theory in an attempt to locate the critical and crucial contradiction of capitalist economic development.

Drawing from Marx's law of the tendency of a falling rate of profit, and from the underconsumption theory found in Marx's discussions of periodic crises, Strachey concludes that capitalism cannot continue due to the contradictory need for both accumulation and consumption. The falling rate of profit, which Strachey claims to be an 'observed fact,' requires an expansion of markets, accomplished through imperialist policies, and a contraction of wage payments, accomplished through reductions in employment and the maintenance of minimal wage rates. According to Strachey, this minimization of employment levels and wage rates creates a realization problem that blocks further accumulation and ultimately offsets the expanded mass of profits.[46] The depression of the 1930s, he argues, indicates that Marx's 'predictions' concerning the fate of capitalism are fully accurate.

Although Strachey remained convinced that the breakdown of capitalism would soon occur, he no longer placed full faith in the inevitability of social revolution. In 1935, Strachey concluded that the future held two possibilities. Profit rates might be restored through increased exploitation, but the use of force required to increase exploitation would feed fascism and signal the onset of barbarism. Alternatively, economic hardship and the brutality of the fascist regimes might trigger revolution, followed by a transition to socialism. Strachey concludes, in fully apocalyptic tones, that 'the inevitable decline of civilization can only be interrupted by revolution.'[47]

Twenty years later, Strachey returned to the problem of breakdown in a book written while he was a Member of Parliament, and simply entitled *Contemporary Capitalism*. Capitalism had survived the depression of the 1930s that Strachey had once predicted would be its 'last and most monstrous form.' With earlier political expectations and theoretical speculations again defeated, Strachey reformulated his ideas in a last attempt to reconcile his lifelong commitment to breakdown theory with the realities of capitalism's seeming invulnerability. Finally, Marx's thought, as Strachey understood it, was subjected to critical examination, followed by a partial and hesitating rejection.

In *Contemporary Capitalism*, Strachey's reading of Marx no longer relies on Volume III of *Capital* and the concept of a falling rate of profit, but shifts its full focus to Volume I and Marx's statements on revolution provoked by the increasing exploitation of the working class. Strachey argues that Marx did not believe that real wages could rise under capitalism; this was Marx's 'fatal error.' Marx did not foresee, Strachey claims, that the state, through direct and indirect means, would reverse the downward trend in real wages in order to reinforce the economic system. Strachey locates the source of this 'error' in Marx's 'partially deductive, anti-empirical approach, which made him believe that he had determined and defined the value of labor-power as subsistence. . . .'[48] The real threat to capitalism, Strachey now argues, arises from the contradiction between the desire for democratic government and the continuation of an economic structure which, with its inclination towards concentration and imperialism, is basically opposed to democracy. The future, he claims, lies in democratic socialism, the inevitable victor in the 'coming struggle for power' that Strachey still saw as the undeniable course of history. Once again, unfulfilled expectations of mechanical collapse and spontaneous revolution prompted a turn to revisionism and reformism.

The resurrection of neo-orthodoxy after 1930 spread to the Continent, where Strachey's thought found its parallel in the works of Otto Bauer. In *Between Two Wars?*, published in 1936, Bauer produced the most sophisticated argument for underconsumption theory to appear in Marxist scholarship. Bauer had studied the reproduction schemes of *Capital*, and had argued against Luxemburg's emphasis on outside markets. He combined the notion of a rising organic composition of capital, taken from profit theory, with disproportionality theory, to produce a version of underconsumptionism that linked crises to the overaccumulation of constant capital. Crises are inevitable, Bauer argues, because the accumulation of constant capital always exceeds the increase in commodity consumption that results from population growth and expanded employment. Bauer locates the primary contradiction of capitalism in the realization problem created by commodity underconsumption. Although he never subscribed to a definitive concept of breakdown, those neo-orthodox theorists who came under his influence combined his underconsumptionist thesis with ideas taken from Luxemburg and Grossmann to produce a new series of empirically based breakdown studies.

The most successful of these studies, and the most extensive defense of neo-orthodoxy in the post-war period came from Ernst Mandel, a Belgian Trotskyist who was prominent in the Fourth International. In 1962, Mandel published his two-volume *Marxist Economic Theory*, the most complete commentary on *Capital* to appear in the post-war years. A decade later, Mandel produced *Late Capitalism*, the first global treatment of capitalist development to appear in the West since Hilferding's *Finance Capital*, and the definitive neo-orthodox work on the 'new capitalism.'

In *Marxist Economic Theory*, Mandel attempts to integrate his own reading of Marx with an enormous amount of empirical data on the development of capitalism since the publication of *Capital*. Mandel concludes that Marx's theories are still adequate and accurate, and that capitalism cannot endure the contradictions inherent in its structure as a mode of production. Mandel, however, does not offer a definitive explanation of the course of events that will lead to the collapse he clearly anticipates, but suggests several scenarios, with no indication of their relative probability. He discusses the role of state intervention in an economy that cannot survive crises induced by overproduction and falling profit rates unaided. At this point, Mandel seems to indicate that the most immediate threat to capitalism arises from a tendency towards long-term stagnation and inflation that the state is unable to influence.[49] Mandel later argues that this tendency, '[o]n the purely economic plane . . . need not lead to an automatic collapse of capitalism,' but that the tendency does lead to 'a *potential enhancement* and sharpening of the class struggle.'[50]

The capitalist class, according to Mandel, can respond to intensified class antagonisms through the expansion of the 'Welfare State,' or through the expansion of the 'Fascist State,' which, as Strachey had argued earlier, would reinforce falling profit rates through increased exploitation. Mandel indicates that capitalism will increasingly rely on a combination of 'Welfare State' and 'Fascist State' policies to reduce economic instability and class conflict, but that 'this increasing economic role of the state means at the same time the violent compression of social and international contradictions, and so intensifies the advance of capitalism towards explosive outbreaks of war and revolution.'[51] This argument eventually leads Mandel to the spectre of 'collective destruction, of nuclear war,' that also haunted Strachey's works, as the most probable form of collapse.[52] The threat of nuclear war, touched off by imperialist policies and competition for markets, is a recurring theme in Mandel's works.

A more sustained consideration of the development of capitalism and the potential for economic breakdown appeared ten years later in Mandel's *Late Capitalism*, a book of enormous scope and scholarship. This work attempts to reconstruct the development of capitalism since 1930 'within the framework of classical Marxist categories' initiated by Marx and refined by Lenin.[53] Mandel describes 'late capitalism' as a distinct phase of economic development which 'began when fascism and the Second World War generated a significant increase in the rate of surplus value, which was prolonged by a substantial reduction in the price of important elements of constant capital,' and resulted in upward economic movement during the post-war years.[54] Late capitalism is, then, a phase of development within the broader epoch of monopoly capitalism, the epoch that began at the turn of the century and was first described in Lenin's *Imperialism*.

Although Mandel views late capitalism as a distinct historical phase, the term 'in no way suggests that capitalism has changed in essence, rendering the analytical findings of Marx's *Capital* and Lenin's *Imperialism* out of date.'[55] He notes that his intention in *Late Capitalism* is to reconstruct economic history, to explicate 'the basic laws of motion of capitalism discovered by Marx in *Capital*,' and 'to demonstrate that the "abstract" laws of motion of this mode of production remain operative and verifiable in and through the unfolding "concrete" history of contemporary capitalism.'[56]

Mandel directly addresses the unresolved problem of the relationship between the laws and conditions of capitalism. He equates the 'abstract laws of motion' with the 'essence' of capitalism, and argues that Marx resolved the problem of the relationship between the laws and conditions of capitalism through a dialectical mediation that Mandel describes as an oscillation between theoretical and empirical knowledge. Althusser is sharply attacked for his 'attempt to escape the spectre of empiricism and its theory of knowledge – a spectre of his own making – by establishing a basic dualism between "objects of knowledge" and "real objects",' and falling into idealism.[57]

This separation between 'objects of knowledge' and 'real objects' led Marx to the discourse of the open dialectic and directed later Marxists to the anti-positivist position that characterizes anti-orthodox Marxist thought in the post-war period. According to Mandel, however, the separation has no foundation in Marx's thought. Moreover, he argues that this separation has stimulated misinterpretations of the tendential laws found in *Capital*, and a subsequent defusing of Marx's profit theory. The error of the anti-positivist position, Mandel claims, lies in its attempt to reproduce the disjuncture between 'appearance' and 'essence' within concrete economic reality at the epistemological level, so that theoretical knowledge and empirical knowledge exist within a similar state of disjuncture.

112

Mandel turns to Hegel to validate his claim that 'the essence, together with its mediations to the appearance, forms a unity of abstract and concrete elements.'[58] According to Mandel the dialectical method can grasp this unity in its entirety. For Mandel, then, Marx postulated a unity of opposites at the level of concrete reality, and an identity of opposites at the level of conceptual understanding. This argument allows Mandel to reconstruct what he refers to as the 'real history' of capitalism without the epistemological difficulties that Marx encountered when he rejected the Hegelian assumption of identity and voiced this rejection through the discourse of the open dialectic.

According to Mandel, earlier Marxist theorists have failed to understand the 'development and the inevitable collapse of the capitalist mode of production' because they have attempted 'to reduce this problem *to a single factor.*'[59] Mandel claims that breakdown, like any economic event, must be seen as a combination of historical forces and variables that exist in an 'interplay constantly articulated through the laws of development of the whole capitalist mode of production.'[60] The key to Mandel's concept of breakdown lies in his notion of the falling rate of profit, combined with the idea of realization problems stimulated by overproduction:

> Fluctuations in the rate of profit are the seismograph of this history, since they express most clearly the result of this interplay in accordance with the logic of a mode of production based on profit, in other words, the valorization of capital.[61]

Mandel claims that 'late capitalism' is characterized by significant increases in the rate of surplus value, and by large discrepancies between the average rate of profit and the rate of profit in monopoly sectors of the economy. Mandel argues, however, that high rates of profit in the monopoly sector do not invalidate the law of the falling rate of profit, since the constant expansion of the monopoly sector increases the organic composition of capital and eventually results in reduced profit rates in both sectors. The role of the state in late capitalism is to protect profit rates during increased monopolization by regulating currency and credit, underwriting investments and creating additional markets. The increase in surplus value and the state's absorption of the realization costs 'can merely retard' the law of value and the corresponding law of profit, but cannot 'abolish it.'[62]

The empirical information provided by Mandel is intended to demonstrate that monopolization and state regulation cannot circumvent the law of value. Mandel argues that if the law of value has ceased to be valid, as some theorists have claimed, then

113

'contemporary society has ceased to be capitalist,' a hypothesis that Mandel flatly rejects.[63] Moreover, Mandel argues that,

[i]f the 'regulation of the economy' by government and monopolies . . . is simply an attempt to deflect and temporarily attenuate (i.e., ultimately merely postpone) the effects of the law of value, then the operations of this law must inevitably prevail in the end.[64]

Consequently, Mandel refuses to consider the issue of a shift in structural/superstructural relations, and argues that '[n]o arbitrary separation of the social or socio-political sphere from the economic sphere can provide a satisfactory answer to the question of the overall nature of late capitalism.'[65] State regulation is merely a symptom of the 'incurable malady' of the system. The continuation of economic crises indicates that regulations generated in the superstructure have not been and will not be able to overpower structural flaws.

Mandel further argues that the state has been thwarted in its attempts 'to "integrate" the worker into late capitalist society,' and in its attempts to 'divert any rebellion into reforms containable within the system.'[66] Class conflict, then, still remains a threat to the continuation of capitalism:

The essential and intrinsic consequence of the end of the long wave of post-war expansion, and the intensified struggle over the rate of surplus-value unleashed from the second half of the 60s onwards, is a world-wide tendency towards qualitatively sharpened class conflicts, which will bring the endemic crisis of capitalist relations of production to explosion point.[67]

Like Strachey, Mandel remains loyal to the neo-orthodox position, and impervious to the anti-orthodox concept of breakdown that dominated European Marxist thought during his lifetime. Mandel's perception of a changing capitalist reality exists within a broader perception of fundamental continuity. Although Mandel recognizes the role of state intervention, he rejects the anti-orthodox perception of a reversal in the relationship between economic structure and political superstructure, and the massive theoretical and practical shifts entailed in that reversal. Mandel does not share the anti-orthodox assessment of ideological forces, or their critique of the concept of value, or their indeterminate form of breakdown theory. He has no sympathy for their anti-positivist ideology, or for their political passivity and pessimism.

But at points, Mandel's description of late capitalism coincides with the anti-orthodox vision. Mandel writes:

Late capitalism is characterized by the *simultaneous* combination of the directly economic role of the bourgeois State, the drive to depoliticize the working-class and the myth of a technologically determined, omnipotent economy which can allegedly overcome class antagonisms, ensure uninterrupted growth, steadily raise consumption and thereby bring forth a 'pluralistic' society.[68]

The descriptive elements in both Mandel's *Late Capitalism* and Habermas's *Legitimation Crisis* form a point of overlap between the neo-orthodox and anti-orthodox positions. The radical differences between these two works, written in the same year and in the same language, are found beyond their descriptive content, in their theories of knowledge and their theories of history.

Despite their common vision of their common world – the irresistible present – Mandel and Habermas diverge in their thoughts about the past and the future, and in their explanatory forms, duplicating once again the diverse discourses of *Capital*, and exaggerating tendencies within a text they seek to clarify. Each turns away from the other and, in doing so, broadens the range of theoretical possibilities arising from *Capital*. This range of theoretical possibilities forms the conceptual context for the works of the American Marxists who confronted the concept of breakdown in the post-war period.

7 Breakdown theory and the American Marxists:
Abandonment and retrieval in the post-war period

The one-dimensional society is such only ideologically; in every other respect it is still the capitalism of old. Ideological conformity depends on conditions of prosperity; it has no staying power of its own. But unless all theoretical reasoning should be entirely valueless, in so far as it allows for predictability it points to the demise not only of capitalistic prosperity but also to the end of capitalism itself.

Mattick, *Critique of Marcuse*

I have not taken the oath I have just taken in order to preside over the dissolution of the world's strongest economy.

Ronald Reagan, *Inaugural Address*, 1981

The restoration of prosperity, the systematic repression of working-class movements, and the institutionalization of McCarthyism in the United States after World War II posed conceptual and political obstacles for the development of Marxist economic analysis. The popular genre of crisis literature that flourished during the depression years dissipated as growth resumed during World War II; the social contract between labor and capitalists derailed resistance. McCarthyism silenced many of those who maintained a Marxist position. Others retained their freedom only by virtue of the shift to superstructural analysis that effectively defused the radical posture of their critique of capitalism. The commitment to the concepts of crisis and collapse was maintained, in many cases, only at the sacrifice of economic analysis, and the abandonment of Marx's texts.

The four post-war American Marxist theorists studied in this chapter – Paul Baran, Paul Sweezy, Paul Mattick and James O'Connor – do not form a homogeneous group. Instead, their lives and their works are characterized by the same theoretical and practical diversity that marked the lives and works of the early American theorists. Baran, a Russian immigrant, was the leading Marxist scholar in American universities in the post-war period. Although he maintained significant ties to both neo-orthodox and anti-orthodox European Marxist theorists, his influence was largely felt in the United States. Soon after he arrived in the United States, Baran joined forces with Sweezy, an American-born Harvard scholar. Together they constructed a neo-orthodox perspective that spoke to the non-communist American left of the 1960s and to the growing number of Third World dependency theorists. Consistently concerned with contemporary events in the Soviet Union and the developing socialist nations, and with the concrete fluctuations of the American economy, Baran and Sweezy struggled to maintain a position that spanned theory and praxis, orthodoxy and anti-orthodoxy. Ever faithful to their original reading of Marx, and yet pressured to construct a new theory for a new social order, Baran and Sweezy pressed the question of the fate of capitalism until a theoretical impasse was reached.

Paul Mattick and James O'Connor, Marxist theorists who wrote during the political turbulence of the Vietnam War era, responded to a different set of demands. Both were fully familiar with the works of Baran and Sweezy, but both turned to Europe in their attempt to revitalize a neo-orthodox position that could accommodate the political and economic issues of late capitalism and the ideological questions generated by the growing presence of the state in economic and social affairs. Their formulations of the theory of breakdown differ significantly from those produced by Baran and Sweezy. In this chapter, the works of these four theorists are discussed as part of the continued expansion of the range of theoretical possibilities arising from the breakdown controversy.

The tenuous nature of post-war neo-orthodoxy

The works of Baran and Sweezy recast the terms of Marxist analysis in the United States for a whole generation of scholars, and provided a solution to the problem of breakdown that maintained the concept of collapse by silencing the basic Marxist concepts that proved problematic in the post-war era. *Monopoly Capital: An Essay on the American Economic and Social Order*, co-authored by Baran and Sweezy, is perhaps the single most influential Marxist analysis of capitalism to appear in the United States in the post-war period. *Monopoly Capital* is a more extreme and less substantial version of Baran's earlier works, and clearly derives its inspiration from Baran's only published monograph,

The Political Economy of Growth.[1] Sweezy's own writings were conceptually overshadowed by the force of Baran's analyses. Baran was born in 1910 in Russia, but educated in Germany, where he joined the Young Communist League. In 1926, he began a two-year course of study at the Plekhanov Institute in Moscow. Disillusioned by Stalinism, Baran ended his association with the Communist Party in 1930, joined the SPD in Germany, and wrote a series of articles for the SPD organ. Baran worked under Pollock at the Frankfurt Institute and completed a dissertation in Berlin before his migration from Germany in 1933. He had no party affiliation after this point. Baran moved to Paris, then to Moscow where he was soon deported as a Trotskyite sympathizer, then to Poland, to London, and finally to the United States in 1939. He received a Master's degree from Harvard in 1941, and worked for the United States government until 1949, when he accepted a position at Stanford University. Baran remained at Stanford until his death in 1964.[2] During his tenure at Stanford, Baran was a consistent contributor to *Monthly Review.*

Political Economy of Growth grew out of a series of lectures delivered at Oxford University in 1953, and quickly established Baran as one of the foremost Marxist economists in the West. Translated into nine languages and praised by Third World leaders like Che and Castro, *Political Economy of Growth* was highly influential in the developing dependency theory movement. *Political Economy of Growth* contains the most sustained and consistent formulations of the concepts that remained central to Baran's later works.[3] Most importantly, the book introduces the concept of 'economic surplus,' which provides the framework for the abandonment of the most central and yet the most demanding of Marx's concepts: the theory of surplus value. Although the book is usually categorized as a contribution to the corpus of works concerning the economics of underdevelopment, most of its pages are devoted to an analysis of advanced capitalist societies, and to a reformulation of Marx's theory of capitalist development.

In *Political Economy of Growth*, Baran's immediate concern lies with the economic and political forces that affect economic growth in underdeveloped countries. His assessments, however, draw him into a detailed consideration of theories of the breakdown of capitalism. The economic growth of underdeveloped countries is restricted, Baran contends, primarily by the institutions of advanced capitalism, which suffer from the economic stagnation of world capitalism. An understanding of the political economy of growth, then, is contingent on an understanding of the political economy of stagnation and breakdown in advanced capitalism. For this reason, the theories of colonialism and imperialism generated by Hobson and Lenin play a less important role in the book than Marx's theories of surplus value and capital accumulation. The most significant contemporary references consist largely of works by the British and American Marxists and non-Marxists who have studied advanced capitalism. Strachey, Dobb, Kalecki, Sweezy, Schumpeter, Robinson, Keynes and Bettelheim are frequently cited.

The central theoretical role of Marx's texts in *Political Economy of Growth* is foreshadowed in Baran's first chapter. According to Baran, '[m]uch if not all we know about the complex mechanism responsible for the development (and stagnation) of productive forces, and for the rise and decay of social organizations is the result of the analytical work undertaken by Marx and those whom he inspired.'[4] Bourgeois economics, he argues, abandoned 'both reason and history' when the limitations of capitalism were revealed through economic analysis. This self-induced blindness ended only with Keynesian analysis, which 'advanced to the very limits of bourgeois economic theorizing, and exploded its entire structure.'[5]

Keynesian analysis, Baran continues, forced economists to admit 'that instability, a strong tendency towards stagnation, chronic underutilization of human and material resources, are inherent in the capitalist system.'[6] With this admission, Baran argues, conventional economics opened itself to a dialogue with Marxist analyses. Baran utilizes both models in his conceptual scheme. Drawing from Marx's theory of surplus value, especially as it appears in *Grundrisse*, and Keynes's theory of income from *Theories of General Wealth*, Baran constructs his concept of economic surplus. The development of this concept entails a detailed consideration of accumulation and breakdown.

Baran distinguishes between two types of economic surplus: actual and potential. Actual surplus is the difference between society's actual current output and its actual current consumption, and is equal to savings and accumulation. It is that part of surplus value that is accumulated rather than consumed by the capitalist class or by government spending, and cannot be equated with profits, which are only a small part of surplus. Potential economic surplus is the difference between the output that could be produced given full utilization of productive resources, and essential, or rational, consumption.[7] The concept of potential economic surplus is of little importance in breakdown theory, but the concept of actual surplus, as the measure of accumulation, forms the basis for Baran's analysis of capitalist stagnation and breakdown.

Baran claims that the rate and direction of economic development depend on the size and utilization of actual economic surplus. The decline of the economic growth rate in the United

States is caused by and expressed in fluctuations in economic activity, employment, and, in a more general sense, the availability and nature of surplus. The problem of breakdown, then, is posed as the problem of locating

> what it is in the structure of advanced capitalism, and in such changes in the investment process as have occurred in the course of the last five to eight decades, that renders the employment of the economic surplus in the realization of these projects difficult, if not downright impossible.[8]

According to Baran, these changes in the investment process threaten the ability of capitalism to reproduce and expand itself as a system. They are not random disturbances in an otherwise harmonious order, but are inherent in the 'laws of motion' of capitalism. The disruptive changes are the result of 'a process that is deeply rooted in the basic structure of capitalism,' and its development over time. This process includes 'the growth of large-scale enterprise, of monopoly and oligopoly, and their ever-increasing sway over all sectors and branches of the capitalist system.'[9]

Under the conditions of advanced capitalism, Baran argues, the distribution and mode of utilization of the actual economic surplus shifts dramatically, decreasing the volume of investment in the face of defeated profit expectations, and increasing the amount of unabsorbed surplus. Consequently, there is a chronic tendency towards underemployment and stagnation of the sort predicted by Marx in his discussions of excess accumulation. According to Baran, then, the threat to capitalism in its advanced stage of development does not stem from falling rates of profit or social revolution but from an inability to convert profits and surplus into lucrative investments, a problem of realization rather than production. Only direct state intervention in the economy, through unproductive government spending and the protection of foreign markets, can absorb surplus and alleviate stagnation. 'The very existence of monopoly capitalism,' Baran contends, 'now depends on the ability of capitalists to control the state.'[10] In Baran's analysis, the economic problems of stagnation and breakdown become political problems of state action under the conditions of monopoly capitalism, and the terms of breakdown theory are redefined to meet this development.

Consequently, Baran shifts his emphasis from the structural dysfunctions of capitalism to the superstructural forces that mitigate and conceal these dysfunctions. Consistent and continuous state intervention in the economy began, Baran finds, not at the turn of the century or during World War I, but with the New Deal, in a massive effort to legitimize and stabilize an economic system that had moved to the brink of collapse. The New Deal constituted a fundamental change in the sources of legitimation as it 'removed the onus for the malfunctioning of the economy from the capitalist class and placed it upon society at large and its expendable political functionaries.[11] Control over the state's economic programs, however, remained with the capitalists as they assumed government posts and brought influence to bear within the Roosevelt administration.[12] 'The drive of monopoly capital to secure control over the state, to concentrate in its hands the conduct of such government intervention in economic affairs as may be required,' Baran continues, is motivated by the fact that 'what is at stake is the most vital interests of monopoly capital, which concern, indeed, its very existence.'[13]

Stagnation may be alleviated through government spending in social welfare programs and public works programs. But, Baran argues, these forms of spending have side-effects that are not favorable to monopoly capitalism. Only two forms of government spending can assist monopoly capitalism without creating competition or boosting wage payments – both are found in government spending outside the commercial realm. The first form consists of state expenditures for research and development in areas that are not subject to immediate commercial exploitation. Expenditures for projects like atomic energy development absorb surplus without creating the conditions for increased competition in a monopoly sector. The second and most important form consists of unproductive government spending for foreign aid and national defense. This form provides the outlet for surplus that permits the continuation of monopoly capitalism.[14]

Baran argues that the most significant absorption of surplus through direct or indirect state intervention occurs in this international arena, where intervention insures that the necessary foreign markets are created and remain open to monopoly investments. Markets are created and protected by extending aid and loans to foreign countries, exerting political and military pressure, and promoting stability in foreign governments. State intervention absorbs surplus through government spending abroad and military expenditures at home, and also creates the conditions necessary for corporate disposal of surplus through foreign investments.[15]

According to Baran, the success of this program depends on the continuation of cold war relations and public acquiescence in imperialist policies. Public acquiescence has been achieved through the 'systematic ideological "processing" of the population to assure its loyalty to monopoly capitalism.'[16] Ideology, or what Baran defines as a conscious belief system, has been largely displaced by an administrative logic that resembles Habermas's depoliticized technical rationality. In advanced capitalist countries, Baran argues,

> [t]he stress on crude pragmatism, on the 'science' of control and manipulation kills any preoccupation with the purposes and goals of human activity, and elevates efficiency to an end in itself regardless of what is to be 'efficiently' accomplished.[17]

The parallel to Habermas's idea of depoliticization extends to the idea of possible repoliticization when Baran notes that the alliance of 'feudal elements' and labor interests forced concessions from the capitalists in the 1930s.[18]

According to Baran, monopoly capitalism does not strive to end crises and unemployment through state regulation, but only to prevent total collapse caused by unmitigated stagnation.[19] Baran indicates that cyclical crises cannot be avoided and may not be subject to long-term control.[20] He also indicates that state intervention may induce collapse indirectly through excessive militarism, which could trigger catastrophic international conflict, or the loss of mass loyalty at home.[21]

Although Baran concludes that 'the stability of monopoly capitalism is highly precarious,' and ends his analysis with an apocalyptic note, he does not give an explicit and detailed account of the processes that would lead to breakdown. With Baran, as with earlier neo-orthodox theorists, the breakdown of capitalism remains the necessary end of an unexplained process. But Baran departs from the neo-orthodox position long enough to make a significant if ambiguous concession to anti-orthodoxy, a concession necessitated by his perceptions of the contemporary capitalist order, and facilitated by his abandonment of the concept of surplus value.

Baran shifts from an economic and mechanistic conception of breakdown to a conception that relies on social revolution as the inevitable but unsituated response to a decaying economic order.[22] But Baran does not believe that the development of capitalism over the last hundred years constitutes a new economic order, or a reversal in structural and superstructural relations.[23] The ambiguity of Baran's initial concession to the anti-orthodox position arises when he defends the concept of continuity in capitalism and its contradictions. When Baran's confidence in mechanical structural collapse falters, he turns to superstructural analysis. Collapse then becomes contingent on the development of the 'subjective factor,' or the possibility for social revolution.

Baran's confidence in the ability of the masses to challenge the 'ideological stability' of advanced capitalism, however, falls quickly, and what little remains of a theory of breakdown falls with it.[24] Although he denies that a reversal in structural and superstructural forces has occurred, Baran finds that the 'manipulative ability' of the ruling class and the state have 'increased dramatically over the last few decades,' a time span that merges the depression years with the war years, and obliterates the massive working class uprisings of the 1930s.[25] The New Deal, Baran's point of origin for large-scale state intervention, 'was able to avert political and social upheavals that might have shaken the foundations of capitalism itself.'[26]

Baran's pessimism concerning the 'subjective factor' disintegrates into a recitation of ruling class victories, speculations about the potential for fascism, and a final retreat into 'faith in the spontaneity of rational and socialist tendencies in society.'[27] But Baran's proclamations of 'faith' are undermined by his consistent references to the 'weakness' of the subjective factor, and the 'ideologically overpowering impact of bourgeois, fetishistic consciousness on the broad masses of the working population.'[28] 'Social psychology and political experience,' Baran finds, suggest that the prospects for social change 'are bleak.'[29]

Baran's treatment of Veblen further exemplifies his refusal to recognize his own anti-orthodox leanings and his distance from Marx. When Baran turned to Veblen, he studied *The Theory of the Leisure Class*, Veblen's long discourse on culture and society. *The Theory of Business Enterprise*, Veblen's primary economic work, was left to Sweezy. Veblen incites some of the most forceful and condemning prose to be found in Baran's work, and yet at points Baran's commentary would qualify as self-inspection. Despite Baran's distaste for Veblen's works, the similarities between Baran and Veblen cannot be overlooked. Veblen's works converge with those of Marx at crucial points, but Veblen refused the recognition and the indebtedness; Baran's works depart from Marx at crucial points, and yet he steadfastly retained a false and shallow commitment to the texts. Veblen and Baran both rejected the notion of a structural/superstructural shift, but both were preoccupied with the elucidation of ideology and mass cultures.

Baran's determination that Veblen's 'economic determinism is of a peculiarily vacillating, bloodless nature,'[30] is more accurately applied to his own work. His criticism of Veblen's psychological approach arrives on the heels of his own preoccupation with psychoanalysis and the most subjective elements of ideological rule. He attacks Veblen for failing to realize that the misery of capitalism 'carries in itself the objective chance of its abolition,' while drafting manuscripts which give little or no hope for the future. Baran's analysis of Veblen – the master of waste and surplus, of ideology and fetishism – rejects findings that closely parallel or complement his own. A full confrontation with Veblen

123

would have produced the self-recognition necessary to turn Baran's anti-orthodoxy into a self-conscious critique of capitalist ideology. Instead, the confrontation was blocked by a dismissive review, cast off in a few printer's pages, and lost in the long months of *Monthly Review*.

Baran's early associations with the Frankfurt School, his continuing interest in Freud and in superstructural phenomena like advertising, and his long-range commitment to theoretical rather than empirical studies, combine to create a receptivity to anti-orthodox concepts that exceeds the actual assimilation of anti-orthodox concepts in Baran's writings. Baran adopts many of the analyses and conclusions of the anti-orthodox position while holding at arm's length the anti-orthodox premises of a fundamental change in capitalism, a radical shift in structural and superstructural relations, and a critical reassessment of Marx required by the perception of a new social order. With a significant but reluctant glance at the anti-orthodox interpretations, and yet a fast determination to defend his reading of Marx and the concept of economic primacy, Baran fills his works with ambiguities that cannot be resolved. A full confrontation of neo-orthodox premises and anti-orthodox conclusions was forestalled throughout Baran's intellectual life. The consistency with which Baran avoided that confrontation gives his works the static quality that characterizes those written during his most prolific periods. Baran's writings eventually form a repetition of an ambiguous litany: continuity, with change; structural determination, with superstructural control. This ambiguity was not minimized but compounded by Baran's long collaboration with Paul Sweezy.

When Baran arrived at Harvard in 1939 he met Paul Sweezy and their collaborative efforts began. Sweezy had studied at Exeter, Harvard, and the London School, and taught at Harvard until 1946, when he began his long tenure as editor of *Monthly Review*. Sweezy did not share Baran's immigrant status or political background, but he was intimately familiar with the European theorists who informed Baran's thought, and concerned with the same issues. In 1942, Sweezy published *The Theory of Capitalist Development: Principles of Marxian Political Economy*, which provides long and studious summaries of Marx's economic thought and the development of Marxist theory during the pre-war period.[31] Sweezy concludes the book with a detailed examination of the growth of monopolies and imperialist policies and their impact on Marxist theory. This section of *Theory of Capitalist Development* provides the conceptual basis for Sweezy's later collaborations with Baran.

In *Theory of Capitalist Development*, Sweezy explicitly rejects the distinction between crises and breakdown.[32] Marx's writings on underconsumption, disproportionality, and the falling rate of profit are all treated as aspects of crisis theory. The law of the tendency of falling rates of profit is discussed as an explanation of a cyclical movement in capitalism that generates realization problems like underconsumption and disproportionality and results in crises followed by partial recovery.[33] Falling rates of profit are not treated as the basis for decisive breakdown, but as the basis for stagnation or 'chronic depression.'[34] Sweezy provides a detailed account of the 'breakdown controversy' during the 1890–1920 period, with special attention given to underconsumption theorists. He concludes by endorsing underconsumption theory as the most sufficient explanation of crises, and Kautsky's notion of 'chronic depression' as the most probable speculation concerning the fate of capitalism.

These endorsements, Sweezy argues, do not run counter to Marx's thought. Marx's scattered references to underconsumption, Sweezy claims, are 'advance notice of a line of reasoning' which, had Marx completed his work, 'would have been of primary importance in the overall picture of the capitalist economy.'[35] Sweezy then constructs his own theory of underconsumption, but claims that he does not draw from concepts that 'are not implicitly or explicitly present in the main body of Marx's theory.'[36] With this claim to loyalty completed, Sweezy outlines the theory of underconsumption and stagnation that marks all his writings on capitalist development, and anticipates Baran's work in *The Political Economy of Growth*.

Sweezy argues that the underconsumption of consumer goods – the result of the inherent gap between production and consumption in capitalism – induces stagnation. Stagnation is the result of anticipation that increased production cannot be absorbed.[37] This is the basis for Sweezy's theory of crises, which he grounds in Marx's passages on underconsumption in *Capital*. Marx assumes, however, that 'all productive forces are continuously fully utilized,' an assumption that, Sweezy argues at a later point, does not apply under the conditions of advanced capitalism. In the last third of *Theory of Capitalist Development*, Sweezy explores the ways in which monopolization and imperialism have mitigated the applicability of crisis theories derived from Marx's thought. Sweezy adopts Lenin's term, 'monopoly capitalism,' to describe the new economic structure. The full investigation of 'monopoly capitalism,' however, was reserved for a later work, *Monopoly Capital*.

Monopoly Capital: An Essay on the American Economic and Social Order was the culmination of the long and productive collaboration of Baran and Sweezy. The book was first published by Monthly Review Press in 1966, two years after Baran's death, but was the result of a combined effort. The first outlines for the book were drafted in 1956, as Baran prepared *The Political Economy of Growth* for publication. *Monopoly Capital* is in many ways a continuation of Baran's work in *Political Economy of Growth* and of Sweezy's work in *Theory of Capitalist Development*. It was well-received and widely read, and adopted as a seminal text by sectors of the American left of the 1960s. With its dedication to Che, its hopeful glance towards the Third World, and its invocation of political activism, *Monopoly Capital* seemed to offer a bridge between theory and praxis that was largely absent from the texts of other Western Marxist theorists writing during the same period. And yet the book, like the political movement that it served, failed to fulfill its many theoretical and practical promises.

In *Monopoly Capital*, Baran and Sweezy claim that the changes in capitalist society over the last hundred years necessitate a reformulation of Marx's thought. This reformulation, however, is not directed at the understanding of the relationship between structure and superstructure or at the concept of economic primacy. Although they agree that state intervention in the economy reached new levels in the twentieth century, Baran and Sweezy reject the anti-orthodox contention that this development demands a reconsideration of structural and superstructural relations. The state, Baran and Sweezy argue, has always played a significant role in the economy, 'and while this role has certainly increased quantitatively we find the evidence of a qualitative change in recent decades unconvincing.'[38]

According to Baran and Sweezy, the qualitative change in capitalism that has occurred over the last century and necessitates a reformulation of Marx's thought lies in the structural realm alone. The growth of monopolies, rather than the state intervention spurred by this growth, constitutes the most significant development in capitalist societies. Marxist theorists have failed, they argue, to respond to this structural change. Hilferding and Lenin sensed the significance of the growth of monopolies, but erred in effecting only 'quantitative modifications of the basic Marxian laws of capitalism,' rather than qualitative reformulations required by the qualitative changes in the nature of capitalism.[39] Baran and Sweezy seek 'to remedy this situation and to do so in an explicit and indeed radical fashion.'[40] The remedy involves 'amending the competitive model' which, they claim, forms the basis for Marx's economic theories.[41] The amended model must fit the conditions of monopoly capitalism, where monopolies and oligopolies have become the 'typical economic unit.'[42]

Although Baran and Sweezy note that the remedy they propose is a 'radical' revision of Marx's thought, Marx remains a constant reference in the text. Baran and Sweezy insist that their reformulation of Marx's economic theories consists of modifications and substitutions rather than refutations. The tension between their loyalty to Marx and to the neo-orthodox tradition of Lenin, and their perception of the theoretical demands generated by a qualitatively new economic order, destabilizes the text as a whole, and creates a series of contradictions and ambiguities in *Monopoly Capital.*

A qualitative change in the economic structure of capitalism, induced by the growth of monopolies and initiated in the last quarter of the nineteenth century, is assumed throughout *Monopoly Capital.* But the nature of the change is never fully explicated, despite the centrality of the assumption in the arguments presented. Baran and Sweezy indicate in a rather brief and confusing passage that the change is marked by two developments. First, monopoly capitalism does not follow competitive pricing, but is characterized by its ability to fix prices at a certain level. Competitive behavior now appears primarily in marketing.[43] Secondly, monopoly capitalism is characterized by a consistent ability to reduce the costs of production.[44] Most of the assumptions involved in Baran and Sweezy's modification of Marx's 'competitive model' are related to this second characteristic of monopoly capitalism. But Baran and Sweezy do not indicate that the consistent reduction of costs under monopoly conditions differs significantly from the reduction of costs under competitive conditions. The motivation for their modification of Marx's model, then, does not seem to be fully justified. The difficulties that arise with the introduction of the new monopoly model of capitalist development begin with this initial ambiguity in the text.

In their attempt to construct a model that will accommodate monopoly conditions, Baran and Sweezy adopt a version of Baran's concept of economic surplus from *Political Economy of Growth.* In *Monopoly Capital,* the concept of economic surplus is the basis for the analysis of monopoly capitalism and for speculations concerning its future as an economic system. Baran and Sweezy argue that the concept of economic surplus constitutes a clarification of Marx's concept of surplus value. The clarification, they claim, is necessitated by the multiplicity and obscurity of forms that surplus assumes under monopoly conditions.[45] In *Monopoly Capital,* however, the concept of economic surplus signals a radical departure from the basic tenets of Marx's economic thought and from the conception of capitalist development that occurs in Volume III of *Capital.*

According to Baran and Sweezy, Marx's law of the tendency of the rate of profit to fall, the only tendential law of capitalist development that receives full theoretical elaboration in *Capital,*

127

THE AMERICAN MARXISTS: THE POST-WAR PERIOD

presupposes a competitive system.[46] In an attempt to formulate a substitute for this law, Baran and Sweezy propose 'as a law of monopoly capitalism that the surplus tends to rise both absolutely and relatively as the system develops.'[47] The substitution, they argue, does not constitute a break with Marxist theory:

> By substituting the law of rising surplus for the law of falling profit, we are therefore not rejecting or revising a time-honored theorem of political economy: we are simply taking account of the undoubted fact that the structure of the capitalist economy has undergone a fundamental change since that theorem was formulated. What is most essential about the structural change from competitive to monopoly capitalism finds its theoretical expression in this substitution.[48]

Despite this disclaimer, the law of rising surplus stands as a rejection of Marx's law of the falling rate of profit and of the labor theory of value upon which Marx's profit theory is based. The law of rising surplus depends on the assumption of decreased costs of production. Baran and Sweezy assert that overhead costs per unit decline under monopoly conditions. If prices and the cost of labor and materials remain constant, profits rise. Marx's distinction between constant and variable capital – a distinction that places Marx outside the classical tradition and forms the basis for the theory of surplus value – is ignored in *Monopoly Capital*.

Baran and Sweezy include the cost of materials as a part of variable capital.[49] Marx, however, clearly states that variable capital consists of wage payments alone, and that living labor is the only source of the surplus value from which profits are derived.[50] The organic composition of capital, or the relationship between constant and variable capital, accounts for the falling rate of profit but is not treated in *Monopoly Capital*. The formulations offered by Baran and Sweezy indicate that profits may be derived from sources outside the realm of variable capital as Marx defined it. This constitutes a rejection of Marx's profit theory and of the labor theory of value. Additional confusion is created when Baran and Sweezy discount any attempt to equate surplus with profits, but then refer to surplus as aggregate profit.[51]

Baran and Sweezy provide a detailed refutation of Schumpeter's theory of monopoly competition, which runs counter to the concept of rising surplus.[52] They also defend the concept against Kaldor's formulation of a theory of falling profits.[53] In both cases, Baran and Sweezy construct arguments that are incompatible with Marx's profit theory and the labor theory of value. But when they refute Strachey's claim that increases in variable capital have cut profits, Baran and Sweezy adopt a terminology that implicitly accepts the labor theory of value.[54] The confusion generated by these discrepancies in *Monopoly Capital* is compounded by the fact that Baran and Sweezy never provide a sustained discussion of the text of *Capital* itself. References to Marx are frequent but prove to be largely rhetorical. The presence of Marx in *Monopoly Capital* is explicitly established and implicitly undermined by the arguments presented.

The law of rising surplus forms the basis for the conception of economic breakdown in *Monopoly Capital*. With Marx's theory of the falling rate of profit displaced by the new law of rising surplus, Baran and Sweezy locate the potential cause of economic collapse in the realm of circulation and investment rather than the realm of production. As an economic problem, the breakdown of capitalism receives only a brief treatment in *Monopoly Capital*. Breakdown is defined as a realization problem, a threat arising from the difficulties associated with a shortage of profitable investment opportunities for economic surplus.[55] With breakdown redefined as a realization problem, Baran and Sweezy argue that the unbearable stagnation and 'chronic depression' caused by a rising surplus would destroy capitalism if 'counteracting forces' did not exist.[56] These 'counteracting forces' arise largely from the various forms of state intervention described by Baran in *Political Economy of Growth*. Baran and Sweezy indicate that state intervention, especially in the form of military expenditures, can absorb surplus and postpone economic collapse, but not indefinitely.[57]

Following Baran's reasoning in earlier works, Baran and Sweezy discount the possibility for revolution or political action in the United States. Industrial workers have been 'integrated as consumers and ideologically conditioned members of society.'[58] With mechanical collapse left in an indefinite state, and class struggle in capitalist countries an unlikely possibility, Baran and Sweezy turn to the Third World. Capitalism, they argue, is threatened by developments in the Third World that might trigger social revolution or international conflict. The continuation of the monopoly order depends on the maintenance of appropriate state intervention and a supportive ideological system. Although Baran and Sweezy reject the anti-orthodox claim that a major shift in structural and superstructural relations has occurred, their formulation of breakdown theory implicitly accepts this conclusion.

The concern with superstructural phenomena in *Monopoly Capital* overwhelms the economic analysis, despite the initial defense of the concept of economic primacy. Indeed, Baran and Sweezy devote a disproportionate part of the book to a critique of the 'quality of life' under monopoly capitalism. More space is allotted to a discussion of the educational system in the United States than to the discussion of the sources of economic surplus.

The effects of mass media are more closely studied than the behavior of profit rates. A full chapter is devoted to race relations, while the assumption of decreased production costs under monopoly conditions remains unexplored.

Baran and Sweezy place themselves within the Marxist tradition and claim a neo-orthodox position within that tradition. They reject the anti-orthodox claim that a radical shift in the relationship between structure and superstructure has occurred, and requires a new theory of superstructural determination. Their reformulation of Marx's thought, however, cannot be accommodated within the text of *Capital*. When the members of the Frankfurt School attempted to respond to the theoretical demands of monopoly capitalism, they infused Marx's thought with Hegelian and Freudian concepts and reversed the roles of structure and superstructure. In doing so, they pushed the conceptual boundaries of *Capital* to their logical extreme. The anti-orthodox theorists were critical of Marx, but thoroughly indebted to him. When Baran and Sweezy attempted to respond to the theoretical demands of the new capitalist order, however, they infused Marx's thought with contemporary sociology and Keynesian economics. This infusion generates a series of contradictions that ultimately undermine the Marxist content of the text, and cripple the arguments presented.

Ultimately, the text of *Monopoly Capital* breaks under the weight of the impossible combination of Marxist and classical modes of analysis, a combination which is present but silent throughout much of the book. In their attempt to reformulate Marx's concept of capitalist development in the light of monopoly control and pricing, Baran and Sweezy abandon the concept of surplus value and detemporalize the business cycle in favor of the notion of chronic depression. In their attempt to maintain Marx's emphasis on the economic structure of society, Baran and Sweezy succeed only in undermining the theoretical elaborations of *Capital* and the concepts that form the basis for the elaboration. In their attempt to preserve the concept of breakdown, they succeed only in duplicating the inarticulate and unsituated call to revolution found in the deterministic discourse initiated by Kautsky. In their attempt to revitalize Marxist theory, Baran and Sweezy succeed only in duplicating and exaggerating the contradictions contained within the Western Marxist tradition.

There is, however, no 'radical paradox,' as one commentator has claimed, at work within the text of *Monopoly Capital*.[59] The tension that lies between the neo-orthodox and anti-orthodox positions and fills the pages of *Monopoly Capital* is not a paradox, but a tension that arises from particular appropriations of *Capital* itself, as the discourse of the general statements on contradiction are wrenched from their strategic locations and thrown into comparison with the discourse of the open dialectic. In this sense, the parallels to *Capital* suggested by the title of *Monopoly Capital* fall far short of those intended by Baran and Sweezy. But then intention and recognition, as the neo-orthodox and anti-orthodox Marxists demonstrate, do not fully account for the history of ideas.

Neo-orthodox mediations

In the same year that Baran and Sweezy completed the draft of *Monopoly Capital*, Herbert Marcuse published *One-Dimensional Man: Studies in the Ideology of Advanced Industrial Society.* Marcuse worked closely with Horkheimer and Adorno during the early Frankfurt School shift to an anti-orthodox position. Marcuse, however, did not return to Germany with his colleagues after the war, but remained in the United States and began an extensive examination of late capitalism in what seemed to be its most complete stage of development. The conclusions drawn from this examination are detailed in the pessimistic pages of *One-Dimensional Man*, where Marcuse pushes the anti-orthodox position to its most extreme and hopeless conclusions.

One-Dimensional Man was the first book to be written in English by a Frankfurt scholar, and its focus, like that of *Monopoly Capital*, was directed towards the superstructural conditions of advanced capitalism in the United States. In *Monopoly Capital*, Baran and Sweezy, with Keynes at hand, undermined the potential for a breakdown theory based on Marx's understanding of the structural contradictions of capitalism. Marcuse, in *One-Dimensional Man*, laid to rest all hope for a structural breakdown or for the overthrow of capitalism by a social revolution. According to Marcuse, little stands in the way of the continued development of advanced capitalism.

Marcuse argues that the structural contradictions of capitalism have been circumvented by technological developments and state interventions. Economic crises and the potential for structural collapse have been effectively minimized, he argues, by a fundamental change in the relationship between the economy and the state and by a technological revolution in the machine process. According to Marcuse, Marx's concepts of the organic composition of capital, surplus value, and profit are no longer applicable in a society where automation exists on such a massive scale.[60] Production and consumption are regulated in a way which mitigates and conceals structural flaws in the system.

Moreover, Marcuse argues that the same processes that produce economic stability lead to a thoroughgoing depoliticization of the working class. The superstructural manifestations of structural contradictions are collapsed into one-dimensional patterns of thought and behavior. Class consciousness and the potential for revolutionary upheaval are lost in a society where all oppositions have been canceled. Much like Baran and Sweezy, Marcuse concludes his study with a clear but unsupported call for a return of 'the historical subject.'

The implicit refutations of breakdown theory proffered by Baran and Sweezy and, from a different perspective, Marcuse, were soon challenged by Paul Mattick. Before his emigration to the United States in 1926, Mattick developed close ties to the neo-orthodox theorists in Europe, including Korsch and, more importantly, Grossmann. After his arrival in America, Mattick worked as the editor of *Living Marxism* and conducted a study of unemployment in the United States for the Frankfurt Institute. Many of his findings are incorporated in *Marx and Keynes: The Limits of the Mixed Economy* (1969), where Mattick refutes the Keynesian analysis of capitalism and its infusion into Marxist theory, and attempts to restore a theory of breakdown based on Marx's concept of the falling rate of profit. In doing so, he constructs an argument that runs counter to the position adopted by Baran and Sweezy in *Monopoly Capital*.

A few years later, Mattick published *A Critique of Marcuse* (1972), a short book that moves quickly to the heart of the anti-orthodox position and confronts the assumptions entailed. In many ways, Mattick's brief treatment of Marcuse provides the best argument against anti-orthodoxy to appear among the neo-orthodox defenders. Mattick concludes that the anti-orthodox position is simply an inversion of orthodox assumptions that reflects the distorted economy and ideology of late capitalism.

In *Marx and Keynes* and *Critique of Marcuse*, Mattick initially constructs a theory of breakdown that combines Marx's law of the tendency of the rate of profit to fall, taken from Volume III of *Capital*, with the statements on general contradiction found in Volume I:

> According to Marx . . . capital accumulation leads necessarily to a decline of profitability relative to the growing mass of capital, and therewith to crises and depressions devastating enough to produce social convulsions and, eventually, the overthrow of the capitalist system.[61]

The structural contradictions of capitalism have not been resolved in the 'mixed economy' of the post-Keynesian period, Mattick argues. State intervention does not provide a solution to the falling rate of profit in the private sector. Eventually, the tendency for the rate of profit to fall 'must turn into its actual decline at a certain stage in capital expansion.'[62] Once this occurs, the degree of state intervention required to reverse the tendency will eliminate the private and 'mixed' sectors of the economy in favor of a fully planned system.[63] According to Mattick, the contradictions of late capitalism simply reproduce the contradictions of liberal capitalism on a higher level:

> There are, then, within the capitalist relations of production, limits set to both private production and government induced production; the limits of the latter are the limits of capital production itself.[64]

Mattick rejects the idea that a transition to a post-capitalist stage of development has occurred. He also rejects the anti-orthodox claim that the relationship between structure and superstructure has been reversed. The structural contradictions of capitalism, he argues, may not bring a quick end to the system. The effects of accumulation have not yet reached a point where profitability is seriously threatened. But, Mattick claims, the structural flaws of capitalism have produced a sufficient level of misery to spark social revolution, and the working class is still capable of mobilization. Economic instability threatens to destroy the ideological hegemony of the ruling class.

According to Mattick, ruling class hegemony and the one-dimensional quality of life and thought that characterize its present state are not determinative factors in the continuation of capitalism. Superstructural forces, he argues, are still determined and maintained by structural conditions. Mattick provides an apocalyptic image of the end of the capitalist order, prompted by economic breakdown and concretized in the failure of ideological integration:

> Integration in death is the only integration really given to capitalism. Short of this final integration, one-dimensional man will not last for long. He will disappear at the first breakdown of the capitalist economy – in the bloodbaths the capitalist order is now preparing for him. Capitalism, at the height of its powers is also at its most vulnerable; it has nowhere to go but to its death.[65]

Mattick's rejection of the anti-orthodox reversal of structural and superstructural roles is explicit and self-conscious. In this sense, his defense of the concept of economic primacy differs significantly from the defense produced by theoretical default in the works of Baran and Sweezy, Boudin and Corey. Moreover, Mattick attempts to situate the anti-orthodox position in the context of bourgeois thought, and to relate it to general ideological developments in late capitalist societies. Marcuse's theory of technological domination, he argues, is not a true rejection of

133

Marx or proof of Marx's inapplicability, but 'implies an unconscious acceptance' of Marx's theory of increasing productivity brought about by the rising organic composition of capital, which is followed by a falling rate of profit.[66]

According to Mattick those who, like Marcuse, speak of technological or political solutions to economic problems have simply fallen prey to the irrationalities produced by the system itself. 'It is productive labour on which the whole social edifice rests,' Mattick argues, and '[t]o deny this fact is the main job of bourgeois ideology.'[67] Anti-orthodoxy does not offer a 'functional equivalent' to Marx's theory of breakdown, but an inversion of the theory infused with bourgeois ideology and deluded in its rejection of the concept of economic primacy. With Mattick, the return to the concept of economic primacy is a self-conscious attempt to restore the original text of *Capital*.

Mattick's reading of the original text and his defense of its efficacy are aimed at the refutation of anti-orthodoxy. Mattick's commitment to the concept of economic primacy and his rejection of the anti-orthodox position, however, are largely unsupported. No full-blown analysis of contemporary capitalism is provided as evidence of the continuing centrality of economic forces or as an alternative to the anti-orthodox characterization. Moreover, Mattick's claim that the working class will respond to collapse with focused political activity is not provided with any specification of the objective conditions for social revolution.

While Mattick attempts to refute the claims of anti-orthodoxy, James O'Connor attempts to integrate anti-orthodox findings into a neo-orthodox study of state capitalism. His book, *The Fiscal Crisis of the State* (1973), is probably the best example of the attempt to utilize anti-orthodox concepts while rejecting the anti-orthodox assumption of a reversal in structural and superstructural roles. In *The Fiscal Crisis of the State*, O'Connor applies European anti-orthodox theory to the analysis of advanced capitalism in the United States. O'Connor, a professor at California State University at San Jose, studied at the Max Planck Institute and acknowledges his indebtedness to German theorists like Claus Offe. Although American and British neo-orthodox theorists like Baran, Sweezy, Dobb and Hobsbawm are cited throughout the book, the references are largely confined to empirical points. O'Connor's theory of capitalist development and crises is an amalgamation of both neo-orthodox and anti-orthodox theories. Although his tools are taken from *Capital*, his conclusions resonate most clearly with the works of later Frankfurt theorists like Habermas.

Advanced capitalism, O'Connor determines, is characterized by a 'fiscal crisis of the state,' an economic and political condition that reflects and determines the development of monopoly capitalism. The basic cause of the fiscal crisis lies in the central contradiction of capitalist production as presented by Marx in Volume I of *Capital*, the contradiction between socialized production and private appropriation.[68] This contradiction and the particular form of crisis it generates in the post-war period can only be understood, O'Connor argues, in terms of 'basic Marxist economic categories.'[69] *Fiscal Crisis* is an attempt to enlarge the scope of these categories so that the economic and political peculiarities of advanced capitalism can be accommodated. The labor theory of value, the concept of surplus value, and the notion of a falling rate of profit all remain intact, but are given much broader application. Marx's concepts are used to interpret phenomena like taxation, regulation and subsidization, all of which post-date nineteenth-century liberal capitalism, but remain, as O'Connor demonstrates, within the theoretical reach of *Capital*.

According to O'Connor, the fiscal crisis of the state occurs when the state expenditures required to maintain monopoly capital exceed state revenues. Under advanced capitalism, O'Connor argues, the state must fulfill the two basic but often contradictory functions of insuring continued accumulation and legitimating the economic order. State expenditures related to accumulation, or 'social capital' expenditures, are required to insure profitable private accumulation and to expand surplus value. These expenditures include 'social investments,' which increase productivity in the private sector, and 'social consumption,' which lowers the costs of variable capital, the costs of reproducing labor. State expenditures related to legitimation, or 'social expenses,' are required to insure social harmony and ideological hegemony. The combined costs of social capital and social expenses rise as the monopoly sector grows and places an increasing demand on the state to subsidize production costs.[70] Since the profits derived from socialized production are privately appropriated, there is a tendency for state expenditures to increase at a higher rate than revenues, and a fiscal crisis results. The fiscal crisis, according to O'Connor, is manifested in inflation, tax increases, and unemployment, and may stimulate social unrest which, in turn, aggravates the crisis and threatens legitimation.

O'Connor argues that economic stability since World War II has depended on economic expansion and control abroad, harmonious labor relations in the monopoly sector at home, and the socialization of monopoly sector production costs.[71] These policies, he claims, are inflationary, and create economic burdens that the state can finance only through deficit spending and high rates of taxation. The resulting tendency towards crisis can be counteracted by a significant reduction in state spending, but this option is largely precluded by the demands of the monopoly sector. Significant tax increases can offset the expenditures, but often generate legitimation problems. According to O'Connor, the only viable and effective counter-tendency is a rapid acceleration in the growth of the 'social-industrial complex.'[72] This growth, however, increases the economic pressures brought to bear on the working class and state employees. Divisiveness and conflict among groups within the working class may result. Alternatively, increased pressures may stimulate unity and militancy within the working class and among state employees and state dependents. Class conflict may then appear as a threat to the continuation of the capitalist order.[73]

According to O'Connor, then, the structural demand for continued accumulation is satisfied only through massive state intervention, a superstructural response to structural contradictions. State intervention, however, does not constitute a final politicization of the economy. Contradictions that are originally generated in the economic structure are first displaced onto the political superstructure. O'Connor argues that '[m]onopoly capital and organized labor have, in effect, "exported" their conflicts to the competitive and state sectors.'[74] Conflict in the competitive sector is defused through the dominance of monopoly sector trends, and conflict in the state sector is administratively processed and depoliticized. Although the state responds to demands that are structurally determined, the response consists of a series of political decisions that soon lose their nature as such: 'the interpenetration of private economy and the state and the growth of the federal bureaucracy have transformed political economic issues and conflicts into problems of administration.'[75]

This conclusion clearly resembles Habermas's discussion of depoliticization and administrative processing. O'Connor, however, does not call for a 'functional equivalent' to Marx's theories, or for a radical reformulation of Marx's theory of capitalist development. Instead, he explains state intervention in terms of profit theory and works close to the text of *Capital*. O'Connor's understanding of accumulation is adopted largely from Volume I of *Capital*, but he supplements this understanding with the profit theory from Volume III. With respect to the breakdown of capitalism, he combines the general statements on class conflict in Volume I with the undeterministic discourse of the open dialectic from the discussion of profits in Volume III. O'Connor does not claim that breakdown and revolution are inevitable, or that continued accumulation can be guaranteed. Instead, he presents an open-ended repetition of crises assuming various forms and intensities, potentially decisive or indecisive.

O'Connor's conscious utilization of both neo-orthodox and anti-orthodox theories far exceeds the ambiguous marriage of the two found in Baran's and Sweezy's *Monopoly Capital*. His analysis of contemporary capitalism, however, relies on several untested assumptions. O'Connor assumes that large-scale deficit spending can be directly correlated with the occurrence of economic crisis, but provides only brief documentation for the correlation, and does not scrutinize the supporting data. The correlation is questionable and without it, O'Connor's thesis falls. Moreover, although O'Connor argues that the working class has been depoliticized, he seems to assume that it can and will be repoliticized, and that repoliticization will take a socialist direction. He does not indicate, however, at what point, or under what conditions, repoliticization might occur, or why Habermas's fears of repoliticization in a fascist direction are unfounded.

Despite these difficulties, O'Connor's work suggests many possibilities for a mediation of the neo-orthodox/anti-orthodox schism in Western Marxist theories of breakdown. Although O'Connor's scheme does not present an original theoretical contribution to theories of breakdown or to Marxist scholarship, his self-conscious blending of two distinct approaches, with critical modifications completed, demonstrates an understanding of Marx's thought that goes far beyond the claims of loyalty issued by Baran and Sweezy. With O'Connor and Mattick, the range of theoretical possibilities generated by the breakdown controversy is once again expanded, and *Capital* resumes its position as an explosive text in twentieth-century thought.

8 Conclusions

The theory of the growth of the means of production, of the
sequence of the various modes of production, and of the task of
the proletariat is neither a historical painting to be gazed upon
nor a scientific formula for calculating future events. It
formulates the adequate consciousness for a definite phase of
struggle and as such can be recognized again in later conflicts.

Horkheimer, 'The Authoritarian State'

Once a discourse is thus driven by its own momentum into the
backwater of the 'unreal', exiled from all gregarity, it has no
recourse but to become the site, however, exiguous, of an
affirmation.

Barthes, *A Lover's Discourse*

Debates among Western Marxist scholars fill countless volumes.
Few attempts have been made, however, to conceptualize the
development of Western Marxist thought over the last century.
Although theories of the breakdown of capitalism form a
significant aspect of Western Marxist thought, the history of those
theories has rarely been studied by those who made it. Paul
Mattick provided a brief exception to this general rule in an article
published in 1959. In this short piece, Mattick reviews and laments
the confusion that surrounds the status of the laws of capitalism in
Marxist thought. He criticizes those Marxists for whom 'the "law
of value," as the economic counterpart of the dialectics, seems to
assure the breakdown of capitalism.' When theorists like Grossmann assumed that the apparent development of capitalism is
determined by its laws, 'Marx's critique of political economy
became the ideology of the inevitability of socialism.' With the
tendential laws of capitalism tied to actual events in capitalist
economies, 'the theory of breakdown waxed and waned with the

capitalist movement from depression to prosperity, from relative stability to general crisis.'[1]

According to Mattick, then, the development of Marxist theories of breakdown has followed a pattern of growth and decline that parallels the cycle of economic growth and decline in capitalism itself. According to this characterization of the history of theories of breakdown, the theories flourished when capitalism faltered. Mattick's discernment of a cyclical pattern in the history of breakdown theories provides a useful characterization of the development of popular literature concerning the fate of capitalism. General, speculative works on the breakdown of capitalism have flourished during periods of perceived and publicized economic decline. Corey's popular articles are only one example of a genre of 'worry' literature that appeared during the depression of the 1930s. During the most recent recession, this genre was revitalized in the United States, fed by the federal government, the popular press and by what seemed to be a national obsession with the state of the economy. The contemplation of economic crises became something of a popular pastime. Early in the recession, the 'collapse of capitalism' received cover-story treatment in *Time* magazine.

Mattick's characterization of a theory that may rise and fall in a perfect inversion of the business cycle can also be applied to the history of theories of breakdown in the works of revisionist, orthodox and neo-orthodox Marxists like Bernstein, Kautsky, Strachey and Mandel. When empirical conditions failed to produce the catastrophic events that Bernstein described as elements in breakdown theory, he dismissed breakdown theory and the theory of capitalist development as well. When Kautsky received empirical reports of continued economic growth, he surrendered his concept of 'chronic depression' and abandoned all work on breakdown theory. Strachey's hopes for empirical verification were lost as capitalism climbed out of the depression in the 1930s; he renounced breakdown theory shortly thereafter. Mandel has continued to defend his theory of collapse by piling reams of empirical data supporting the idea of breakdown against the reams that do not, and pushing his predictions forward in time.

When theories of breakdown are tied to immediate empirical correlations, they blow with the shifting winds of 'given facts.' Mandel, and the faithful Corey, stitch their sails accordingly. But the empirical economic developments of the last century – the realities of prosperity and decline – are difficult to identify. There is little agreement among the economists who study fluctuations in capitalist economies. The periodization and interpretation of the second Great Depression, its magnitude and its effects, are still widely debated. Seemingly unending disagreements concerning

139

economic indicators and their meanings continue in discussions of the present state of capitalist economies. The theories of breakdown that rely on these indicators have suffered from the inconsistency of their sources, and waivered with them. But the rise and fall of crisis literature in popular journals bears little connection to the development of Marxist theories of breakdown in systematic treatises. The popular literature on breakdown may ebb and flow, but the production of systematic treatises has been fairly constant over the last century. It would be difficult to locate a decade since 1890 that has not witnessed the publication of several major contributions to breakdown theories, or a decade that was not marked by controversy among serious Marxist scholars about the fate of capitalism. Volume III of *Capital*, published in 1894, was soon followed by the breakdown controversy of the Second International, the debates between Bernstein and Kautsky, Boudin's orthodox defense, and Veblen's monumental *Theory of Business Enterprise*. Hilferding's *Finance Capital*, released in 1910, was followed by Lenin's and Luxemburg's massive works. The 1920s saw the publication of Grossmann's long statement on breakdown; the 1930s witnessed the beginnings of the anti-orthodox perspective in Germany, and the labors of Corey and Strachey in America and England. Sweezy's huge *Theory of Capitalist Development* appeared in 1942, followed by another book by Strachey and by Baran's *Political Economy of Growth* in the 1950s. *Monopoly Capital* was completed by 1965, one year after the works by Althusser and Balibar. The fate of capitalism has been discussed since that time in numerous works by Habermas, Mattick, Mandel, Baudrillard and O'Connor, each with their very different approach and perspective.

There is nothing to suggest that theories of breakdown will soon disappear; many of the post-war theorists discussed here are still writing, and new scholars appear as the years pass. The history of the theories is not marked by an ebb and flow that corresponds to any accepted pattern of economic development, but by a fairly consistent expansion of the range of theoretical possibilities generated by Marx's theory of capitalist development, and by a consistent retreat from the political conclusions of that text. The relative autonomy of theories of breakdown has insured their continued existence despite the consistent failure of their predictive powers.

The phenomenal recoveries that followed both the first Great Depression and the second Great Depression forced deep shifts in the substance of the theories, but not, in most cases, the abandonment of the theories. The first Great Depression and the subsequent recovery called into question the concepts of temporal crises and cycles, and gave rise to the idea of chronic depression and the concept of a politicized economy, forcefully represented in Luxemburg's works. The second Great Depression and the subsequent recovery consolidated the idea of a full reversal in structural and superstructural relations, and the concept of political and ideological collapse. In both cases, perceived shifts in the economy initiated reformulations of theories of breakdown, but not complete reconsiderations of the validity of the theories themselves.

Over the last century, the shifting positions of dominance and subordination assumed by each of the three forms of breakdown theory, and the multiplicity of ideas related to breakdown, have created enormous movement within the history of the theories as a whole. The admission of superstructural considerations, the infusion of non-Marxist ideas, the changing perceptions of capitalist reality, and the continued controversy over interpretations of *Capital* have fed this movement, and regenerated questions concerning the fate of capitalist societies. The theories have not waxed and waned, but have marked sharp shifts in Western Marxist thought as a whole.

Marx's points of reference in the formulation of his theory of capitalist development were defined by what he learned from Hegel and Ricardo. His attempt to modify and combine the tenets of classical political economy and German idealism resulted in the creation of an explosive text, so rich in its range of possibilities that it has supported a full century of work by some of the finest minds of Europe and the United States. The seeming autonomy and relative durability of theories of breakdown derives, in part, from their common grounding in this complex text. The self-referentiality of the theories, their imperviousness to empirical defeat, and their isolation from popular perceptions do not, however, indicate that the theories grew and survived outside the broader social and economic context of their creation. The social functions of theories of breakdown – realized or potential – tie them to the capitalist societies in which they were produced and received.

Marxist theories of breakdown, and Western Marxist thought in general, have often been perceived as a critical force in capitalist societies. The original site of Marx's theory of capitalist development – the discovery of the temporality of capitalism as a mode of production – was a necessary and radical corrective to the classical assumption that capitalism is atemporal. Although Marx certainly intended this discovery to be an impetus for further inquiry and analysis, the opposite effect has too often occurred in the history of theories of breakdown. The classical assumption was easily replaced by its simple inversion – the assumption that uncontrollable and inevitable collapse would occur. Mandel and Strachey, Boudin and Corey, all show signs of this failure. Moreover, the

141

classical assumption of apparent facts is reproduced in their uncritical use of technical data. Classical assumptions about history and knowledge resurface in subsequent theories of breakdown, and defeat their critical potential.

Marx also intended his discovery of the temporality of capitalism to be an impetus to political action. In other hands, however, his discovery has often failed to produce the intended effect. In Kautsky's and Grossmann's writings, the mechanistic interpretation of breakdown theory led to political passivity and to a diminished role for class action in social change. The link between mechanical theories of capitalist development and political fatalism is a familiar problem in the history of Western Marxist theory and practice – one that has been fueled by the continued existence of theories of breakdown.

The conservative effects of breakdown theories are not limited to the orthodox and neo-orthodox schools. Breakdown theories have also led to conservative conclusions in the hands of anti-orthodox Marxists. The breakdown of capitalism was contemplated with sober but hopeful anticipation by those theorists who adopted structural conceptions of capitalism and its impending collapse. When capitalism and its future were conceived in broader, superstructural terms by writers like Veblen and Habermas, the conception of breakdown expanded accordingly, and came to carry far more ominous associations.

In the works of the anti-orthodox theorists, the breakdown of capitalism comes to mean the collapse of the state, all forms of intellectual life, even language itself. The apocalyptic imagery surrounding the theories assumes more dramatic forms. With the threat of barbarism or fascism raised as a possible or even probable aftermath to collapse, breakdown becomes something to be feared rather than desired. As desire turns to fear, theories of breakdown become a conservative force, protective of the *status quo* or nostalgic for a liberal past, and hesitant to endorse any call for change. Marxist scholars like Marcuse are left on a strange footing when they condemn capitalist societies, and yet support their survival. Veblen's reticence in joining with the political movements of his day and Habermas's uneasy relationship to the German student movement are both, in part, products of their conservative interpretation of the end of capitalism.

Apart from the nature of the anticipation that fills each theory, and the fear or desire that surrounds it, the incessant talk of the breakdown of capitalism has reinforced the image of capitalism as a fragile, vulnerable, yet irreplaceable, social system. The recurrent themes of crisis and collapse, when combined with the chaotic imagery of breakdown, deter any inclination to place demands on the economy or the state. The preoccupation with the economy as an entity in need of technical understanding and treatment displaces broader considerations of possibilities and alternatives. As theorists become immersed in models and data involving rates of inflation and interest, price indices and tax structures, the larger social questions of choice and control are repressed. Mandel, Baran and Sweezy are examples of theorists who have confined themselves to the sort of technical rationality that perpetuates the capitalist order; their occasional calls to revolution are resoundingly superficial. Now that President Reagan's staff and advisers have openly discussed the politics of declaring an 'economic emergency,' the critical status of theories of breakdown seems even more dubious. When auto workers vote to further reduce their earnings in order to 'save Chrysler,' the superstructural interpretation of collapse no longer suffices. When Marxists openly fear the end of a system they so disparage, theory is very much amiss.

Marxist theories of breakdown, like the broader Western Marxist perspective of which they are a part, have led a marginal life in the history of ideas. Held at the edge of the intellectual world, they have been barred from entry into mainstream economic and social thought. Excluded from the social discourse on the nature of capitalism and distanced from class struggles, Marxist theorists turned in upon themselves, and conducted a long, intense, and largely self-referential monologue about the fate of a system from which they remained estranged. The monologue was conducted in the context of a profound silence on the part of mainstream theorists – a systematic refusal to contemplate the contradictions of capitalism and the potential for an end to the system.

This silence has now twice been broken – first by Keynes and those who saw the depression of the 1930s as evidence of a weakened economy, and more recently by a group of theorists and commentators captivated by the economic crisis of the last decade. Marxist theories of crisis and collapse are now paralleled, as they were in the 1930s, by a mainstream intellectual movement. Western Marxist and mainstream theorists offer comparable analyses of the most recent recession. But the Marxist monologue remains a monologue; there is little exchange between the Marxist and mainstream counsels of despair.

The concept of contradiction has finally been admitted into mainstream economic thought. The anticipation of crisis and the image of collapse have been normalized and domesticated. Theories of breakdown, once dismissed from social discourse, have been reincorporated. In the incessant chatter of 'crises, conflicts, and catastrophes,' Kautsky's 'lovely alliteration' continues. It seems that mainstream theorists, in an independent

143

fashion, have finally reached the same conclusions, the same admissions of contradiction, that have formed a litany in Western Marxist thought for the last century. In the 1930s, Corey viewed Keynesian theory as a belated vindication of Marx's tired truths. The new, if unnoticed, consensus between Western Marxist and mainstream theorists appears to be a final validation of particular readings of *Capital*.

But it might be argued that while the underlying reality of a continuing capitalist order remains, the illusion of infinite economic stability has simply been transformed into the illusion of utter instability. It may well be that the normalization of theories of breakdown represents a simple reversal, so that the exiled idea and the unseen reality are now those of capitalism's continued existence. The new consensus between Western Marxist and mainstream ideas may simply reflect their mutual captivation by a common ideology. If so, it is time to reverse the question posed by Western Marxists for the last century, and to direct our focus away from the 'impending collapse.'

In theories of breakdown, the apocalyptic vision and the morbid fascination with decline and decay displace analyses of historically specific movements in the economy as the objective context for shifts in the balance of class forces. With the image of crises and cycles transformed into the image of chronic depression and stagnation or the anticipation of final collapse, breakdown theories fail to measure periods of recovery and expansion, or to comprehend new terms for exploitation. As such, breakdown theories cannot serve the purpose Horkheimer once outlined for theories of capitalist development: to formulate an adequate consciousness for a definite phase of struggle. While distracted critics passively await the end of the system, capitalism lives on, and the working class looks elsewhere for history and political economy.

Notes

2 Points of reference in Marx's theory of capitalist development

1 A. Smith, *An Inquiry into the Nature and Causes of the Wealth of Nations*, New York, Random House, 1937, pp. 87–98.

2 D. Ricardo, *Principles of Political Economy and Taxation*, Harmondsworth, Penguin Books, 1971, pp. 139, 142–3.

3 On the Physiocratic and classical conceptions of economic development see generally M. Dobb, *Political Economy and Capitalism: Some Essays in Economic Tradition*, London, Routledge & Kegan Paul, 1937, ch. 4; and H. Grossmann, 'Marx, classical political economy, and the problem of dynamics', translated by P. Burgess, *Capital and Class: Bulletin of the Conference of Socialist Economists*, no. 2, Summer, 1977, pp. 32–55, and no. 3, Autumn, 1977, pp. 67–100.

4 *Theories of Surplus Value* was published in a mutilated edition edited by Karl Kautsky in 1905–10, and in its full original form in 1956–62. The first full English translations were published in Moscow by Progress Publishers in 1963 (vol. 1), 1968 (vol. 2), and 1971 (vol. 3). *Theories* is particularly useful when read in conjunction with the sections on surplus value found in Marx's *Grundrisse: Foundations of the Critique of Political Economy*, translated by M. Nicolaus, New York, Random House, 1973, pp. 549–602, 614–18.

5 Marx, *Theories of Surplus Value*, vol. 1, p. 44.

6 Ibid., p. 46.

7 Ibid., pp. 44–5.

8 Ibid., vol. 3, p. 55. Although *Theories* constitutes Marx's most extended critique of classical political economy, many of the ideas found in *Theories* are prefigured in earlier works. The critique of the notion of capital as an atemporal, material condition, for example, is found in the *Economic and Philosophic Manuscripts of 1844*, where Marx writes: 'Political economy starts with the fact of private property; it does not explain it to us. It expresses in general, abstract formulas the *material* process through which private property passes, and these formulas it then takes for laws.' *Marx-Engels Collected Works*, New York, International Publishers, 1975, vol. 3, p. 270.

145

9 Marx, *Theories of Surplus Value*, vol. 3, pp. 71, 270, 272, 294 and 427–8.
10 Ibid., p. 265.
11 Ibid., p. 274.
12 Ibid., p. 265.
13 Ibid., p. 55.
14 Ibid., vol. 2, p. 501.
15 It is common practice among Marxist scholars to limit Marx's critique of classical political economy to the critique of the notion of capitalism as eternal and absolute. The best example of this is found in R. Eagly, *The Structure of Classical Economic Thought*, New York, Oxford University Press, 1974, pp. 103–5, where Marx's relationship to classical political economy is seen as the simple process of 'dynamizing' the static classical models. A more sophisticated example is found in the debate between L. Sève and M. Godelier in *International Journal of Sociology*, vol. 2, nos 2–3, Summer/Fall, 1972, pp. 178–314, where the attempt to combine structuralism and the dialectic in the context of Marx's critique results in the creation of an objectless dialectic, a merging of the dynamic and static models.
16 F. Engels, Preface to *Capital: A Critique of Political Economy*, New York, International Publishers, 1975, vol. 1, p. 5.
17 Marx, *Theories of Surplus Value*, vol. 1, p. 92.
18 Ibid., vol. 2, p. 106.
19 Ibid., vol. 3, p. 87; and see vol. 2, p. 191.
20 Ibid., vol. 1, p. 89.
21 Ibid., vol. 1, p. 205; and see vol. 3, p. 87.
22 Ibid., vol. 3, p. 265; and see p. 272 for an exemplary passage on the reification process which lies at the root of empiricism in classical political economy and other forms of positivistic thought.
23 Ibid., vol. 2, p. 400. For examples of Marx's reading of these gaps, see the discussion of Smith, vol. 1, pp. 78–82; of Ricardo, vol. 2, pp. 501–2; and of Malthus, vol. 3, pp. 29–34.
24 Ibid., vol. 3, p. 88; and see vol. 2, p. 529. The critique of the philosophy of identity in classical political economy is a constant theme in *Theories of Surplus Value*, and is discussed in the final section of this chapter in more general terms.
25 Marx, *Capital*, vol. 1, pp. 8–9 (Preface to the first German edition).
26 Ibid., p. 763.
27 Ibid.
28 According to J. Seigel, *Marx's Fate: The Shape of a Life*, Princeton, Princeton University Press, 1978, pp. 339–43, the sequence of these chapters was rearranged by Engels and their titles were provided by him. After an examination of Marx's original manuscripts at the Institute for Social History in Amsterdam, Seigel concludes that Engels created these chapter divisions by shifting some of the pages in the original manuscript to different locations, and in doing so, altered the focus of Marx's argument in a way which gives greater weight to the discussion of counteracting tendencies than Marx had intended. Although Seigel's findings should be taken into account, I do not think that they clarify Marx's position to the extent that Seigel claims.

Seigel's contention that Marx did not recognize the 'internal contradictions of the law' is misleading. Marx specifically and explicitly characterized the law as a 'double-edged law.' See Marx, *Capital*, vol. 3, p. 220.

29 Marx, *Capital*, vol. 3, p. 250.
30 Ibid.
31 Ibid.
32 Ibid., p. 213.
33 Ibid., p. 242, and see Marx, *Theories of Surplus Value*, vol. 3, p. 447. See also R. Rosdolsky, *The Making of Marx's Capital*, translated by P. Burgess, London, Pluto Press, 1980, ch. 26.
34 See Marx, *Capital*, vol. 1, p. 612.
35 Ibid., p. 216.
36 Ibid., vol. 3, p. 49.
37 Ibid., pp. 211–12. For a standard technical treatment of the law see H. Dickenson, 'The falling rate of profit in Marxian economics', *Review of Economic Studies*, vol. 24, no. 64, February, 1957, pp. 120–31. A thorough discussion of the law is found in D. Yaffe, 'The Marxian theory of crisis, capital, and the state', *Economy and Society*, vol. 2, no. 2, May, 1973, pp. 186–232. Standard criticisms of the law are found in: L. von Bortkiewicz, 'On the correction of Marx's fundamental theoretical construction in the third volume of Capital', reprinted in Paul Sweezy's edition of E. von Böhm-Bawerk, *Karl Marx and the Close of His System*, New York, Augustus M. Kelly, 1949, pp. 197–221, and 'Value and price in the Marxian system', *International Economic Papers*, no. 2, 1952; J. Robinson, *An Essay on Marxian Economics*, London, Macmillan, 1966, ch. 5; and P. Sweezy, *The Theory of Capitalist Development: Principles of Marxian Political Economy*, New York, Monthly Review Press, 1970, ch. 6. See also Rosdolsky's response, *The Making of Marx's Capital*, pp. 398–411.
38 Marx, *Capital*, vol. 3, p. 219.
39 Ibid., p. 218.
40 Ibid., p. 247.
41 Ibid., pp. 232, 234–5, 239.
42 Ibid., p. 239.
43 The most thorough considerations of the status of the law and its counteracting influences are found in A. Cutler, B. Hindess, P. Hirst and A. Hussain, *Marx's Capital and Capitalism Today*, Boston, Routledge & Kegan Paul, 1977, vol. 1, pp. 157–65; Balibar's treatment in L. Althusser and E. Balibar, *Reading Capital*, translated by B. Brewster, second edition, New York, NLB, 1977, pp. 283–302; A. Hussain, 'Crises and tendencies of capitalism', *Economy and Society*, vol. 6, no. 4, November, 1977, pp. 436–60; and P. Mattick, 'Value theory and capital accumulation', *Science and Society*, vol. 23, no. 1, Winter, 1959, pp. 27–51. See also G. Hodgson, 'The theory of the falling rate of profit', *New Left Review*, no. 84, March-April, 1974, pp. 55–84.
44 Marx, *Capital*, vol. 3, p. 225; see also p. 231.
45 Ibid., p. 235.
46 Marx, *Theories of Surplus Value*, vol. 3, p. 122.

47 Ibid., vol. 2, pp. 495–6, 528–9, 534–5.
48 On the problem of disproportionality, see Marx, *Capital*, vol. 2, pp. 466–9, 494–5. This section of *Capital* was pieced together by Engels in 1885. The primary purpose of the reproduction schemes is to illuminate the difference between gross and net profit, not to formulate a theory of crises or breakdown.
49 Marx, *Theories of Surplus Value*, vol. 3, p. 497.
50 Ibid.
51 Ibid., vol. 3, p. 500; and see pp. 403, 505, 512–13.
52 Ibid., vol. 2, p. 509.
53 Ibid., pp. 512–13.
54 Marx, *Capital*, vol. 2, pp. 410–11.
55 Marx, *Theories of Surplus Value*, vol. 2, p. 495.
56 The most extensive discussion of Marx's critique of underconsumptionism is found in M. Bleaney, *Underconsumption Theories: A History and Critical Analysis*, New York, International Publishers, 1976, pp. 102–19.
57 Marx, *Theories of Surplus Value*, vol. 2, pp. 534–5.
58 Marx, *Capital*, vol. 2, p. 316.
59 Ibid., vol. 3, p. 484.
60 M. Foucault, *The Order of Things: An Archaeology of the Human Sciences*, New York, Random House, 1973, p. 176.
61 Marx, *Theories of Surplus Value*, vol. 3, p. 88.
62 Ibid., vol. 1, p. 409.
63 Ibid., p. 408.
64 Foucault, op. cit., p. 261.
65 See Marx, *Capital*, vol. 1, pp. 35–6, 50, 57, 60–1, 65.
66 T. Adorno, H. Albert, R. Dahrendorf, J. Habermas, H. Pilot, K. Popper, *The Positivist Dispute in German Sociology*, translated by G. Adey and D. Frisby, New York, Harper & Row, 1976, p. 9.
67 Marx to Engels, January 18, 1858, *Marx-Engels Correspondence*, New York, International Publishers, 1967, vol. 3, p. 91.
68 Marx, *Capital*, vol. 3, p. 239.
69 Seigel's reading of this passage is unnecessarily psychological, and misled by his earlier erroneous interpretation of the internal contradictions of the law. See Seigel, *Marx's Fate*, pp. 345–6. For a more reliable and general interpretation, see Cutler, *et al.*, op. cit., vol. 1, pp. 161–5.

3 **Breakdown theory in the Second International:**
The political construction of the orthodox concept

1 See generally M. Dobb, *Studies in the Development of Capitalism*, New York, International Publishers, 1981, pp. 300–19.
2 F. Engels, *Herr Eugen Dühring's Revolution in Science (Anti-Dühring)*, edited by C. Dutt, translated by E. Burns, New York, International Publishers, 1966, p. 302.
3 Ibid.
4 Ibid., p. 312.
5 Ibid., p. 395.

6 Ibid., p. 290.
7 F. Engels, Preface to the first German edition of K. Marx, *The Poverty of Philosophy*, New York, International Publishers, 1975, p. 11.
8 Ibid., p. 20.
9 F. Engels, 1886 Preface to K. Marx, *Capital*, New York, International Publishers, 1975, vol. 1, p. 6.
10 Dobb, op. cit., p. 307.
11 K. Kautsky, *The Class Struggle (Erfurt Program)*, translated by W. Bohn, Chicago, Charles H. Kerr and Co., 1910, pp. 136, 87.
12 F. Engels, note in Marx, *Capital*, vol. 3, p. 489.
13 Ibid.
14 Marx, ibid., vol. 3, pp. 437–8.
15 Ibid., vol. 2, chs. 15 and 16.
16 E. von Böhm-Bawerk, *Karl Marx and the Close of His System*, edited by P. Sweezy, New York, Augustus M. Kelly, 1949.
17 Published as E. Bernstein, *Evolutionary Socialism: a Criticism and Affirmation*, translated by E. Harvey, New York, Schocken Books, 1975. For a general account of Bernstein's life and work, see P. Gay, *The Dilemma of Democratic Socialism: Eduard Bernstein's Challenge to Marx*, New York, Collier Books, 1962. See also L. Colletti, *From Rousseau to Lenin*, translated by J. Merrington and J. White, New York, Monthly Review Press, 1974, pp. 48–92.
18 Bernstein, *Evolutionary Socialism*, p. xxiv.
19 Ibid., pp. 208–11.
20 Ibid., p. 87.
21 Ibid., pp. 40–54, 73–94.
22 Ibid., p. xxiv. The International Socialist Congress of 1896 passed a resolution stating that 'the economic and industrial development is going on with such rapidity that a crisis may occur within a comparatively short time,' and called for workers to prepare to assume positions of power. Ibid., p. 80.
23 Ibid., pp. xxiv-xxx.
24 Ibid., p. xxviii.
25 Ibid., p. xxiv.
26 Ibid., pp. 43–9.
27 Ibid., pp. 34–9.
28 Ibid., p. 39.
29 Ibid., p. 6.
30 Ibid., p. 16.
31 Ibid., pp. 15–16.
32 Ibid., p. 25.
33 For the political context of the debates see generally G. D. H. Cole, *A History of Socialist Thought*, vol. 3, *The Second International*, part 1, London, Macmillan, 1974, pp. 273–7.
34 H. Cunow, 'Zur Zusammenbruchstheorie', *Die Neue Zeit*, jhrg. 17, bd. 1, 1898–99, pp. 356–64, 396–403, 424–30.
35 Bernstein, op. cit., p. 176.
36 K. Kautsky, *The Economic Doctrines of Karl Marx*, translated by H. Stenning, Westport, Connecticut, Hyperion Press, 1977. The best

reference on Kautsky is M. Salvadori, *Karl Kautsky and the Socialist Revolution, 1880–1938*, translated by J. Rothschild, New York, NLB, 1979.
37 K. Kautsky, *Bernstein und das Sozialdemokratische Programm*, Stuttgart, J. H. W. Dietz, 1899, p. 42.
38 Ibid., p. 49.
39 Ibid., p. 43.
40 K. Kautsky, 'Krisentheorien', *Die Neue Zeit*, jhrg. 20, bd. 2, 1901–02, pp. 140–1.
41 Ibid., p. 143.
42 *Engels-Kautsky Correspondence*, Kautsky's commentary dating from 1935, quoted in Colletti, op. cit., p. 58.

4 Neo-orthodoxy and the general analysis of a politicized economy

1 R. Hilferding, *Böhm-Bawerk's Criticism of Marx*, in E. von Böhm-Bawerk, *Karl Marx and the Close of His System*, edited by P. Sweezy, New York, Augustus M. Kelly, 1949.
2 Ibid., p. 130.
3 R. Hilferding, *Finance Capital: The Latest Stage of Capitalist Development*, translated by M. Watnick and S. Gordon, Boston, Routledge & Kegan Paul, 1981.
4 Ibid., p. 334.
5 Ibid., pp. 332–6.
6 Ibid., p. 295.
7 Ibid., p. 335.
8 Ibid.
9 Ibid., p. 366.
10 Ibid., pp. 366–70.
11 Ibid., p. 370.
12 V. I. Lenin, *The Development of Capitalism in Russia*, Moscow, Progress Publishers, 1977.
13 V. I. Lenin, 'Marxism and Revisionism', in *Against Revisionism*, Moscow, Progress Publishers, 1976, p. 114.
14 Ibid.
15 V. I. Lenin, *Imperialism: The Highest Stage of Capitalism*, New York, International Publishers, 1969, p. 46.
16 Ibid., pp. 17–27.
17 Ibid., p. 127.
18 V. I. Lenin, *What Is To Be Done?*, New York, International Publishers, 1973, p. 63.
19 D. Howard (ed.), *Selected Political Writings of Rosa Luxemburg*, New York, Monthly Review Press, 1971, pp. 48–9.
20 E. Bernstein, *Evolutionary Socialism: A Criticism and Affirmation*, translated by E. Harvey, New York, Schocken Books, 1975, pp. 80–94.
21 R. Luxemburg, *Reform or Revolution*, New York, Pathfinder Press, 1973, p. 35.
22 Ibid., p. 55.
23 Ibid., p. 11.

24 Ibid., p. 17.
25 Ibid., p. 18.
26 R. Luxemburg, *The Accumulation of Capital*, translated by A. Schwarzschild, New York, Monthly Review Press, 1968, p. 36. New York, Monthly Review Press, 1968, p. 36.
27 Luxemburg, *Reform or Revolution*, p. 17.
28 Ibid., p. 11.
29 Luxemburg, *The Accumulation of Capital*, p. 417.
30 Ibid., 417.
31 Ibid., p. 467.
32 Ibid., p. 466.
33 G. Lukács, *History and Class Consciousness: Studies in Marxist Dialectics*, translated by R. Livingstone, Cambridge, Mass., MIT Press, 1971, p. xxi.
34 Ibid., p. 11.
35 Ibid., p. 182.
36 Ibid., pp. 38–9.
37 Ibid., p. 35.
38 Ibid., pp. 36–7, 40–1.
39 Ibid., p. 182.
40 Ibid., p. 183.
41 Ibid., pp. 66–7.
42 Ibid., p. 75.
43 Ibid., p. 40.
44 Ibid., p. 76.
45 See R. Day, *The 'Crisis' and the 'Crash': Soviet Studies of the West (1917–1939)*, London, NLB, 1981.
46 H. Grossmann, *The Law of Accumulation and Collapse in the Capitalist System*, Leipzig, J. Gortz, 1929.
47 The best account of the debate between Grossmann and Pollock is G. Marramao, 'Political economy and critical theory', *Telos*, no. 24, Summer, 1975, pp. 56–81. See also Marramao's more general article on Grossmann, 'Theory of crisis and the problem of constitution', *Telos*, no. 26, Winter, 1975–6, pp. 143–64.
48 For the history of the Institute and of Grossmann's relationship to the other members, see generally M. Jay, *The Dialectical Imagination: A History of the Frankfurt School and the Institute of Social Research, 1923–1950*, Boston, Little, Brown, 1973, especially pp. 16–20.

5 Breakdown theory and the American Marxists: The theoretical spectrum of the early years

1 See, for example, M. Jay, *The Dialectical Imagination: A History of the Frankfurt School and the Institute of Social Research, 1923–1950*, Boston, Little, Brown, 1973; and P. Anderson, *Considerations on Western Marxism*, London, NLB, 1977.
2 See generally G. D. H. Cole, *A History of Socialist Thought*, vol. 3, *The Second International*, part 2, New York, St. Martin's Press, 1963, pp. 775–819; and A. Kraditor, *The Radical Persuasion, 1890–1917: Aspects of the Intellectual History and the Historiography of Three*

American Radical Organizations, Baton Rouge, La., Louisiana State University Press, 1981, pp. 205–20.

3 The best source of biographical information on Boudin is T. Draper, *The Roots of American Communism*, New York, Viking Press, 1957. For an introduction to Boudin's theoretical work see P. Sweezy, 'The influence of Marxian economics on American thought and practice', in D. Egbert and S. Persons (eds.), *Socialism in American Life*, Princeton, N. J., Princeton University Press, 1952, vol. 1, pp. 453–86.

4 L. Boudin, *The Theoretical System of Karl Marx, In the Light of Recent Criticism*, Chicago, Charles H. Kerr, 1907.

5 R. Luxemburg, *The Accumulation of Capital*, pp. 319–20.

6 Boudin, *Theoretical System*, p. 120.

7 Ibid., p. 125.

8 Ibid., p. 127.

9 Ibid., p. 157.

10 Ibid., p. 254.

11 Ibid., p. 163.

12 Ibid.

13 Ibid.

14 Ibid., p. 157.

15 Ibid., p. 153.

16 Ibid., pp. 227–8.

17 Ibid., pp. 152–3.

18 Ibid., p. 165.

19 Ibid., p. 250.

20 Ibid., pp. 240–1.

21 Ibid., p. 252.

22 Ibid., p. 253.

23 Ibid., p. 254.

24 L. Boudin, *Socialism and War*, New York, New Review Publishing Association, 1916.

25 T. Veblen, 'The socialist economics of Karl Marx', in M. Lerner (ed.), *The Portable Veblen*, New York, Viking Press, 1972, pp. 279–83, 294–5.

26 T. Veblen, 'Why economics is not an evolutionary science', in Lerner, *The Portable Veblen*, p. 236. Veblen completed a Ph.D. in philosophy at Cornell, and taught at a number of universities during his long but tenuous academic career. The best source of biographical information on Veblen is J. Dorfman, *Thorstein Veblen and His America*, New York, Augustus M. Kelly, 1966. For an analysis of Veblen's works, see J. Diggins's *The Bard of Savagery: Thorstein Veblen and Modern Social Theory*, New York, Seabury Press, 1978.

27 Veblen, 'Why economics is not an evolutionary science', p. 236.

28 Veblen, *The Theory of Business Enterprise*, New York, Augustus M. Kelly, 1965 (1904). For the purposes of this study, Veblen's most significant works include *The Theory of the Leisure Class*, New York, Modern Library, 1934 (1899); *The Instinct of Workmanship*, New York, Augustus M. Kelly, 1964 (1914); *Imperial Germany and the Industrial Revolution*, New York, Augustus M. Kelly, 1964 (1915); *The Engineers and the Price System*, New York, Augustus M. Kelly,

1965 (1921); and *The Theory of Business Enterprise*, which is discussed here in detail.
29 Veblen, *The Theory of Business Enterprise*, p. 185.
30 Ibid., pp. 200–1.
31 Ibid., pp. 200–1, 206.
32 Ibid., pp. 193–4.
33 Ibid., pp. 191–2.
34 Ibid.
35 Ibid., p. 254.
36 Ibid., p. 234.
37 Ibid., p. 263.
38 Ibid.
39 Ibid., p. 284.
40 Ibid.
41 Ibid., pp. 361, 369, and see p. 371.
42 Ibid., p. 338.
43 Ibid., p. 351.
44 Ibid., p. 337.
45 Ibid., p. 341.
46 Ibid., pp. 305–6.
47 Ibid., pp. 345–6.
48 Ibid., p. 400.
49 See Veblen, 'The socialist economics of Karl Marx'.
50 Sweezy, op. cit., p. 477.
51 Veblen, p. 275.
52 Ibid., p. 285.
53 Ibid., p. 292.
54 Ibid., pp. 292–3.
55 Ibid., p. 294.
56 Ibid., pp. 294, 296, and see pp. 292–3.
57 Veblen, 'Note', *Journal of Political Economy*, March, 1895, p. 78.
58 See generally Draper, op. cit., pp. 293–302.
59 L. Corey, *The Decline of American Capitalism*, New York, Covici Friede, 1934, p. 113.
60 Ibid., p. 485.
61 Ibid.
62 Ibid., p. 218.
63 Ibid., pp. 42, 44.
64 Ibid., p. 193.
65 Ibid., p. 452.
66 Ibid., p. 45.
67 Ibid., pp. 116–17.
68 Ibid., p. 130.
69 See ibid., pp. 150, 191, 479.
70 L. Corey, *The Crisis of the Middle Class*, New York, Covici Friede, 1935, p. 9.
71 Ibid., p. 200.
72 Ibid., pp. 164–5.
73 Ibid., pp. 148–9.
74 Ibid., p. 11.

75 Ibid., p. 296.
76 Ibid., pp. 195–6, and see pp. 316, 331, 347.
77 Ibid., p. 12.
78 Ibid., pp. 12–13.
79 Ibid., p. 191.
80 L. Corey, 'Veblen and Marxism', *Marxist Quarterly*, vol. 1, January–March, 1937, pp. 162–8.
81 Ibid., p. 163.
82 Ibid.
83 Ibid., p. 167.

6 **The anti-orthodox response to crash and recovery: Superstructural models of collapse**

1 Horkheimer quoted in R. Jacoby, 'Marxism and the critical school', *Theory and Society*, vol. 1, 1974, p. 235. See also Horkheimer's essays in his *Critical Theory: Selected Essays*, translated by M. O'Connel *et al.*, New York, Seabury Press, 1972, particularly 'Traditional and critical theory', where Horkheimer attempts to define critical theory, the basis of West German anti-orthodox Marxism.
2 Adorno quoted in Jacoby, op. cit., p. 238.
3 F. Pollock, 'State capitalism: Its possibilities and limitations', in A. Arato and E. Gebhardt (eds.), *The Essential Frankfurt School Reader*, New York, Urizen Books, 1978, pp. 71–94, at pp. 74–5; first published in *Studies in Philosophy and Social Sciences*, vol. 9, no. 2, 1941.
4 Ibid., pp. 71–2.
5 Ibid., p. 74.
6 Ibid., pp. 72–5.
7 Ibid., p. 78.
8 Ibid., p. 87.
9 Ibid., pp. 86–7.
10 Ibid., pp. 89–90.
11 The central works here include, in the field of methodology, Marcuse's *Reason and Revolution* (1941); Adorno's *Negative Dialectics* (1966) and *Minima Moralia* (1951); Horkheimer's essays in *Critical Theory* (2 vols.); and Habermas's *Knowledge and Human Interests* (1968) and *Theory and Praxis* (1971). In the field of aesthetics, see Adorno's *Philosophy of Modern Music* (1949) and *Aesthetic Theory* (1970); Benjamin's *Illuminations* (1968) and *Charles Baudelaire: A Lyric Poet in the Era of High Capitalism* (1969). Treatments of ideology and consciousness include Marcuse's *Eros and Civilization* (1954) and *One-Dimensional Man* (1964); Adorno's *The Authoritarian Personality* (1950); and Horkheimer's and Adorno's *Dialectic of Enlightenment* (1947).
   For a history of the Frankfurt School, see generally M. Jay, *The Dialectical Imagination: A History of the Frankfurt School and the Institute of Social Research, 1923–1950*, which is useful but overestimates the extent to which the Institute members abandoned Marxism. Like many commentators, Jay fails to see Marx's discussions of

fetishism and dialectics as the source for many of the ideas associated with the Institute's most 'non-Marxist' works. See also Jay's update, 'Some recent developments in critical theory', *Berkeley Journal of Sociology*, vol. 18, 1973–4, pp. 27–44. R. Jacoby's 'Marxism and the critical school', *Theory and Society*, vol. 1, 1974, pp. 231–8, provides a necessary corrective to Jay's perspective. The shift in Marxist thought discussed here is the subject of P. Anderson's short but eloquent study, *Considerations on Western Marxism*, New York, NLB, 1977. Like Jay, Anderson exaggerates the extent to which the Frankfurt School moved away from Marxism, but Anderson provides a context for the shift which minimizes overestimations of its effects. See also the treatment of the shift in A. Wellmer, 'Communications and emancipations: Reflections on the linguistic turn in critical theory', in J. O'Neill (ed.), *On Critical Theory*, New York, Seabury Press, 1976, pp. 231–63, and A. Wellmer's *Critical Theory of Society*, translated by J. Cumming, New York, Seabury Press, 1974.

12 Habermas's most important works are *Theory and Praxis* (1971); *Knowledge and Human Interests* (1968); *Legitimation Crisis* (1973); and the essays reprinted in *Communication and the Evolution of Society* (1976). The definitive reference on Habermas is T. McCarthy's *The Critical Theory of Jürgen Habermas*, Cambridge, Mass., MIT Press, 1979.

13 J. Habermas, *Towards a Rational Society: Student Protest, Science, and Politics*, translated by J. Shapiro, Boston, Beacon Press, 1970, p. 97. See also pp. 98–9.

14 Ibid., p. 101.

15 Ibid.

16 Ibid.

17 Ibid., p. 103.

18 Ibid., pp. 102–3, and see the interview with Habermas by A. Bolaffi in *Telos*, no. 39, Spring, 1979, pp. 163–72, at 171–2.

19 J. Habermas, *Communication and the Evolution of Society*, translated by T. McCarthy, Boston, Beacon Press, 1979, p. 195.

20 Ibid., p. 194.

21 J. Habermas, *Legitimation Crisis*, translated by T. McCarthy, Boston, Beacon Press, 1975, pp. 52–3.

22 Ibid., pp. 92–4.

23 Habermas, *Telos* interview, p. 163.

24 Ibid., p. 167.

25 Ibid.

26 Habermas, *Towards a Rational Society*, pp. 100–1.

27 Habermas, *Telos* interview, p. 168.

28 Ibid.

29 See, for example, J. Habermas, 'Towards a theory of communicative competence', *Inquiry*, no. 13, Winter, 1970, pp. 360–75; and T. Veblen, *The Theory of the Leisure Class: An Economic Study of Institutions*, New York, New American Library, 1953.

30 See L. Sève, 'The structural method and the dialectical method', and 'Reply to Maurice Godelier', *International Journal of Sociology*, vol. 2, nos. 2–3, Summer, Fall, 1972, pp. 195–240, 281–314; and M.

Godelier, 'Comments on the concepts of structure and contradiction', and 'Dialectical logic and the analysis of structures: A reply to Lucien Sève', in the same issues, pp. 173–88, 241–80.

31 Althusser's most important works are *For Marx* (1965); *Reading Capital* (1965); and *Lenin and Philosophy and Other Essays*, a collection of articles written between 1964 and 1970. For a short, simple account of Althusser's theoretical work, see A. Callinicos, *Althusser's Marxism*, London, Pluto Press, 1976. See also M. Glucksmann, *Structuralist Analysis in Contemporary Social Thought: A Comparison of the Theories of Claude Lévi-Strauss and Louis Althusser*, Boston, Routledge & Kegan Paul, 1974.

32 See L. Althusser, *For Marx*, translated by B. Brewster, London, Verso Press, 1979, pp. 111–20; and Callinicos, *Althusser's Marxism*, pp. 39–53.

33 E. Balibar, 'On the basic concepts of historical materialism', in Althusser, *Reading Capital*, p. 286 and part 3 in general.

34 Ibid., p. 291.

35 Ibid., p. 293.

36 The relevant work here is L. Althusser, 'Ideology and ideological state apparatuses', in *Lenin and Philosophy and Other Essays*, translated by B. Brewster, New York, Monthly Review Press, 1971.

37 J. Baudrillard, *The Mirror of Production*, translated by M. Poster, St Louis, Telos Press, 1975, p. 144.

38 Ibid., p. 139.

39 Ibid., pp. 125–8.

40 Ibid., p. 130.

41 Ibid., p. 143.

42 Ibid., p. 146.

43 J. Strachey, *The Coming Struggle for Power*, New York, Covici, Friede, 1933, p. 244.

44 Ibid., p. 245.

45 Ibid.

46 J. Strachey, *The Nature of Capitalist Crisis*, New York, Covici, Friede, 1935, pp. 321–42.

47 Ibid., p. 393.

48 J. Strachey, *Contemporary Capitalism*, London, Victor Gollancz, 1956, pp. 129–30.

49 E. Mandel, *Marxist Economic Theory*, translated by B. Pearce, New York, Monthly Review Press, 1970, vol. 2, pp. 530–3.

50 Ibid., p. 536.

51 Ibid., p. 539.

52 Ibid., p. 543.

53 E. Mandel, *Late Capitalism*, translated by J. De Bres, London, Verso, 1978, p. 557.

54 Ibid.

55 Ibid., p. 9.

56 Ibid., p. 10.

57 Ibid., p. 19.

58 Ibid., p. 21.

59 Ibid., p. 34.

60 Ibid., p. 39.
61 Ibid.
62 Ibid., p. 535.
63 Ibid., p. 526.
64 Ibid., p. 527.
65 Ibid., p. 525.
66 Ibid., pp. 485–6.
67 Ibid., p. 571.
68 Ibid., pp. 486–7.

7 Breakdown theory and the American Marxists: Abandonment and retrieval in the post-war period

1 P. Baran, *The Political Economy of Growth*, New York, Monthly Review Press, 1957.
2 The best source of biographical information on Baran is Sweezy's eulogy in P. Sweezy and L. Huberman (eds.), *Paul A. Baran: A Collective Portrait*, New York, Monthly Review Press, 1965.
3 Many of Baran's important articles are found in J. O'Neill (ed.), *The Longer View*, New York, Monthly Review Press, 1969.
4 Baran, *The Political Economy of Growth*, p. 5.
5 Ibid., p. 7.
6 Ibid., pp. 7–8.
7 Ibid., pp. 22–8. See also Baran, 'Economic progress and economic surplus', *The Longer View*, pp. 271–307, written in 1953.
8 Baran, *The Political Economy of Growth*, p. 71.
9 Ibid., p. 72.
10 Ibid., p. 100.
11 Ibid., p. 98.
12 Ibid., p. 99.
13 Ibid., p. 100.
14 Ibid., pp. 108–9. For an earlier formulation of Baran's analysis of forms of intervention see Baran, 'National economic planning', *The Longer View*, pp. 115–81, at pp. 122–38, written in 1952.
15 Baran, *The Political Economy of Growth*, pp. 118–19.
16 Ibid., p. 129.
17 Ibid., pp. 104–5.
18 Ibid., p. 130, and see p. 97.
19 Ibid., p. 103.
20 Ibid., p. 123.
21 Ibid., pp. 131–2.
22 See, for example, Baran, 'On the nature of Marxism', *The Longer View*, pp. 19–42, at p. 41.
23 See Baran, 'Economics of two worlds', *The Longer View*, pp. 68–91, at pp. 69–70.
24 See Baran, 'Better smaller but better', *The Longer View*, pp. 208–9.
25 Ibid., p. 204.
26 Baran, *The Political Economy of Growth*, p. 97.
27 Baran, 'Better smaller but better', p. 209.
28 Ibid., p. 208.

29 Ibid.
30 Ibid., p. 213.
31 Sweezy's *The Theory of Capitalist Development* has appeared in over a dozen printings by Monthly Review Press. Sweezy's writings over the last thirty years have appeared largely in the form of articles for *Monthly Review*. Many of these articles have been reprinted in collections. See especially *The Present as History: Essays and Reviews on Capitalism and Socialism*, New York, Monthly Review Press, 1953; and *Modern Capitalism and Other Essays*, New York, Monthly Review Press, 1972.
32 Sweezy, *The Theory of Capitalist Development: Principles of Marxian Political Economy*, New York, Monthly Review Press, 1970, pp. 214–15.
33 Ibid., pp. 138–46.
34 Ibid., pp. 214–18.
35 Ibid., p. 178.
36 Ibid., pp. 179–80.
37 Ibid., pp. 180–3.
38 P. Baran and P. Sweezy, *Monopoly Capital: An Essay on the American Economic and Social Order*, New York, Monthly Review Press, 1968, pp. 66–7.
39 Ibid., p. 5.
40 Ibid.
41 Ibid., p. 6.
42 Ibid.
43 Ibid., pp. 57–66.
44 Ibid., pp. 70–1.
45 Ibid., p. 10.
46 Ibid., p. 72.
47 Ibid.
48 Ibid.
49 Ibid., p. 83.
50 See K. Marx, *Capital*, vol. 1, p. 216.
51 Baran and Sweezy, op. cit., pp. 72–6.
52 Ibid., pp. 73–5.
53 Ibid., pp. 75–6.
54 Ibid., pp. 77–8.
55 Ibid., pp. 87–9, 108, 114.
56 Ibid., p. 108.
57 See the explication and critique of this argument in M. Bleaney, *Underconsumption Theories: A History and Critical Analysis*, New York, International Publishers, 1976, pp. 231–3.
58 Baran and Sweezy, op. cit., p. 363, and see pp. 364–7.
59 See P. Clecak, *Radical Paradoxes: Dilemmas of the American Left, 1945–1970*, New York, Harper and Row, 1973, pp. 72–174.
60 H. Marcuse, *One-Dimensional Man: Studies in the Ideology of Advanced Industrial Society*, Boston, Beacon Press, 1968, p. 28.
61 P. Mattick, *Critique of Marcuse*, New York, Herder and Herder, 1972, p. 15; and see P. Mattick, *Marx and Keynes: The Limits of the Mixed Economy*, Boston, Porter Sargent, 1969, pp. 57–65, 70–2,

87–95, 99–100.
62 Mattick, *Critique of Marcuse*, p. 55.
63 Ibid., pp. 50–3.
64 Ibid., pp. 51–2.
65 Ibid., p. 107.
66 Ibid., pp. 55–6.
67 Ibid., p. 97.
68 J. O'Connor, *The Fiscal Crisis of the State*, New York, St Martin's Press, 1973, p. 40.
69 Ibid., p. 6.
70 Ibid., pp. 6–9.
71 Ibid., pp. 45–8.
72 Ibid., pp. 48–58.
73 Ibid., pp. 249–55.
74 Ibid., p. 41.
75 Ibid., p. 67.

8 Conclusions

1 Mattick, 'Value theory and capital accumulation', *Science and Society*, vol. 23, no. 1, Winter, 1959, pp. 27–51, at p. 33.

Bibliography

ADORNO, T., et al., The Positivist Dispute in German Sociology, translated by G. Adey and D. Frisby, New York, Harper & Row, 1976.

ALTHUSSER, L., Lenin and Philosophy and Other Essays, translated by B. Brewster, New York, Monthly Review Press, 1971.

ALTHUSSER, L., For Marx, translated by B. Brewster, London, Verso Press, 1979.

ALTHUSSER, L. and BALIBAR, E., Reading Capital, translated by B. Brewster, second edition, New York, NLB, 1977.

AMIN, S., Dynamics of Global Crisis, New York, Monthly Review Press, 1982.

ANDERSON, P., Considerations on Western Marxism, London, NLB, 1977.

ARATO, A. and BREINES, P., The Young Lukács and the Origins of Western Marxism, New York, Seabury Press, 1979.

ARNDT, H., The Economic Lessons of the 1930s, London, Frank Cass, 1972.

BARAN, P., 'Veblen's Theory of the Leisure Class', Monthly Review, vol. 9, nos 3–4, July-August, 1937, pp. 83–91.

BARAN, P., The Political Economy of Growth, New York, Monthly Review Press, 1957.

BARAN, P., The Longer View: Essays Toward a Critique of Political Economy, edited by J. O'Neill, New York, Monthly Review Press, 1969.

BARAN, P. and SWEEZY, P., Monopoly Capital: An Essay on the American Economic and Social Order, New York, Monthly Review Press, 1968.

BARTHES, R., A Lover's Discourse, translated by R. Howard, New York, Hill and Wang, 1978.

BAUDRILLARD, J., The Mirror of Production, translated by M. Poster, St Louis, Telos Press, 1975.

BEBEL, A., My Life, New York, H. Fertig, 1973.

BERNSTEIN, E., Evolutionary Socialism: A Criticism and Affirmation, translated by E. Harvey, New York, Schocken Books, 1975.

BLEANEY, M., Underconsumption Theories: A History and Critical Analysis, New York, International Publishers, 1976.

BODDY, R. and CROTTY, J., 'Class conflict, Keynesian policies, and the business cycle', *Monthly Review*, vol. 26, no. 5, October, 1974, pp. 1–17.

BÖHM-BAWERK, E. VON, *Karl Marx and the Close of His System*, edited by P. Sweezy, New York, Augustus M. Kelly, 1949.

BORTKIEWICZ, L. VON, 'Value and price in the Marxian system', *International Economic Papers*, no. 2, 1952.

BOUDIN, L., *The Theoretical System of Karl Marx, In the Light of Recent Criticism*, Chicago, Charles H. Kerr, 1907.

BOUDIN, L., *Socialism and War*, New York, New Review Publishing Association, 1916.

BRAUN, O., '"Value" in Ricardo and Marx', *New Left Review*, no. 99, September-October, 1976, pp. 114–17.

BREWER, A., *Marxist Theories of Imperialism: A Critical Survey*, Boston, Routledge & Kegan Paul, 1980.

CALLINICOS, A., *Althusser's Marxism*, London, Pluto Press, 1976.

CARLO, A., 'The crisis of the state in the thirties', translated by M. Finocchiaro, *Telos*, no. 46, Winter, 1980–1, pp. 62–80.

CLECAK, P., *Radical Paradoxes: Dilemmas of the American Left: 1945–1970*, New York, Harper & Row, 1973.

COGOY, M., 'The fall of the rate of profit and the theory of accumulation: a reply to Paul Sweezy', *Capital and Class: Bulletin of the Conference of Socialist Economists*, no. 3, Winter, 1973, pp. 52–7.

COLE, G. D. H., *A History of Socialist Thought*, vol. 3, *The Second International, 1889–1914*, part 1, London, Macmillan, 1974, and part 2, New York, St Martin's Press, 1963.

COLLETTI, L., 'The theory of the crash', *Telos*, no. 13, Fall, 1962, pp. 34–46.

COLLETTI, L., *From Rousseau to Lenin*, translated by J. Merrington and J. White, New York, Monthly Review Press, 1974.

COLLETTI, L., 'Marxism and the dialectic', *New Left Review*, no. 93, September-October, 1978, pp. 3–29.

COREY, L., *The Decline of American Capitalism*, New York, Covici Friede, 1934.

COREY, L., *The Crisis of the Middle Class*, New York, Covici Friede, 1935.

COREY, L., 'Veblen and Marxism', *Marxist Quarterly*, vol. 1, no. 1, January-March, 1937, pp. 162–8.

COREY, L., 'The costs of depression', *Marxist Quarterly*, vol. 2, no. 3, October-December, 1938, pp. 381–93.

CUNOW, H., 'Zur Zusammenbruchstheorie', *Die Neue Zeit*, jhrg. 17, bd. 1, 1898–99, pp. 356–64, 396–403, 424–30.

CUTLER, A., HINDESS, B., HIRST, P., and HUSSAIN, A., *Marx's Capital and Capitalism Today*, 2 vols., Boston, Routledge & Kegan Paul, 1977.

DAY, R., *The 'Crisis' and the 'Crash': Soviet Studies of the West (1917–1939)*, London, NLB, 1981.

DICKENSON, H., 'The falling rate of profit in Marxian economics', *Review of Economic Studies*, vol. 24, no. 64, pp. 120–31.

DIGGINS, J., *The Bard of Savagery: Thorstein Veblen and Modern Social Theory*, New York, Seabury Press, 1978.

DOBB, M., *Political Economy and Capitalism: Some Essays in Economic Tradition*, London, Routledge & Kegan Paul, 1937.

DOBB, M., *Theories of Value and Distribution Since Adam Smith: Ideology and Economic Theory*, Cambridge, Cambridge University Press, 1977.

DOBB, M., *Studies in the Development of Capitalism*, New York, International Publishers, 1981.

DORFMAN, J., *Thorstein Veblen and His America*, New York, Augustus M. Kelly, 1966.

DRAPER, T., *The Roots of American Communism*, New York, Viking Press, 1957.

EAGLY, R., *The Structure of Classical Economic Thought*, New York, Oxford University Press, 1974.

EGBERT, D. and PERSONS, S., *Socialism in American Life*, 2 vols., Princeton, N.J., Princeton University Press, 1952.

ENGELS, F., *Herr Eugen Dühring's Revolution in Science (Anti-Dühring)*, edited by C. Dutt, translated by E. Burns, New York, International Publishers, 1966.

ENGELS, F., *The Condition of the Working Class in England*, translated by W. Henderson and W. Chaloner, Stanford, California, Stanford University Press, 1968.

ENGELS, F., *Frederick Engels on 'Capital': Synopsis, Reviews and Supplementary Material*, translated by L. Minns, New York, International Publishers, 1974.

FINE, B. and HARRIS, L., 'Controversial issues in Marxist economic theory', *Socialist Register*, 1976, pp. 141–79.

FOUCAULT, M., *The Order of Things: An Archaeology of the Human Sciences*, New York, Random House, 1973.

GAY, P., *The Dilemma of Democratic Socialism: Eduard Bernstein's Challenge to Marx*, New York, Collier Books, 1962.

GERAS, N., 'Rosa Luxemburg: Barbarism and the collapse of capitalism', *New Left Review*, November-December, 1973, pp. 17–37.

GERAS, N., *The Legacy of Rosa Luxemburg*, London, NLB, 1976.

GILLMAN, J., *The Falling Rate of Profit: Marx's Law and Its Significance to Twentieth Century Capitalism*, New York, Dennis Dobson, 1957.

GLUCKSMANN, M., *Structuralist Analysis in Contemporary Social Thought: A Comparison of the Theories of Claude Lévi-Strauss and Louis Althusser*, Boston, Routledge & Kegan Paul, 1974.

GLYN, A. and SUTCLIFFE, B., *Capitalism in Crisis*, New York, Random House, 1972.

GODELIER, M., 'Comments on the concepts of structure and contradiction', *International Journal of Sociology*, vol. 2, no. 2, Summer, 1972, pp. 173–88.

GODELIER, M., 'Dialectical logic and the analysis of structures: A reply to Lucien Sève', *International Journal of Sociology*, vol. 2, no. 3, Fall, 1972, pp. 241–80.

GODELIER, M., *Rationality and Irrationality in Economics*, translated by B. Pearce, New York, Monthly Review Press, 1972.

GOLD, D., et al., 'Recent developments in Marxist theories of the capitalist state', *Monthly Review*, vol. 27, no. 5, October, 1975, pp.

29–43, and no. 6, November, 1975, pp. 36–51.

GOTTHEIL, F., *Marx's Economic Predictions*, Evanston, Illinois, North-western University Press, 1966.

GOULDNER, A., *The Dialectic of Ideology and Technology: The Origins, Grammar, and Future of Ideology*, New York, Seabury Press, 1976.

GROSSMANN, H., *The Law of Accumulation and Collapse in the Capitalist System*, Leipzig, J. Gortz, 1929.

GROSSMANN, H., 'Marx, classical political economy, and the problem of dynamics', translated by P. Burgess, *Capital and Class: Bulletin of the Conference of Socialist Economists*, no. 2, Summer, 1977, pp. 32–55, and no. 3, Fall, 1977, pp. 67–100.

HABERMAS, J., *Towards a Rational Society: Student Protest, Science, and Politics*, translated by J. Shapiro, Boston, Beacon Press, 1970.

HABERMAS, J., 'Towards a theory of communicative competence', *Inquiry*, no. 13, Winter, 1970, pp. 360–75.

HABERMAS, J., *Knowledge and Human Interests*, translated by J. Shapiro, Boston, Beacon Press, 1972.

HABERMAS, J., *Theory and Practice*, translated by J. Viertal, Boston, Beacon Press, 1973.

HABERMAS, J., *Legitimation Crisis*, translated by T. McCarthy, Boston, Beacon Press, 1975.

HABERMAS, J., *Communication and the Evolution of Society*, translated by T. McCarthy, Boston, Beacon Press, 1979.

HABERMAS, J., 'Interview', with A. Bolaffi, *Telos*, no. 39, Spring, 1979, pp. 163–72.

HARDACH, G., *et al.*, *A Short History of Socialist Economic Thought*, translated by J. Wickham, New York, St Martin's Press, 1978.

HARRINGTON, M., *The Twilight of American Capitalism*, New York, Simon and Schuster, 1976.

HILFERDING, R., *Böhm-Bawerk's Criticism of Marx*, edited by P. Sweezy, New York, Augustus M. Kelly, 1949.

HILFERDING, R., *Finance Capital: A Study of the Latest Phase of Capitalist Development*, translated by M. Watnick and S. Gordon, Boston, Routledge & Kegan Paul, 1981.

HODGSON, G., 'The theory of the falling rate of profit', *New Left Review*, no. 84, March-April, 1974, pp. 55–84.

HORKHEIMER, M., *Critical Theory: Selected Essays*, translated by M. O'Connell, *et al.*, New York, Seabury Press, 1972.

HORKHEIMER, M., 'The authoritarian state', *The Essential Frankfurt School Reader*, edited by A. Arato and E. Gebhardt, New York, Urizen Books, 1978.

HOROWITZ, D., 'Reply to Mandel', *International Socialist Review*, vol. 28, no. 4, July-August, 1967, pp. 26–8.

HOROWITZ, D. (ed.), *Marx and Modern Economics*, New York, Monthly Review Press, 1968.

HUSSAIN, A., 'Crisis and tendencies of capitalism', *Economy and Society*, vol. 6, no. 4, November, 1977, pp. 436–60.

ITOH, M., *Value and Crisis: Essays on Marxian Economics in Japan*, New York, Monthly Review Press, 1980.

JACOBY, R., 'Marxism and the critical school', *Theory and Society*, vol. 1,

1974, pp. 231–8.

JACOBY, R., 'The politics of crisis theory: towards a critique of automatic Marxism II', *Telos*, no. 23, Spring, 1975, pp. 3–52.

JACOBY, R., *Dialectic of Defeat: Contours of Western Marxism*, New York, Cambridge University Press, 1981.

JAY, M., *The Dialectical Imagination: A History of the Frankfurt School and the Institute of Social Research, 1923–1950*, Boston, Little, Brown, 1973.

JAY, M., 'Some recent developments in critical theory', *Berkeley Journal of Sociology*, vol. 18, 1973–4, pp. 27–44.

KALECKI, M., *Selected Essays on the Dynamics of the Capitalist Economy*, Cambridge, Cambridge University Press, 1971.

KAUTSKY, K., *Bernstein und das Sozialdemokratische Programm*, Stuttgart, J. H. W. Dietz, 1899.

KAUTSKY, K., 'Krisentheorien', *Die Neue Zeit*, jhrg. 20, bd. 2, 1901–02, pp. 140–56.

KAUTSKY, K., *The Class Struggle (Erfurt Program)*, translated by W. Bohn, Chicago, Charles H. Kerr and Co., 1910.

KAUTSKY, K., *The Economic Doctrines of Karl Marx*, translated by H. Stenning, Westport, Connecticut, Hyperion Press, 1977.

KELLER, R., 'Monopoly capital and the Great Depression: testing Baran and Sweezy's hypothesis', *Review of Radical Political Economy*, vol. 7, no. 4, Winter, 1975, pp. 65–75.

KIERNAN, V., *Marxism and Imperialism*, New York, St Martin's Press, 1974.

KIRKENFELD, T., 'The paradox of profit', *Science and Society*, vol. 12, no. 1, Winter, 1948, pp. 33–41.

KOLKO, J., *America and the Crisis of World Capitalism*, Boston, Beacon Press, 1974.

KRADITOR, A., *The Radical Persuasion, 1890–1917: Aspects of the Intellectual History and the Historiography of Three American Radical Organizations*, Baton Rouge, La., Louisiana State University Press, 1981.

LEFEBVRE, H., *The Survival of Capitalism: Reproduction of the Relations of Production*, translated by F. Bryant, London, Allison & Busby, 1978.

LENIN, V. I., *The State and Revolution*, New York, International Publishers, 1943.

LENIN, V. I., *Imperialism: The Highest Stage of Capitalism*, New York, International Publishers, 1969.

LENIN, V. I., *Materialism and Empirio-Criticism*, Peking, Foreign Languages Press, 1972.

LENIN, V. I., *What Is To Be Done?*, New York, International Publishers, 1973.

LENIN, V. I., *Against Revisionism*, Moscow, Progress Publishers, 1976.

LENIN, V. I., *The Development of Capitalism in Russia*, Moscow, Progress Publishers, 1977.

LUKÁCS, G., *History and Class Consciousness: Studies in Marxist Dialectics*, translated by R. Livingstone, Cambridge, Mass., MIT Press, 1971.

LUXEMBURG, R., *The Accumulation of Capital: A Contribution to the Economic Elucidation of Imperialism*, translated by A. Schwarzschild, New York, Monthly Review Press, 1968.

LUXEMBURG, R., *Rosa Luxemburg Speaks*, edited by M. Waters, New York, Pathfinder Press, 1970.

LUXEMBURG, R., *Selected Political Writings of Rosa Luxemburg*, edited by D. Howard, New York, Monthly Review Press, 1971.

LUXEMBURG, R., *Reform or Revolution*, New York, Pathfinder Press, 1973.

LUXEMBURG, R., *Rosa Luxemburg, Selected Political Writings*, edited by R. Looker, translated by W. Graf, New York, Grove Press, 1974.

MANDEL, E., *Marxist Economic Theory*, 2 vols., translated by B. Pearce, New York, Monthly Review Press, 1970.

MANDEL, E., *The Formation of the Economic Thought of Karl Marx, 1843 to Capital*, translated by B. Pearce, New York, Monthly Review Press, 1971.

MANDEL, E., *Late Capitalism*, translated by J. De Bres, London, Verso, 1978.

MANDEL, E., *The Second Slump: A Marxist Analysis of Recession in the Seventies*, translated by J. Rothschild, London, NLB, 1978.

MARCUSE, H., *One-Dimensional Man: Studies in the Ideology of Advanced Industrial Society*, Boston, Beacon Press, 1968.

MARRAMAO, G., 'Political economy and critical theory', *Telos*, no. 24, Summer, 1975, pp. 56–81.

MARRAMAO, G., 'Theory of crisis and the problem of constitution', *Telos*, no. 26, Winter, 1975–6, pp. 143–64.

MARX, K., *Theories of Surplus Value*, 3 vols., Moscow, Progress Publishers, 1963, 1968, 1971.

MARX, K., *Contribution to the Critique of Political Economy*, New York, International Publishers, 1970.

MARX, K., *Critique of the Gotha Program*, New York, International Publishers, 1973.

MARX, K., *Grundrisse: Foundations of the Critique of Political Economy*, translated by M. Nicolaus, New York, Random House, 1973.

MARX, K., *Capital: A Critique of Political Economy*, 3 vols., New York, International Publishers, 1975.

MARX, K., *The Poverty of Philosophy*, New York, International Publishers, 1975.

MARX, K., *Economic and Philosophic Manuscripts of 1844*, in K. Marx and F. Engels, *Collected Works*, vol. 3, New York, International Publishers, 1975.

MARX, K., and ENGELS, F., *The German Ideology*, in K. Marx and F. Engels, *Collected Works*, vol. 5, New York, International Publishers, 1976.

MATTICK, P., 'Value theory and capital accumulation', *Science and Society*, vol. 23, no. 1, Winter, 1959, pp. 27–51.

MATTICK, P., 'Marxism and "monopoly capitalism"', *Progressive Labour*, vol. 6, no. 1, July-August, 1967, pp. 34–49.

MATTICK, P., *Marx and Keynes: The Limits of the Mixed Economy*, Boston, Porter Sargent, 1969.

MATTICK, P., *Critique of Marcuse*, New York, Herder and Herder, 1972.

McCARTHY, T., *The Critical Theory of Jürgen Habermas*, Cambridge, Massachusetts, MIT Press, 1979.

McLELLAN, D., *Marxism After Marx: An Introduction*, New York, Harper and Row, 1979.

MEEK, R., *Studies in the Labour Theory of Value*, second edition, London, Lawrence and Wishart, 1973.

MEILLASSOUX, C., 'From reproduction to production', *Economy and Society*, vol. 1, no. 1, February, 1972, pp. 93–105.

MILIBAND, R., *The State in Capitalist Society*, New York, Basic Books, 1969.

NAPOLEONI, C., *Smith, Ricardo, and Marx*, translated by J. Gee, New York, John Wiley and Sons, 1975.

O'CONNOR, J., '"Monopoly capital"', *New Left Review*, no. 40, November-December, 1966, pp. 38–50.

O'CONNOR, J., *The Fiscal Crisis of the State*, New York, St Martin's Press, 1973.

OFFE, C., 'Political authority and class structures – an analysis of late capitalist societies', *International Journal of Sociology*, Spring, 1972, pp. 242–68.

O'NEILL, J. (ed.), *On Critical Theory*, New York, Seabury Press, 1976.

PANNEKOEK, A., 'The theory of the collapse of capitalism', translated by A. Buck, *Capital and Class: The Bulletin of the Conference of Socialist Economists*, no. 1, Spring, 1977, pp. 59–81.

PILLING, G., 'The law of value in Ricardo and Marx', *Economy and Society*, vol. 1, no. 3, August, 1973, pp. 281–307.

PILLING, G., *Marx's 'Capital': Philosophy and Political Economy*, Boston, Routledge & Kegan Paul, 1980.

POLLOCK, F., 'State capitalism: Its possibilities and limitations', *The Essential Frankfurt School Reader*, edited by A. Arato and E. Gebhardt, New York, Urizen Books, 1978, pp. 71–94.

POSTER, M., *Existentialist Marxism in Postwar France*, Princeton, New Jersey, Princeton University Press, 1975.

POULANTZAS, N., *Political Power and Social Classes*, translated by T. O'Hagan, London, NLB, 1975.

RICARDO, D., *Principles of Political Economy and Taxation*, Harmondsworth, Penguin Books, 1971.

ROBERTS, P. and STEPHENSON, M., *Marx's Theory of Exchange, Alienation, and Crisis*, Stanford, California, Stanford University Press, 1973.

ROBINSON, J., *An Essay on Marxian Economics*, London, Macmillan, 1966.

ROSDOLSKY, R., *The Making of Marx's Capital*, translated by P. Burgess, London, Pluto Press, 1980.

RUBIN, I., *Essays on Marx's Theory of Value*, translated by M. Samardzija and F. Perlman, Montreal, Black Rose Books, 1975.

SALVADORI, M., *Karl Kautsky and the Socialist Revolution, 1880–1938*, translated by J. Rothschild, New York, NLB, 1979.

SARTRE, J.-P., *Critique of Dialectical Reason, Theory of Practical Ensembles*, edited by J. Rice, translated by A. Sheridan-Smith, London, NLB, 1978.

SCHLESINGER, R., 'The general law of capitalist accumulation: past and future', *Science and Society*, vol. 31, no. 4, Fall, 1967, pp. 515–26.

SCHORSKE, C., *German Social Democracy, 1905–1917: The Development of the Great Schism*, New York, Russell, 1970.

SCHROYER, T., 'Marx's theory of crisis', *Telos*, no. 14, Winter, 1972, pp. 106–26.

SEIGEL, J., *Marx's Fate: The Shape of a Life*, Princeton, New Jersey, Princeton University Press, 1978.

SÈVE, L., 'The structural method and the dialectical method', *International Journal of Sociology*, vol. 2, no. 2, Summer, 1972, pp. 195–240.

SÈVE, L., 'Reply to Maurice Godelier', *International Journal of Sociology*, vol. 2, no. 3, Fall, 1972, pp. 281–314.

SHERMAN, H., 'Marx and the business cycle', *Science and Society*, vol. 31, no. 4, Fall, 1967, pp. 486–504.

SHONFEILD, A., *Modern Capitalism*, New York, Oxford University Press, 1965.

SMITH, A., *An Inquiry into the Nature and Causes of the Wealth of Nations*, New York, Random House, 1937.

STRACHEY, J., *The Coming Struggle for Power*, New York, Covici Friede, 1933.

STRACHEY, J., *The Nature of Capitalist Crisis*, New York, Covici Friede, 1935.

STRACHEY, J., *Contemporary Capitalism*, London, Victor Gollancz, 1956.

SWEEZY, P., *The Present as History: Essays and Reviews on Capitalism and Socialism*, New York, Monthly Review Press, 1953.

SWEEZY, P., *The Theory of Capitalist Development: Principles of Marxian Political Economy*, New York, Monthly Review Press, 1970.

SWEEZY, P., *Modern Capitalism and Other Essays*, New York, Monthly Review Press, 1972.

SWEEZY, P. and HUBERMAN, L. (eds.), *Paul A. Baran: A Collective Portrait*, New York, Monthly Review Press, 1965.

SWEEZY, P. and MAGDOFF, H., *The Dynamics of US Capitalism*, New York, Monthly Review Press, 1972.

TRIBE, K., 'Remarks on the theoretical significance of Marx's "Grundrisse"', *Economy and Society*, vol. 3, no. 2, May, 1974, pp. 180–210.

VEBLEN, T., 'Note', *Journal of Political Economy*, March, 1895, pp. 73–9.

VEBLEN, T., *The Theory of the Leisure Class: An Economic Study of Institutions*, New York, New American Library, 1953.

VEBLEN, T., *Imperial Germany and the Industrial Revolution*, New York, Augustus M. Kelly, 1964.

VEBLEN, T., *The Instinct of Workmanship, and the State of the Industrial Arts*, New York, Augustus M. Kelly, 1964.

VEBLEN, T., *The Engineers and the Price System*, New York, Augustus M. Kelly, 1965.

VEBLEN, T., *The Theory of Business Enterprise*, New York, Augustus M. Kelly, 1965.

VEBLEN, T., 'The socialist economics of Karl Marx', *The Portable Veblen*, edited by M. Lerner, New York, Viking Press, 1972, pp. 275–96.

VEBLEN, T., 'Why economics is not an evolutionary science', *The Portable*

Veblen, edited by M. Lerner, New York, Viking Press, 1972, pp. 215–40.

WELLMER, A., *Critical Theory of Society*, translated by J. Cumming, New York, Seabury Press, 1974.

WOLFE, B., 'New aspects of cycle and crisis', *Marxist Quarterly*, no. 1, January-March, 1937, pp. 99–114.

WRIGHT, E., *Class, Crisis, and the State*, New York, NLB, 1979.

YAFFE, D., 'The Marxian theory of crisis, capital, and the state', *Economy and Society*, vol. 2, no. 2, May, 1973, pp. 186–232.

Index

Printed in the United States
by Baker & Taylor Publisher Services